EXPERIENCE AND CONFLICT:
THE PRODUCTION OF URBAN SPACE

Work on good prose has three steps:
a musical stage when it is composed,
an architectonic one when it is built,
and a textile one when it is woven.
Walter Benjamin (1979b [1928]: 61)

What we observe is not nature itself, but nature exposed to our method of
questioning
Werner Heisenberg 1959, quoted in Sandercock 1998: 67

An Icarus flying above these waters, he can ignore the devices of Daedalus
in mobile and endless labyrinths below.
Michel de Certeau 1993: 152

We have to relearn to think about space.
Marc Augé 1995: 36

Experience and Conflict:
The Production of Urban Space

PANU LEHTOVUORI
Estonian Academy of Arts, Tallinn, Estonia

ASHGATE

Published by
Ashgate Publishing Limited
Wey Court East
Union Road
Farnham
Surrey GU9 7PT
England

Ashgate Publishing Company
Suite 420
101 Cherry Street
Burlington, VT 05401-4405
USA

www.ashgate.com

British Library Cataloguing in Publication Data
Lehtovuori, Panu.
  Experience and conflict : the production of urban space.
  1. Public spaces--Design. 2. Public spaces--Case studies.
  3. City planning--Social aspects. 4. Architecture and
  society. 5. Lefebvre, Henri, 1901-1991--Influence.
  I. Title

  711.4'01-dc22

Library of Congress Cataloging-in-Publication Data
Lehtovuori, Panu.
  Experience and conflict : the production of urban space / by Panu Lehtovuori.
      p. cm.
  Includes bibliographical references and index.
  ISBN 978-0-7546-7602-7 (hardback)
  1. City planning. 2. Public spaces. 3. Spatial behavior. I. Title.
  HT166.L456 2009
  307.1'216--dc22

                                                                2009033059

ISBN 9780754676027

Printed and bound in Great Britain by
MPG Books Group, UK

Contents

List of Figures

Acknowledgements

I have been lucky to be able to write this book in a variety of inspiring academic communities. I wish to thank my colleagues in the Centre for Urban and Regional Studies at the Helsinki University of Technology, in Manchester Institute for Popular Culture at the Manchester Metropolitan University and in the Faculty of Architecture at the Estonian Academy of Arts in Tallinn. The professors, students and alumnae of Polis, the European Masters for Urban Cultures, have been a constant source of new perspectives.

Besides people, certain cities have shaped my work. Berlin, Barcelona, Brasília, Manchester, Lisbon and Helsinki are the key points of a certain 'geography of writing'. Encounters, atmospheres and night-time soundscapes of these cities, as well as careful studies and mappings of their features, are an important element of the intellectual exploration.

Special thanks to Mark Gottdiener, Simo Haanpää, Saara Hannula, Klaske Havik, Jean Hillier, Tuula Isohanni, Mikko Mälkki, Sampo Ruoppila and Anne Stenros who helped in different ways, making the book possible. I wish to extend my warmest thanks to the editors of Ashgate and the blind referees who helped to sharpen the arguments and find new sources.

Finally, without the continued support, constructive criticism and fresh ideas of my wife Hille Koskela, this work would have been of much less quality. A big thank you to her!

Helsinki, 20 May 2009
Panu Lehtovuori

Foreword

Possessing unique, distinctive skills for an urbanist, Panu Lehtovuori is both an accomplished architect and a PhD in urban theory, planning, and policy from the Helsinki University of Technology where he once served as director of its Centre for Urban and Regional Studies.

Using Lefebvrian, semiotic, participatory planning, and Nordic design theory melded to brilliant insights he has written a definitive analysis of Helsinki urban development over the last two decades. Dr Lehtovuori's focus concentrates on the constructive criticism of existing urban planning practices and architectural design for cities, especially those concerned with preserving the traditional downtown for public use. In the process he attacks the narratives disconnected from people's real needs that underlie the exclusive boosterism, spectacular architecture and locational hype so essential to pushing real estate and such international designations as 'European cultural capital'.

By bringing to the surface recognition of conflict, experimental living, environmental alternatives, and inclusive participatory planning he forges a new synthesis of up-to-date urban theories about space and contemporary activist planning for livable and sustainable urban environments. Most distinctive is Lehtovuori's insistence that the grand narratives of planning and architectural urban design be replaced through an understanding of, what Lefebvre called, 'lived space', i.e., the everyday space of conflict, innovation, change, decay, embodied in quotidian practices of residents. This bottom up vision of multiple agencies creating a lived space melds with the top down 'illusion of transparency' defined in contemporary professional practices to produce an inclusive, malleable, living approach to urban planning and policy.

At the opening of his treatise, Lehtovuori frames three questions:

> Why do new urban spaces lack feeling, power and sensory quality?
> Why does 'urbanness' retreat from the newly produced public spaces?
> Why does the political significance of urban space seem to be lost?

From this inquisitive beginning, he charts out the issues, problems, 'artificial realities', and ideological delusions of exclusionary planning and architectural practices. Analysis proceeds using case studies of his native Helsinki and two other important urban places – Manchester in the UK and Berlin, Germany. Empirical cases help ground the reader in his discourse as does his clear, readable writing even when complex theoretical ideas are discussed. No doubt users of this text will appreciate the latter qualities and learn, through reading, the straightforward means of applying Lehtovuori's critical ideas for inclusive, creative urban design.

This book begins with a critical discussion of urban planning and design ideologies that are not exclusive to the Nordic countries alone. Covered are examples ranging from Le Corbusier's International Style as practiced in Europe to urban design in Brazil. A new chapter applies the same investigation of reified concepts applied to the production of public space. UK and Finnish cases are used as examples.

A second section of the book lays out in sharp detail the concepts developed for the critique of contemporary urban planning, design and policy. Lehtovuori presents a comprehensive examination of space and place theory coupled with a critique of contemporary urban architecture. Emphasis here is on how professional practices miss the more malleable aspects of lived space, of inclusive, sustainable environments.

In a penultimate section the author provides a detailed investigation into the two decades effort to preserve the central city of Helsinki. Equally applicable to urban places in America as well as Europe, case study material and analysis provide a wealth of information regarding what to do and not to do in order to promote a 'user friendly' city environment.

A final section supplies a comprehensive guide to the author's own tools developed for a more participatory planning practice along with further detailed examples of case studies including references to Lehtovuori's own architectural and planning practice.

I like this book immensely. I have found it profoundly refreshing to read. In one place, the author provides overviews of the most trenchant arguments against traditional urban planning and architectural design from the perspective of activism, inclusivity and the theoretical Lefebvrian ideas about space. Lehtovuori has produced a text at once applicable to discussions of urbanism, planning, design and public policy with ample case study material that suits the varied courses in these areas. Professionals, academics and students of urbanism will all benefit from absorbing the insights and penetrating wisdom offered by Lehtovuori in this text.

Mark Gottdiener
28 March 2009

Introduction

The Problem of Public Urban Space in the Contemporary City

In cities, different, contradictory and conflictual actors, practices and agendas co-exist. Richard Sennett claims that while there probably are as many ways to define 'city' as there are cities, a simple definition stating that 'city is a human settlement in which strangers are likely to meet' is quite powerful (Sennett 1974: 39). Hartmut Häussermann detects the normative essence of cities' urban character in 'confrontation with diversity, the un-expected, the non-planned and the resistant moment' (Häussermann 1995, quoted in Groth and Corijn 2005: 513). These ideas suggest that to be urban in a true sense, cities should cater for diversity and alterity, allowing for articulation and integration of the Other. Conflicts are no exception but rather a constitutive part of cities' 'urbanness' (Rajanti 1999).

Public urban space is the key site of the coming-together of different actors and influences, thus becoming the 'soul' of the city and breeding ground of its urban character. In contemporary cities, however, the rich, multifaceted public urban space and the continued production of 'urbanness' in negotiations and conflicts are not self-evident. Steven Graham and Simon Marvin suggest that the 'splintering' of technical infrastructures would also fragment the urban social space (Graham and Marvin 2001, see also Castells 1996: 423–8). Michael Sorkin warns about the foreseeable 'end of public space', saying that 'throughout America, city planning has largely ceased its historic role as the integrator of communities in favour of managing selective development and enforcing distinction' (Sorkin 1992: xiv). In Europe, Marc Augé has discussed the proliferation of 'non-places', the a-historic and identityless realm of highways, airports and malls (Augé 1995). Zygmunt Bauman, developing Sennett's thesis about the importance of meeting strangers and the corollary need to rehearse 'civility', claims that many contemporary urban spaces, such as La Défense in Paris or Itäkeskus mall in Helsinki, are 'public, but not civil'. Those spaces for organised movement, organised consumption and organised entertainment are characterised by a 'redundancy of interaction', lack of friction, togetherness and any deeper reason to communicate (Bauman 2001: 27).

It seems that while urban populations are in general becoming multicultural and multi-ethnic, with increasingly divergent lifestyles, preferences and rhythms, public urban space is paradoxically segregated, simplified and sanitised (Smith 1992). Increasingly, developers and other powerful actors treat cities as commodities. Entrepreneurial planning and the manifold glocal effects of inter-urban competition and image marketing tend to homogenise public urban space on consumerist and aestheticised grounds (Groth and Corijn 2005: 513). Commercial projects and issues of private security eat up the public realm, eroding spatial justice. 'Zero-friction' is secured by zero-tolerance, 'spatial interdictions' making the access of the Other less likely (Hajer 1999, Flusty 1994). Even largely benevolent efforts towards 'urban renaissance' and planning that ostensibly cherishes the European model of dense city and lively urban space tend to produce artificial and bleak images of public space, stage-sets for imagined use and exclusionary 'outdoor rooms' (Doron 2002). The emphasis is on 'design space', and the public space creation fails to tap complex and emerging social and cultural potentials.

Weak Places – Urban Conflicts

The picture is not simple, though. Contemporary cities do provide counter-examples. New forms of deeply lived public urban space emerge and existing spaces are constantly challenged. It is possible to resist and divert the 'emic' and 'phagic' strategies of 'non-civic' public space (Bauman 2001: 24). Interesting, too, is to look at the potential of forgotten, sidetracked, vacant and under defined urban spaces. To me it seems that more than in neat and regulated centres, a genuine, idiosyncratic experiencing is possible in urban wastelands, nameless strips, under utilised structures, 'contingent' backsides (Wilson 2001) and 'empty' spaces that fall outside one's mental map (Bauman 2001). Strange actions and clandestine disuses, as well as carnivals, events and urban art, may momentarily offer different and surprising experiences.

Throwing meaning in unlikely sites, creates ephemeral attachments or deeply felt moments that I call 'weak place'. Weak place is the moment of signification. The idea entails a redefinition of the notion of place so that it is not closed and physically bounded but rather open and porous, more about experiential nearness than physical proximity. These experiences are idiosyncratic, weak places singular. This means that the experiences cannot be shared. Weak places remain private, and one cannot easily 'operationalise' them in the public realm, in planning debates, for example. Only the coming-together, juxtaposition and collision of many people and experiences – the resulting conflict – lends weak places a public form. Conflict gathers and ties together a tensioned community of those 'who care', becoming a producer of socially significant public urban space. In conflict the personal, ephemeral, hardly tangible feelings may gain momentum and political significance.

I have discovered the importance of the link between experience and conflict in the context of aesthetic contemplation in architectural and urban settings. It concerns material spaces that can be locally felt, walked upon, touched, smelled and seen, and thus spaces that can also in principle be designed (in the sense that design can define the local conditions of experience). However, I believe that the links between personal signification, attachment, care and action play a role in a wide variety of conflicts and for different kinds of 'public'. While 'non-local' values, political inclinations and solidarity to a group do inspire devoted action, a personal, local trigger is also important. Therefore, if urban conflict in the Fordist era was largely played out along institutionalised lines, with organised actors and clearly definable antagonistic positions, now urban struggles are fragmented, particular and differentiated. The disputed frontiers cross all spheres of life and society, including feelings and knowledge (Lefebvre 1991 [1974]: 418). Today's conflicts do not follow class boundaries, but rather produce new and surprising societal divisions and *ad hoc* coherences. Mark Gottdiener has argued that contemporary urban conflicts would be played out between 'growth' and 'no-growth' (Gottdiener 1994 [1985]: 165). They are against the lack of urban life forms in the city (Schmid 2005: 153), against experiential poverty and limits of appropriation. Individual activists, conservation movements and protest groups thus get, in a new sense, a constitutive role in the production of 'urbanness' and public urban space. Important from the point of view of architecture and planning is that conflicts are embedded in a specific site or spatial structure, as the case of Makasiinit (Chapter 8) shows. The notion of 'quasi-object' suggests that none of the actors can exclusively claim such site but nevertheless they all have a stake in it.

Urban Events Producing Space

Since the mid 1980s, Helsinki has witnessed a remarkable urban cultural change. Together with new sites and forms of consumption and leisure, new cultural institutions and new local media (Cantell 1999, Eskola and Ruoppila 1999, Mäenpää 1993, 2000), the re-appropriation of the city's central public urban spaces has been an important arena and facilitator of the change. Entirely new public urban spaces, taking unprecedented forms, have also been created. *Urban events* have had a key role in the process of public space creation. From the Night of the Arts (since 1989) to the Human Wall demonstration in Makasiinit (2000), events have brought something new: a new reading of space, a new use or a novel vision of the future. Events have nurtured the Other.

After pioneering soundings and experiments in the late 1980s and early 1990s, two major events in Senate Square, the Total Balalaika Show (1993) and its tenth anniversary the Global Balalaika Show (2003), roughly mark the beginning and end of a period of establishing a new use-culture of public urban spaces. During these years, Finland recovered from the worst economic depression since the 1930s, joined the EU and the European monetary union. Helsinki searched for a new, independent role as the gateway to the post-1989 East, became the global window of IT led futures, celebrated as the European City of Culture in 2000 and again fell back into relative invisibility in the first years of the new millennium. The decade from 1993 saw a wave of urban cultural innovation, followed by an inability to nurture further innovation and build on it. During these years, several urban events were important with respect to the production of public space. Besides the Total Balalaika Show and the City of European Culture project, Charles Landry, a consultant who analysed the 'urban creativity' of Helsinki, names the Night of the Arts, the Forces of Light and the Huvila tent of the Helsinki Festival (Landry 1998: 65–79). Timo Cantell argues for the importance of events in changing the public perception of the city and in offering glimpses of a utopia of a European city, a 'would-be Helsinki' (Cantell 1999: 90, 187–9).

My interest in events dates back to an empirical pilot study in summer 1997. This study suggested that specially arranged urban events are, by their sheer number, an important part of Helsinki summer culture in streets and parks. According to the observations of the documentation tours[1], the events were not an exception but an important factor strongly characterising the otherwise somewhat quiet and conventional use of urban spaces in Helsinki. During each observation session, there was at least one major public event taking place, from rock and skating parties to the Naisten Kymppi women's jogging event and the DTM car race (Lehtovuori 2001: 68). Clearly, the event policy of the City of Helsinki, formulated in the Development Scenario of the 1992 General Master Plan, had already succeeded in the mid 1990s. At present, the number of urban events is large, and their popularity is still growing. The city centre spawns beer tents for collective viewing of sports events. There are wine festivals, samba carnivals, mass religious gatherings and annual snow boarding events, many of which attract tens of thousands of viewers and participants. Currently, Helsinki is updating its policy. It will draft a special 'events strategy', which fully recognises the role of events in the economic development.

Appropriation vs Domination of Space

When participating in events, experiencing their atmosphere, observing other people and sounding my own feelings, I realised that events not only take place in public urban space, but *partake in its production*. In events, however, the production of public urban space was something very different from the production of architectonic space I was somewhat familiar with through my education. Various personal, momentary and invisible aspects felt important: the production of space was about feelings, surprises, new points of view, sudden changes of perception, new sites or places to be found and visited, new uses and new meanings one could attach to those sites. Sometimes the new practices or practice-based visions led to conflicts with the ideas and points of view held in the official city planning. For the ephemeral and quite complex processes of space-creation, the understanding of public urban space in architecture and planning seemed to be distant, external and even counter-productive. A dialectic of domination, appropriation and diversion (cf. Lefebvre 1991 [1974]: 167) was taking place.

However, events were not a-spatial, but had their own spatial patterns and locational logics. I came to the conclusion that, with regard to the subtle phenomena of events, the main problem in architecture and planning's space-conception is that space is conceived of as something separate both from the meanings people give to it and the actual uses and practices taking place 'in space'. Despite a rich

---

1   Documentation was conducted by Pekka Lehtinen, Mikko Mälkki and the author.

texture of relational space-theorising, planning and architectural practitioners understand public urban space predominantly as a visualisable stage or stage-set, not as a socially rich entity or realm, even less a process. Space is objectified – and sometimes even subjectified, so that architects can claim that space has a 'will', with themselves as its priests and oracles.

Furthermore, the objectification makes it impossible to grasp the classical idea of public space as a political constellation and a vehicle of a specific community. This aspect has become increasingly complex and contested with the rise of consumerism, electronic media and the horizon of a global community, so that it is possible to argue that urban space has fundamentally lost its role as a political arena. Even though there is no way back to the classical world, I believe that this view can also be proved to be mistaken in the present societal condition. For example, eventual public spaces and their tensioned communities can influence urban agenda setting (*Shadow City* 2004).

Rethinking space, place, event and conflict, I wish to formulate a theory about public urban space, which would do justice to my observations and introspections about the production of public urban space in Helsinki. My aim is to compile a theory, which would include physical space, its use and, as the most difficult aspect, the personal, singular moments of invention and existentially important experiences that are indispensable elements of the lived urban space. The theory could be called *the experiential approach to the production of public urban space*. At its core is an effort to address in a novel, dialectical way the relations between the physical, social and mental aspects of space.

The Space-concept in Planning

The focus on the theory of space reflects my belief that the shortcomings of the planning and design of public urban space cannot be solved on the level of institutions or on the level of an agency (cf. Giddens 1984: 24, Dear and Häkli 1998: 60). Rather, a relevant criticism needs to address the structural level, which in this work entails re-thinking the conceptual foundations of the practice of planning and urban design. I consider the way space and its public aspect are conceptualised, with the epistemological ramifications of the conceptualisation, to be the key from which to start. My hypothesis is that while the theories of space in architecture, planning and other space-related sciences have advanced, the relationship between the physical, social and mental aspects of space has been articulated inadequately, hampering the application of the new theories in developing design practices.

In finding a new approach, my main source is the idea of dialectics of space, proposed by Henri Lefebvre in *The Production of Space* (1991 [1974]). The new conceptualisation has certain unique characteristics, the most important of which are: 1) space always appears dynamic and processual; 2) space cannot be conceived of generally, but the conceptualisation is always specific, in a society, site and moment in time; 3) the conceptualisation is able to deal with the radical qualitative difference between the various 'elements' or 'moments' of social space, without conflating them to a single plane of representation; and 4) providing the opportunity to think the not-yet-existing, the Becoming is as important as describing the existing things.

The experiential approach provides a transdiscursive and relational theory of public urban space. I will show that, firstly, by introducing the notions of experience and conflict in the theory of public urban space and, secondly, by treating them as 'dynamists' of the theory, it is possible to understand the production of public urban space better than with the current theories. Instead of abstractly classifying different aspects of space or assuming structural similarities between them, the dynamic theory of space entails a dialectic understanding of the relations between its physical, social and mental aspects. Only after such work on the level of the structures of thinking is it possible to evaluate and reform the planning and design practice – a task, which I hint at in the last chapters of the book.

The need for my undertaking is underlined by the surprising lack of a well-founded and relevant theory of space in the disciplines of architecture, urban design and planning. Dictionaries of planning and architecture[2] do not even contain the entry 'space'! Madanipour states that the absence of the term 'space' from sociology reference books may be understandable, 'but its absence from architectural reference books is quite noticeable' (Madanipour 1996: 7). In much of architectural and urban research the question of space is understood as the visual and volumetric qualities of buildings, hence mainly described and studied in impressionistic, photographic, hand-gestural or poetic terms. The structure, syntax or morphology of space in relation to social structure have only recently been paid sufficiently serious attention. Even though much used in education and criticism, the notion of space is far from clear. The logic of its complex constituents in urban situations, in particular, should be clarified.

Methodology: Stone, Paper or Scissors

The effort to combine in one theory personal, momentary feelings and insights with other material, which appear to be variably shared and 'provable', warrants a careful methodological consideration. Essentially, the work originates from my own experiences. I am acutely aware that an experience – what is 'right now' – cannot be conceptualised, but rather conceptualisation always comes 'after', it is

---

2   E.g. *Oxford Dictionary of Architecture* by J.S. Curl; the German *Handwörterbuch der Raumforschung und Raumordnung*; and the concise *Arkitekturtermer* by J.T. Ahlstrand. Dictionaries of sociology lack the entry 'space', too. The *Deutsch-Schwedishes Handbuch der Planungsbegriffe* (2001) is the exception of those handbooks I could consult. It does define space, stating that in planning 'space' connotes the areas that people inhabit or influence in some other way. These spaces are characterised by economic, social or political content (p. 278).

in the past tense. This leads to the seemingly paradoxical situation that the theory I am proposing *cannot be a conceptualisation of public urban space as something*, as an idea, a thing or a collection of properties. I will not be able to represent (name, describe, classify) my object of study, stating that 'public urban space is A'. While the theory cannot be a representation, I hope it can provide the reader with a grounded 'intellectual strategy' or 'approach'.

Benjamin, Heidegger and Vattimo are among thinkers who have wrestled with the problem of presenting the non-presentable. They have explored intellectual and literary methods, such as 'dialectical image', 'literary montage' and 'weak thought', that try to do that difficult feat. In this work, I utilise those tools in a rather limited way, nevertheless aiming at 'transdiscursive' or possibly 'rhizomatic' writing (Shields 1996, Hillier 2007), at a mixed and multiple text where the middle is foregrounded instead of the beginning and end. I use three types of text: 1) personal notes, memoirs or 'micrologies' about emotionally strong, important moments; 2) 'excursions' or cases, which represent observations in a traditional way (also images belong to this group); and 3) reflective theoretical text, which I would like to see as a diagram, as the 'mover' or 'intellectual machine' I set in motion. While Helsinki and its evolving public event venues are the focal point of theorising, illustrative parallel phenomena can be found in most cities of the developed West. Because I spent 2001 in Manchester and several shorter periods in Berlin, I will sporadically refer to the harbour reuse in Salford Quays, the renovation of Manchester city centre or Berlin's recreated squares Leipziger Platz and Pariser Platz, as well as events, club nights and solitary wastelands in those cities.

An effort to approach and question the elusive 'boundary' between singular and shared, directly lived and represented, inward-looking and communicable weaves together the moments and cases I discuss. All cases represent a change in social space, a moment suggesting the possibility of meaningful public urban space. All cases are, therefore, about Becoming. Because I develop new theory, I limit my interest to situations and moments where something valuable for the new can be found. By juxtaposing the three types of text, my intention is to open up opportunities for event-like knowledge creation for the reader.[3] Its metaphor might be the ancient game 'paper, stone, scissors', where the players simultaneously hit a table with either a clenched fist, flat open hand or fist with two fingers open, respectively signifying stone, paper and scissors. Paper beats stone because paper can wrap it; scissors beat paper because they can cut it in two, and stone beats scissors because scissors become blunt if one tries to cut stone with them. The micrologies are the 'stones', the representations of facts are 'paper' and the theoretical diagram provides the 'scissors'. These three elements constitute a 'game', process or dialectic, which is the eventual text, the

---

3   The epistemological status of transdiscursive writing is not entirely clear. My effort is to move away from the centuries-long 'perspectival' tradition of thinking towards the emerging 'inspective' mode, which entails that the separation between knower, what is known and the techniques of knowing in-between the two would dissolve (Varto 2000).

non-objectified theory and the specific process of producing a public urban space somewhere, sometime. To continue the metaphor, stone could stand for the non-reflective 'spatial practices' of Lefebvre's *dialectique de triplicité*, paper for his 'representations of space' and scissors for the 'spaces of representation' (Lefebvre 1991 [1974]: 33–9). However, the construction is in movement, and while all the constituents are always needed, any of them may take any position in Lefebvre's diagram. The structurally dominant representations of space may wrap the stone-practice, but likewise the stone can be interpreted as the Moment, the singular Other or the 'weak place', which shifts the game and overcomes the dominant, abstract representation.

I believe that the boundary between lived and represented presents an important challenge for architecture and planning. A new understanding about the 'tools' to work on this boundary may open opportunities to reform planning, think the professional practice of planning in new terms. Clearly, introspection of one's directly lived experience produces unique, irreplaceable knowledge. But how can such knowledge be used in planning? How, as a planner, to be subtler towards individual experiences? How to support soft phenomena? In the proposed inspective mode, the object-ness of knowledge and, therefore, its transferability are placed in question. The collapse of the distance between knower and the 'object of knowledge' foregrounds action, doing something in the world one is in – or immersed. Like the studies on events, the design projects are an integral part of my being in the world. This is the methodological reason to refer to my own design work in the last chapters. In a sense, my own work provides an extended set of cases. Furthermore, the above-formulated hypothesis about the need to address the space-conception of architecture and planning before proposing changes in the institutions or practices cannot be proved or disproved in one study. While my focus is on the structures of thinking, I would, nevertheless, like to make an opening from the theory to the practice and to test aspects of the theory. This is the practical and rhetorical reason for including analysis and reflections of a selection of my own projects and interventions. I believe that the lessons drawn from those tests hint about the relevance of the developed theoretical approach.

Notes about Terminology

'Space' is a key term, which will be discussed, defined and redefined throughout the thesis. Because Lefebvre is an important authority in my work, I want at this early stage to note that I have chosen to use simply 'space' as the equivalent of the French '*l'espace*', even though there is also an argument for 'spatialisation' (e.g. Shields 1999: 153–7).

Because my focus is on the structures of thinking, the three terms, which define the area or discipline of the study, namely 'architecture', 'urban design' and 'urban planning', are treated as a single continuum. I do not emphasise the institutional and practical difference that developed between architecture and planning in the

United States and the United Kingdom in the latter part of the twentieth century, because with regards to the notion of 'space' those disciplines share a very similar understanding. While an architect may be concerned with the 3D composition of an architectural object and a planner with a different complex including societal processes, urban economies, party politics and users' preferences, they both imagine space rather similarly as something visualisable and mappable. Leonie Sandercock, for example, claims that 'the articles of faith of these apparently divergent city-building professions [planning and architecture] … bear remarkable similarities' (Sandercock 1998: 23). Furthermore, in the countries of continental Europe and Scandinavia the division is less clear also on the level of praxis: architecture and planning are commonly taught in the same faculties and an architect may design both buildings and cities. In Finland, urban planning has throughout the post-war decades been practiced as physical planning and design (cf. Taylor 1998: 5). Even though there are some developments towards the Anglo-American differentiation, in Finnish 'urban design' and 'urban planning' are both covered by a single word, '*kaupunkisuunnittelu*'. The word '*rakennustaide*' (like the German '*Baukunst*') may refer to aesthetically merited buildings and urban plans alike.

Outline of the Theoretical Construction (Parts 1–3)

Each part is divided into two chapters, the first concerning the theory of space in general and the second public urban space in particular. In Part 1, I discuss the currently dominant visual paradigm in understanding the city, as well as its critiques in social sciences, planning and urban design. Maps and statistics are the main tools, facilitating the mastering of the space-related knowledge. The ordered visual representation, which I call Concept City, is often taken as real, leading to the belief that cities and their public urban spaces can be designed with no deeper problem. Because of this structural reason, the lived city and the many, diverging and conflicting urban experiences become excluded from the planning and design processes. Public urban space is understood either as primarily physical or as primarily social phenomenon, but the links between those realms remain obscure.

In Part 2, I start to build my main theoretical argument. I assert that instead of a lump of matter or a mental category, only, space should be understood as socially produced. I discuss the elements of social space, with emphasis on how the relations between qualitatively different aspects can be conceptualised. I then move to theory of place. Meaning and place cannot be separated. As noted above, relational place-theory views place as the moment of signification. This notion I call 'weak place'. Place becomes personal, temporary and changing. The singular place-experience is triggered by a material condition, but it entails feelings, memories and knowledge. Place is open and porous, and it offers itself as a possible centre or nexus of the physical, social and mental aspects of social space.

In Part 3, I bridge the seeming gap between the individuality and singularity of place-experience and the public, shared aspect of social space. Social space and its production are best understood as a dialectical process, a spatio-temporal dialectic. Social space consists of points of dialectical centrality. Public space emerges in the conflicts between different lived place-experiences, collisions of weak places, which may constitute a temporary community. A public urban space is understood to be a specific, time-bound assembly of qualitatively different elements, a suspended conflict. Physical and architectonic space, too, may take prominent roles as the 'other' in the dynamics of spatial dialectics.

Taken together, the Parts 1–3 form a succession of ideas, from 'paper' to 'stone' and to 'scissors'; or from representation of space to the singular moments of lived space and then to the diagram of the synchronic dialectic, which is the 'dynamist' of the elements of theory. This tensioned diagram provides an alternative – transdiscursive, case-specific and time-bound – way to conceptualise the links between physical, mental and social aspects of space.

Outline of the Empirical Work (Parts 4 and 5)

In Part 4, I report my findings about post-1989 urban events in Helsinki. The key observation is that in the Helsinki inner city, urban events tend to be located centrally but anyhow to spaces, which have a specific symbolic or visual fringe character. This observation about the sources of 'event potential' is confirmed with space syntax modelling of Helsinki. Senate Square is the main event venue, but the old railway warehouses were even more emblematic in this respect before their demolition to make way for the Music Hall scheme. My main interests are, how events can be the 'other', the third element in spatial dialectics, how they can untap urban symbolisms and are able to change them, hi-jacking established meanings attached to spaces. In Chapter 8, I follow the appropriation and diversion of the old railway warehouses, usually called Makasiinit. Between 1998–2002, Makasiinit triggered an influential planning conflict, which opened a new kind of political arena. In the light of spatial dialectics, Makasiinit can be seen as a point of centrality, a carrier of a community and an emerging public urban space.

If Part 4 is a 'game', where paper, stone and scissors perform their tricks in the production of public urban space in events, Part 5 can be seen as the 'limits of the game' in the professional field. In it, I elaborate on new design and planning practices in the light of the developed theory of space. I present a set of 'theses' for the experiential approach and reflect upon projects. I wish to establish a clear analogy between theory and practice. If space is multiple, coming-together, tensioned and event-like, neither thinking nor acting can grasp it in its totality, but the relationship remains 'weak'. Theory can provide new ways to dissect the world, which make new insights possible. Likewise, design can make oblique cuts to the urban potential, actualising something of its possibilities. Space can be understood and acted on dialectically. The primary point of experiential urban design is not to advance better representations of space, a discourse 'on' space. Rather, it is to suggest that planning and design might freshly 'partake' in dialectical discourses 'of' space.

PART 1
Concept City

Chapter 1
Space Distanced and Objectified

Landing Area for UFOs

Vallila, Helsinki. Next to our then home, the huge classisist Hauhontie building, there used to be a small park. Rather the park was a neglected strip of bushes, and the only thing about it worth mentioning was that down and outs liked to hang around there. One spring, the City's Park Department decided to renew the park. The rationale was to beautify the neighbourhood and also to drive out the alcoholics – which was not openly said. Soon the work started. The land was levelled, new earth was brought in, paths were lined and gravelled, most old trees were felled and some new ones were planted. A few slices of granite were installed here and there, with a French public toilet on the most visible corner next to the tram stop. The trimmed strip was given a new name Hauhonpuisto (Hauho Park), and a wooden block in which the name was carved was erected. The public space was supposed to be ready!

Right under our window happened to be the climax of the clumsy compilation. In the middle of an obscure grass area, in between the French toilet, a turning rail for the trams, and a blue, heavily tagged air quality control box, the city's workers laid a stone circle about ten metres in diameter. It was surrounded by a handful of vandalism-proof benches, a few over-sized trash bins, and a bed of pink roses. Only in the autumn, when evenings got dark, I realised its clou*: on the perimeter of the circle there were four low expensive-looking light poles. Their light was very sharp, making the granite circle and the benches unapproachable. The place was like a questioning room in a police station, and, indeed, even the down and outs could no longer use the benches in the evenings. The hideous creation bothered me so much that I thought to buy spray paint to paint the glass domes of the lamps matt grey.*

Gradually I calmed down, I got 'used' to it. My wife and I tried to find the humour in it, and because the only function we could imagine for the place was cosmic and unintelligible, we started to call it the landing area for UFOs.

Helsinki 1997

***

This small incident in a not-that-important neighbourhood in Helsinki serves to open my treatise in relational theory of public urban space. Firstly, I am interested in architects' space-conception and its effects when designs are realised. In Hauhontie, the park design itself clearly was a 'UFO'. The design had been done blindly with respect to the site, its history, as well as the present social life and the cultural prospects of the neighbourhood. Despite good intentions to beautify, the new Hauho Park did not represent a successful production of public urban space. The result was far from the oft-stated ideals of public urban space as, for example, a nice oasis or a social meeting point for a mixed audience. It was a missed opportunity socially, experientially and aesthetically.

Another reading of the incident is political-economical or 'structural'. While the designers most likely would not acknowledge it, the new park was meant to clean up the neighbourhood and to push unwanted people elsewhere. Both the city and at least some of the local residents supported that, because the cleaning is believed to increase property values and lessen crime and the fear of it. The project was a small piece in a large pattern of post-industrial urban change, which entails socio-economic shifts in many neighbourhoods. Vallila, the quintessential working-class area, is slowly becoming – if not hip and trendy – at least a somewhat culturally valued middle-class inner-city area. In this context, the 'spatial interdictions' (Flusty 1994) of the park design can be seen as far echoes from the 'City of Quartz' (Davis 1990).

The example of Hauho Park is not an anecdotal exception, but rather a rule. Specimens of new public space design, which arouse feelings of falseness, blandness, and displacement, are common across the developed West. There seems to be a pattern of the expert planning and design being unable to recognise, never mind accept, experiential qualities, users' practices and subtle symbolic characteristics of the urban environment they are operating in. Likewise, key structural forces remain unaccounted and 'unseen'. As a result, amazing, rich situations and surprising potentials are neglected, and the production of public urban space becomes a dry exercise of implanting stylistic reifications, pieces of generic modernism or pseudo-historicism.

Fire and Water, or the Mutually Repelling Elements of Architects' Space-conception

The myopic space-conception of practising architects, urban designers and planners is an important factor, underpinning this state of affairs. In those practices, space is first and foremost thought to be material. This naïve realistic idea entails that space 'is'; it is out there, naturally, all the time. Secondly, space is seen through the grid of Euclidean coordinates as an endless, three-dimensional continuum. This intellectual device makes space seem translucent and intelligible. Bernard Tschumi condenses this combination of two ideas, saying that architects tend to view space as a 'three-dimensional lump of matter' (Tschumi 1996: 30). Architecture and urban design are then conceived of as modulating the postulated formless Ur-Matter, making it visible through differences (inside-outside, light-shadow), cultivating and dignifying it.[1] The visible space of architectural incarnations is represented in maps, aerial photographs, perspective drawings, axonometries and façade projections – and more often than not those geometric representations are taken for real.

Despite its seducing simplicity and ostensible clarity, this space-conception is inherently confused. The geometric, three-dimensional space is *absolute*. Therefore it does not depend on particular manifestations. Material space, on the other hand, is *particular*. Material space is always *a* space, a specific, unique space. This contradiction could be circumscribed by understanding 'materiality' as a category, as a mental thing.[2] An architectural object or urban design would then consist of material substance and non-material form. In the mainstream thinking this is not the case, though, as the quotation from Ching below will show. Confusion also resides in the idea of visibility. The metaphorical visibility, the idea that space is intelligible and whatever there is in space can be known, assumes that space is translucent. But visibility in the real world can only be attained through the opaqueness of materials. Taken together, the elements of this common space-conception are like fire and water. The ideas of absolute and particular space repel each other, as do the ideas of translucent and opaque space.

Below I will elaborate on the problems of the visibility of urban space, as well as Lefebvre's notion of 'double illusion' of translucency and opacity. Now it suffices to say that in *urban situations* such an understanding of space is glaringly inadequate and impossible to sustain.

During the twentieth century, the theory of space has, fortunately, developed a great deal from the perspectival Enlightenment origins, such as the Euclidean continuum and the one-eyed abstract perceiver of objects in this continuum. The notion of space has received various interpretations, which reflect epistemology, ideologies and the conception of the world of their time (Norberg-Schulz 1971, van de Ven 1978, Stenros 1992, Madanipour 1996, Varto 2000). While there are distinct differences in the space-conception in architecture, planning and other sciences of space, a clear resonance between the theoretical developments can be traced, leading from absolute to relational space-conception.

---

1   It is striking how much this idea resembles the description of Genesis in the Bible.

2   Philosophy is clear on that distinction. The definition of 'space' in the *Oxford Dictionary of Philosophy* starts: 'The classical questions include: is space real, or is it some kind of mental construct, or artefact of our ways of perceiving and thinking? Is it 'substantival' or purely 'relational?' (*Oxford Dictionary of Philosophy*, 1994). Psychology seems bet for the mental construct: 'Fundamentally, space is an abstraction, a geometric characterisation of a system of location of m objects in n dimensions' (*Penguin Dictionary of Psychology*, 1985).

From Absolute to Relational Space-conception

In geography, space is much debated, and therefore the theoretical positions are rather clear. Jouni Häkli, the Finnish geographer, chronicles the notion of space in 20th century geography as follows: 'in the era of regional geography space was conceived as *absolute* – either as position (coordinates), distance (kilometres) or regional framework (for example, administrative areas) ... [With the "quantitative revolution" in the 1950s and 1960s] absolute space received *relative* space as its counterpart ... Space was no longer the stable foundation of reality, but rather its meaning depended on the object of research ... At a general level, as a geographical umbrella concept, space described the geographical reality in which phenomena, objects and people moved and formed various spatial patterns following certain spatial laws. Space was mostly imagined as a homogenous surface, on which different spatial systems acted and organised themselves' (Häkli 1999: 51–4, transl. PL). Furthermore, with the rise of human geography from the 1970s onwards, '... the interpretation of space as a relative (but basically still physical) dimension was accompanied by the notion of *social space*. Space is social and inseparable from society, not a mere physical structure or dimension. In philosophical debates, this notion is called *relational space*' (ibid.: 81–2, Schulman 1990, Harvey 1996, Koskela 1994).

The relationality and complexity of social space can be viewed from two main angles. Firstly, it concerns the personal experience and signification. The renowned human geographer Yi-Fu Tuan valorises the multidimensionality of human spaces by comparing human works to the constructions of animals: 'Compared with the termite's skyscraper, the lean-tos and thatched mud shelters of the human being look crude. If humans nonetheless claim a certain superiority, the claim must rest on grounds other than architectural achievement. It must rest on awareness' (Tuan 1977: 101–2). Human space is hardly ever purely material, but mixed and infused with symbolism and meanings. Secondly, social space is relational in terms of societal structures. Political power and economical relations are invisible but they do affect and indeed produce both the physical and symbolic space. Space is an instrument of power and, therefore, a site of struggle (e.g. Harvey 1973, Gottdiener 1985). The latter point makes clear that space cannot be separated from time: space is socially produced over time. Massey (2005: 18) insightfully states that 'time and space must be thought together ... it influences how we think of both terms'. Time and space are neither 'competing categories', as the postmodern geographers argue (cf. Soja 1989, Dear 2000), nor an undifferentiated 'fourdimensionality' or 'space-time'. 'Conceiving space as a static slice through time, as a representation, as a closed system and so forth are all ways of taming it' (Massey 2005: 59). Relational space is characterised by openness and lack of any essential foundation – an idea which foregrounds negotiations and conflicts as constituents of space.

A corresponding change in the notion of space can be seen in the field of architectural theory. Many textbooks and handouts still contain an outdated 'positivist' assumption, holding that space is a homogeneous, material continuum, which may be modulated and articulated by architecture. F.D.K. Ching, for example, in his much-used *Architecture: Form, Space and Order* states that '[s] pace constantly encompasses our being. Through the volume of space, we move, see forms and objects, hear sounds, feel breezes, smell the fragrances of a flower garden in full bloom. It is a material substance like wood or stone. Yet it is inherently formless. Its visual form, quality of light, dimensions and scale, depend totally on its boundaries as defined by elements of form. As space begins to be captured, enclosed, molded, and organized by the elements of form, architecture comes into being' (Ching 1979: 108). As noted above, this quotation both summarises and confuses two main ideas about space in architecture. Firstly, there is the 'formless' Euclidean/Newtonian space, which is confusedly understood both as material substance (like the ancient 'aether') and as imagined, abstract and therefore by necessity non-material absolute space. This confusion leads to the second, namely the contention that 'elements of form' would be material. In passing, it is seductive to speculate that it is precisely this theoretical double confusion that explains the striving of modern architecture (and many present architectural currents, too) to 'de-materialise' walls and other parts of buildings and simplify their form so that they satisfy the dream of abstract and translucent but nevertheless material reality.

The confusion notwithstanding, the resulting material and particular 'architectural' space is nothing if not experienced by someone. This is the *Raumgefühl* of the German aesthetics (cf. van de Ven 1978: 90). The experience or feeling already starts to relativise the imagined absolute space. Interpretations through phenomenology, semiotics and urban history have drawn in a more complex picture of the 'man' as a thinking, feeling and reflective subject, as well as 'culture', that is, people as members of a certain culture and society and built artefacts as the concrete, collective manifestations of that culture (e.g. Rossi 1982 [1966]). I take as an example Christopher Norberg-Schulz, the phenomenologist, who presents a hierarchy of five notions of space: '… the pragmatic space of physical action, the perceptual space of immediate orientation, the existential space, which forms man's stable image of his environment, the cognitive space of the physical world and the abstract space of pure logical relations' (Norberg-Schulz 1971: 11). From the basis of this historical construction of concepts, he criticises theoreticians, who tend to reduce architectural space to a Euclidean, mathematical space or to an individual perception only. '[Bruno Zevi's] space concept seems to be a combination of action space and Euclidean space, as he says: "Architecture is like a large hollow structure into which man enters and around which he moves"' (ibid.: 12). According to Norberg-Schulz, this is not enough. It is necessary to consider space as a relatively stable and culturally constructed relationship between man and his environment (cf. relational space), as the existential dimension of Being.

In the Finnish context, Anne Stenros has developed a relational space theory, which understands architectural space as a system of three 'levels', those of perception, memory and 'structure' (Stenros 1992). I will discuss Stenros' argument in detail in Chapter 4. Here it suffices to say that she understands the creation of a meaningful space (a space-experience) in a distinctly relational manner, so that space never is fixed or absolute but dependent on the perceiver, her personal history and cultural context. As a development from to Norberg-Schultz, this leads to viewing space-experience as changing and time-dependent.

In urban planning and planning theory, the shift from absolute to relative space-conception was reflected in the emergence of the 'systems view' of cities and regions in the 1960s. The systems view replaced the physical and morphological understanding of cities with a dynamic conceptualisation, stressing that cities are systems of interrelated activities in flux (Taylor 1998: 159). The relational and social understanding of space entered planning theory with the debate around various Marxist analyses of planning in the 1970s (e.g. Castells [1972] 1977, Harvey 1973). Mark Gottdiener in *The Social Production of Urban Space* (1985) synthesised Marxist views, proposing the 'sociospatial approach' to urban analysis. Based on Henri Lefebvre's theory about the production of social space (Lefebvre 1991 [1974]), Gottdiener articulated the Marxist perspective in terms of the 'second circuit of capital' in real-estate, the 'multi-centered metropolitan regions' as the object of analysis and the new, fluctuating antagonisms between 'growth networks' and citizen groups, which he claims have largely replaced the traditional antagonisms between the relatively stable classes. Finally, the currently popular idea of planning as 'communicative action' (e.g. Forester 1989, Healey 1997, Sager 1994, Staffans 2004) seemingly takes as givens the complex social nature of space and the urban process, as well as the need to always keep in mind the political and economic context of planning as an important structural factor behind the actors of the planning process. From this perspective, space is not a pre-existing stable thing, but rather both space and place can be understood as *events*. They are performative entities – coming-together of various human and nonhuman trajectories and elements (Massey 2005: 140) – requiring negotiations.

These short examples show that there are similarities in the developments and emphasis of the notion of space between different arts and sciences of space. In the course of the 20th century, both in geography, architecture and planning, a development towards a more holistic notion of space may be traced, shifting the conceptualisation from absolute to relative (space-movement or space-perceiver) and to relational (space-society or space-culture). However, the new theoretical ideas have been slow in coming to inform the *practices* of planning, urban design and architecture.

The Problems of Applying Relational Theories in Planning Practices

The hallmark of relational understanding of urban space is complexity. In relational theories, there tend to be many elements, aspects, moments, levels, or axis of analysis. This complexity is justified, and reflects the complexity of the object of theorising. In that sense, relational theories about space offer a promise of 'better' and more 'true' theory of space than absolute or relative accounts[3] (Byrne 2001: 9–12).

However, there is a serious problem related to the complexity of relational conceptions of space. Because relational theories are difficult to operationalise, they may seem irrelevant concerning the practices. This often leads to a situation, where the practice of planning and urban space design is totally ignorant of the relevant and up-to-date theory of space and planning. Taylor, for example, notes that already with the introduction of the abstract systems view of urban space[4] in the late 1960s, 'a gap developed between planning theory and the practice of town planning at the local level' (Taylor 1998: 63). So, the everyday planning practitioners in towns and cities, producing development plans, dealing with building permits and valuing urban designs, did not care about new theory, or were even hostile towards it. They continued their work in the older tradition of physical, design-oriented urban planning, with its unproblematised, absolute space-conception.

The Marxist account of planning has also largely remained on the level of critique, with little influence on planning practice. This is partly because Marxist texts *were* stark critiques, and left little positive room for the planner. So, according to Sandercock, the practice-oriented planners and educators in the 1980s denied the relevance of the Marxist analysis of planning and urban space. The lasting value of the political economy model of planning would be in criticism, and models for action should be looked for elsewhere (Sandercock 1998: 92).

The distance between the theoretical space-concept and the conceptualisation underpinning the practice can also be found in the communicative idea of planning. The theory of communicative planning acknowledges the relationality of space, the fact that different people may have fundamentally different views and that those views may reflect particular social spaces. However, because the focus in communicative planning theory is either in the ideal-type of rational communication or in the actual negotiations between actors, space as a concern has been sidetracked and left non-thought. Therefore, the results of communication 'fall back' to physical planners' habitual map space, carried by the traditional ways to represent space, such as maps and site plans. Final decisions of the communicative process are made in a non-relational episteme and space, which, I believe, is an important reason for the frustrations and difficulties of public participation in planning (cf. Häkli 2002).

---

3   The goodness of a single theory depends on the particular interest of knowledge. In certain specific contexts relative and even absolute conceptions may be 'the best'.

4   The systems view of planning is a 'substantive' theory, addressing the object of planning activity. Therefore it is correct to say that the systems view is a theory about urban space rather that the activity of planning *per se*. See Andreas Faludi's *Planning Theory* (1973) for the distinction between 'substantive' and 'procedural' theory, also in Taylor (1998: 66).

To take an example, the work of project managers and city architects in Finland at present is very much about negotiations, consulting, seminars, public meetings and discussions in the media – so much so that the practical role is at times not far from that of 'action planner' (Taylor 1998: 117). The 'real work' of the planner, however, is still primarily understood in terms of drawing plans. In an interview, one architect-planner in the Helsinki City Planning Office complained that 'no-one draws anything anymore' (Lehtovuori 2002b: 23). This dissatisfaction hints towards the fact that professional planners' space-conception does not fit their actual work.

By and large, the ideal-types of planning practice, such as rational-comprehensive, incremental, advocacy, communicative, radical political economy and radical model of planning (Sandercock 1998: 85–104, Taylor 1998), each entail differing ideas about knowledge production, legitimacy of planning and also space, but for a number of reasons the actual practices tend to fall back on an old, simple or 'common sense' understanding of urban space. Let us examine the characteristics of this stubborn space-conception.

The Representation of Space Taken as the Real

> But a map of a geography is no more that geography – or that space – than a painting of a pipe is a pipe. (Massey 2005: 106)

In order to operate, urban planning and the design of public urban space must conceptualise urban space in a manner appropriate to their goals. The structures, institutions and agency of planning are mutually interdependent[5] (Giddens 1984). Therefore, '[p]lanning does not take place in an urban reality that is transparent to the planners and independent of planning, but in the reality of planning that is formed according to planning practices' (Dear and Häkli 1998: 63, transl. PL). Lefebvre uses the term 'true space' about this substitute of the lived reality: 'This *conceived* space is thought by those who make use of it to be *true*, despite the fact – or perhaps because of the fact – that it is geometrical ...' (Lefebvre 1991 [1974]: 361). This 'reality of planning' or 'reality of architectural design' has three interlinked constituents. In elementary terms, the assumption is that: 1) space can be represented; 2) space can be seen; and, as a derivative of the first two, 3) space can be designed.

Firstly, a site, a city or a region is viewed from 'above'. The architect/planner is distanced from it, and the city (region) is thought to be a totality. Likewise, a single urban design project often becomes a 'world' in itself. The arbitrary, contingent boundaries of a project, a new neighbourhood unit, say, or a square renovation, become the boundaries of both knowledge-gathering and form-giving,

---

5   Below, I will also utilise the Giddensian structure-agency idea in treating production of space in events.

repeatedly leading to less than ideal planning and design solutions. This element is epistemological; it is an assumption of knowability and an assumption that the planner-knower is independent of the object of knowledge (Sandercock 1998: 61–2). Secondly, urban space is rendered as something essentially visual, something that can be represented on a map, aerial photograph, axonometric, perspective drawing or façade projection. The visualisation concerns the way the representation of a city or space is constructed. It is about the 'techniques of knowledge', about the method. Importantly, a representation is never neutral, but does carry an idea of space (Lehtonen 1994: 41–6, Pérez-Gómez and Pelletier 1997).

The elements of this dual structure can be termed the 'Concept City' and the 'Visible City'. They mutually support each other, much like the two epistemological 'illusions' Lefebvre discusses in the opening chapter of *The Production of Space*: the 'illusion of transparency' and the 'illusion of opacity'. According to Lefebvre, the illusion of transparency makes space appear 'as luminous, as intelligible, as giving action free rein. What happens in space lends a miraculous quality to thought, which becomes incarnate by means of a *design*' (Lefebvre 1991 [1974]: 27, original italics). Even though the urban, social space is not transparent and intelligible, the illusion of its transparency is nurtured. The illusion of opacity, then, concerns 'natural simplicity'. It is a likewise misleading idea, entailing that things have more of an existence than the thought and desires of a subject (ibid.:29).

I find Lefebvre's 'illusions' interesting, because they offer a persuasive description of the 'playground' of the architect-planner, who understands urban space on the one hand 'opaquely' as physical-visual and on the other 'transparently' as intelligible. The idea that space can be *designed* flows from the 'oscillation' of the two illusions: 'when space is not being overseen by the geometer, it is liable to take on the physical qualities and properties of the earth' (ibid.: 30). Besides being intelligible, space is thought to be mouldable at will, without any problem in principle. Space is naïvely supposed to have no traps, inconsistencies or secret places, and a 1:1 ratio between invention and realisation, thought and action, is assumed. This is extraordinary, because in practice urban plans – and even architectural designs, where the idea of direct realisation is more apt – are realised partly, if at all.[6] Again, the techniques of visual representation play a role, because they nurture an idea of 'endless future' of the projects (Lehtonen 1994: 40).

Concept City

The deceptive pleasure of seeing the whole is the distinctive mark of Concept City. In his essay 'Walking in the City' Michel de Certeau illustrates this totalising

---

6   A fairly wide academic debate concerns the mundane problems of implementation and the actual effects of planning (Taylor 1998: 99–122), but this debate has had little influence on the practices.

conception of city planning by describing his own experience on the 110th-floor lookout terrace of the World Trade Center in New York. Seen through the eyes of a philosopher from the vantage point that disappeared on 11 September, 2001 the vertical waves of Downtown and Midtown, Greenwich Village, the horizon disappearing into the mists of Central Park and Harlem – the immense masses of the metropolis – are all congealed into a single image. The city appears as a texture where ambition and decay, races and styles, the old and the new, one extremity and another meet and converge. De Certeau notes that the feeling of 'seeing the whole' is enjoyable. 'To what erotics of knowledge does the ecstasy of reading such a cosmos belong?', he asks, and answers that the exaltation comes from being lifted out of the city's grasp. The body is no longer hemmed in by the nervous city, its traffic and streets that turn and return. The eye sees everything and the mind flies far away like Icarus (de Certeau 1993: 151–3).

According to de Certeau, the city of urban planning is precisely such a distant image seen from above. Planners look at the everyday bustle of people from a divine perspective, like the tourist on the top of the WTC building. They imagine the city to be a transparent text that can be known, and they are unable to see any practice alien to the geometric, visual city of their own creation. Echoing Lefebvre's flickering, oscillatory effect of the two epistemological illusions, de Certeau claims that 'perspective vision' and 'prospective vision' together constitute the twofold projection of an opaque past and uncertain future onto a surface that can be dealt with (ibid.: 154). De Certeau's principal point is that in the planning discourse the lived urban fact is transformed into the concept of a city.[7] This is possible through a series of conceptual translations, which involve firstly the 'city' producing its own space (*un espace propre*), secondly the substitution of 'nowhen', of synchronic system and scientific strategies, for resistances offered by traditions and tactics of people living in the city, and finally the creation of a universal and anonymous subject – the city itself. When this 'Concept City' (my term) or 'city-subject' (as de Certeau puts it) is established, it permits planners to bypass the complex, unpredictable city of countless actors and instead to understand and create space through finite, isolated properties that are linked to each other in a controlled manner (de Certeau 1993: 153–4).

The highwater marks of the Concept City belief are the post-WW II ideas about 'scientific' planning. Sandercock credits the planning programme in the University of Chicago as having established the modernist 'pillars of planning wisdom'. This rational comprehensive model entails that planning is

---

7   Henri Lefebvre claims that the Bauhaus group of Dessau in early 1920s pioneered this new way of thinking about space and city, originally in a very positive sense. According to him, Bauhaus discovered that '[s]pace opened up to perception, to conceptualisation, just as it did to practical action. And the artist passed from objects in space to the concept of space itself' (Lefebvre [1974] 1991: 125). Later on, the sense about this possibility of creating a unitary space, suited for the new economic and technical realities, would have been lost. Below and in Chapter 3, I will further discuss Lefebvre's notion of space.

concerned with making political decisions more rational, that planning should be comprehensive, that it uses the (narrowly defined) scientific method, which it is a project of state-directed futures, and that planning operates 'above' normal citizens and the democratic process in the public interest (Sandercock 1998: 27, 62, 87–9). The key epistemological assumption of this 'Chicago model'[8] is that planners can maintain a critical distance, be free of self-interest and transcend the specific interests of capital, labour or the state (ibid.: 26). This assumption is in line with the Enlightenment epistemology, interpreted as the idea that an objective knowledge or truth may exist independently of the knower. As in de Certeau's analysis, in the Chicago model planners are supposed to be able to collate the most accurate and best balanced knowledge of the city so that they can legitimately claim to be the 'masters' or moral owners of it, prior to anyone else, including indeed the democratic system.

Visible City

The privileging of the visual, of what can be seen, is apparent already in the pervasive idiom of 'seeing', 'seeing the whole'. Besides being conceived of as a totality, the city of city planning is thought to lend itself to being visualised. If not earlier, the history of the visible city starts with late mediaeval and Renaissance birds-eye views of European cities, which are shown as unified city-objects surrounded by fortifications or water. Jàcopo de Barbari's view of Venice (1500) already utilises perspective techniques. During sixteenth and seventeenth centuries, several series of aerial views were published, for example Braun and Hogenberg's *Civitates Orbis Terrarum* (1572) and Wenceslaus Hollar's *Totius Galliae Metropolis* (1630). The invention and use of hot-air balloons facilitated increasingly photo-realistic prints during the nineteenth century. In the colonisation and urbanisation of North America, aerial views of new towns in the West served both as advertisements and boosters of civic pride (Espuche 1994).

Walter Benjamin, in his *Denkbild* from 1920s Moscow, provides a graphic illustration about the (political) power of map-based visualisation. Benjamin visited the Red Army Club at the Kremlin, where

> a map of Europe hangs on the wall. Beside it is a handle. When this handle is turned, the following is seen: one after the other, at all the places through which Lenin passed in the course of his life, little electric lights flash. At Simbirsk, where he was born, at Kazan, Petersburg, Geneva, Paris, Krakow, Zurich, Moscow, up to the place of his death, Gorki [since 1991 it's been called Nizhni Novgorod]. Other towns are not marked. The contours of this wooden map are rectilinear, angular, schematic. On it Lenin's life resembles a campaign

---

8   The Chicago model is distinct from the inter-war 'Chicago School' of sociology, which established the notion of 'urban ecology'.

of colonial conquest across Europe. *Russia is beginning to take shape for the man of the people.* The map is almost as close to becoming the centre of the new Russian iconic cult as Lenin's portrait. [A]ll Europeans ought to see, on a map of Russia, their little land as a frayed, nervous territory far out to the west. (Benjamin 1979 [1927]: 196, my italics)

Gradually, the aerial photograph and the view from above also became the paradigmatic way of viewing the city in urban planning. Anthony Vidler claims that Le Corbusier played an important role in this process. Le Corbusier was enthusiastic about flight and aeroplanes. For the design of buildings, the aeroplane (and before it also the automobile and the ocean liner) was the metaphor on the one hand of a problem posed and solved scientifically, and of precise industrial production on the other. But for the city and for urban planning it is a metaphor of the *manner of knowing.* 'Here, the idea of airplanes as simply the analogs of house design and their functionality and precision has been supplanted by the idea of the airplane as a central vehicle of knowledge, analysis, conception, and design' (Vidler 2000: 37). Le Corbusier used aerial photographs as instruments in debating – or battling – over the proper nature of urban space, in his case especially against the overcrowding of Paris. According to Vidler, for Le Corbusier the aerial photograph alone 'reveals the whole truth, shows what is invisible from ground level...' (ibid.: 38). This is the same voyeuristic exaltation de Certeau so well describes. According to Lehtonen, Moholy-Nagy further stressed that an aerial view or perspective of a city plan would facilitate a more perfect spatial experience than earlier representations, while also helping to break historical conceptions of architecture (Lehtonen 1994: 89).

In South America Le Corbusier had an opportunity to fly and practise 'planning by flying'. In the Parana delta he discovered the 'law of the meander', which was transferred to his famous Rio de Janeiro plan in the form of a tortuous superstructure. The logic of the visual model, separated from its context, is well described by the fact that Le Corbusier applied this 'South American' idea of form also in his later plans for North African conditions, for example plan Obus for Algiers. After WW II, with the big advances in technology stimulated by the military reconnaissance, the aerial view became institutionalised as a central tool of planning (Vidler 2000: 39–40).

At present, maps and statistics essentially define the 'visible city', the part of urban reality that is taken seriously in the planning and realisation procedures. Dear and Häkli claim that maps and statistics are the key 'technologies of power' utilised in planning. They facilitate the aimed spatial control, they 'gather' space and time (cf. Harvey 1989: 240–44; Latour 1986), they present opportunities to systematically collate data and to make the city visible and intelligible through various theoretical syntheses. Any new area is thought of as and designed as 'a patchwork of infrastructures: buildings, roads, bridges and green zones' (Dear and Häkli 1998: 64, transl. PL). The visual controls the experiential, the paper projection controls what cannot be put on paper, and in the end, from the perspective of modernist urban planning 'the lived and experienced city has become mere invisible noise, even a disturbance' (ibid.: 64). In the absence of humanist and experiential dimensions, land use, its economics and judicial aspects have become the prime concern of planning: 'from statistics it is easy to produce cost-benefit analyses, and the physical planning operates with maps, the iconic representations of the city', Häkli sums up (Häkli 1997: 49, transl. PL). The only experiential dimension, which is left inside the planning discourse – visual aesthetics under the banners of architecture and urban design – also has its own, professional control technology and its masters, the architects.

Satellite cartography, new techniques of distant imaging and geographic information systems merely continue the story. In the latest wave of influential architectural publications, such as *S, M, L, XL* by Rem Koolhaas and Bruce Mau (1995), *Metacity/Datatown* by MVRDV (1999) and the *Mutations* catalogue edited by Koolhaas et al. (2001), aerial and space-borne images and new maps and diagrams based on those serve the same purpose as the first aerial photos of Paris for Le Corbusier. While they look striking and seductive, they are supposed to tell the 'truth' about new mega-cities, continent-wide urban nebulae, or even the whole Earth. They re-tell the story that urban reality is again revolutionised and better knowledge can be obtained from above, paradoxically the further away, the better.

City Designed

By combining the idea of a city as a pseudo-subject and the visual bias in representing that subject, the third aspect of the dominant space-conception becomes understandable. Because the city is a thing, which can be seen, it is possible to extend the seeing to doing, to manipulating, and designing the city. In his own representation of space, in the 'world of images', the architect and planner creates blueprints, images to be realised. To see is to have power 'over the city'.

While the city-subject can conceptually be traced to the Renaissance, the powers to execute designs in city or metropolitan scale date back to the nineteenth century. According to Henri Lefebvre, in the Ancient Vitruvian thinking the city is an aggregate of monuments and private houses, but the 'urban effect' or 'paradigm of civic space' would be non-existent. 'Only in the sixteenth century, after the rise of the medieval town … and after the establishment of "urban systems" in Italy, Flanders, England, France, Spanish America, and elsewhere, did the town emerge as a unified entity – and as a *subject*' (Lefebvre 1991 [1974]: 271). (The Greek city-state clearly was a 'subject', but the emphasis was on the political community of the citizens, not on the city as an image or architectural object.) The tools to rapidly build towns and cities at will (and erase whatever is in the way) were in place only after full-blown industrialisation. Haussmann's projects in Paris are one important watershed, starting three successive 'waves' of planning ideologies and increasing regulation and rationalisation of cities (cf. Schulman 1990: 172, 206).

The idea of one-to-one correspondence between the graphic space of designs and their urban realisations is futile. Architect's space (the empty lot or the empty computer screen) is not innocent, as it almost always has direct economic and social ramifications. But these are easily hidden. When Lefebvre asserts that '[t]alk of city planning refers to nothing at all' (Lefebvre 1991: 389) or that architectural discourse 'no longer has any frame of reference or horizon' (ibid.: 361), he points to how institutionalised notions of space have obtained iconographic status. These distanced and objectified notions or space are not only internally referential, though. What disturbs Lefebvre is the aspect of power: how the abstract systems of representation are violently 'imposed and actualised in the production of urban space' (Liggett 1995: 246).

Space is, indeed, mouldable, and the master's projects do have an effect (who could deny this?). The point is that in the Concept City–Visible City mode the production of space becomes understood narrowly. Therefore, the effect of a plan or design is likely to be different from the planner's expectation.

These hesitations do not aim to say that architecture and urban design as we know them would be false or unimportant. On the contrary, they do have a certain, important cultural value (see pp. 230–31 for further discussion). The mistake is to equate 'space' and the graphic or map space of architecture and planning. View lines, controlled facades and rhythmic treatment of volumes are part of our aesthetic urban culture, but if architects would widen their notion of space, the meaning of 'design' might also positively change.

Excursion 1: Brasília

Brasília, based on a competition entry by Lúcio Costa (1957), is known as a prime example of modern planning along Athens' Charter principles. It is also a product of Corbuserian 'planning by flying', or making a city which turns its best façade up to the air. I had an opportunity to visit the city in 1999. I do not intend to retell here the heroic story of its construction in less than four years nor lament its massive mistakes and social inequalities, but rather share some personal observations about the peculiarities of the Brasílian urban experience. I do believe that Brasília is one of the great human achievements, but simultaneously, in its clarity, it reveals the weird logic of modern planning very well.

Firstly I was amazed that the city was so well kept. I had expected a booming and chaotic South American metropolis, where the original plan would be in many ways modified, overrun or forgotten. But the opposite was true: in many places time had stopped and almost nothing had changed. The administrative and cultural monuments were untouched. So were the meandering superblocks (*superquadra*), as well as the curious retail arrangement of quite small shopping streets in every second free zone between the superblocks. Only in the Central Sectors North and South (everything appears in doubles in Brasília, because the plan is rigidly symmetric; there are even two identical amusement parks facing each other over

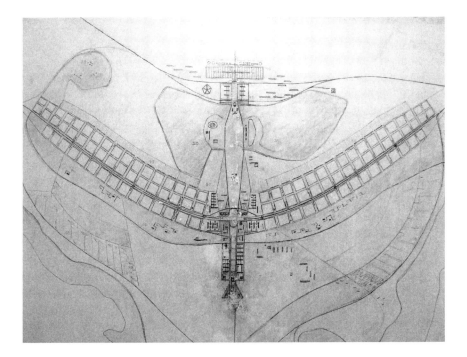

Figure 1.1   Plano Piloto of Brasília

the central axis, Eixo Monumental) were there some new skyscrapers and shopping malls. Some reasons, such as Brasília's unusual symbolic value for the Brazilian state, its status as a UNESCO World Heritage site since 1987, combined with its relatively small and specialised resident population, partly explain the extent of historic preservation, but I still find it rather amazing. (St Petersburg is the only other major city which is, in principle, completely preserved. Quite interestingly, it shares with Brasília the strong feeling of being planned: even the 300 years of history have not been able to erase the singular act of power of Peter the Great.)

Secondly, for a tourist used to 'normal' (historic European or North American cities but also almost any non-or little-planned third world city) Brasília may be literally deadly. Its large-scale, uncompromised functional segregation in the scale of the whole city, and roads designed only for the car, combined with the hot, dry tropical climate make an unusual combination. During the first day of my visit I made the mistake of trying to become familiar with the city by walking. I set out from the hotel in the city centre with the idea of reaching the administrative square, Praça dos Três Poderes, in an hour or two. First I had problems negotiating the main highways with five to eight lanes in each direction crossing the monumental axis with no pavements, traffic lights or pedestrian bridges. But a more serious problem was that there were literally no places to get anything to drink. Between the commercial centre, where outside the air-conditioned, enclosed shopping malls the only place to find a cup of something was the central bus station in the middle of the highway spaghetti, and the Praça dos Três Poderes some five kilometres down the axis is the section dedicated to the ministries. The section is an absolute desert of vast expanses of pampa and very widely spaced office blocks with no-one walking and with no public services whatsoever. After almost three hours of slow walking in the 34°C under the blazing sun, I reached Niemeyer's famous twin-tower, the congress and the parliament. But even they had no café! I was saved only by the two or three refreshment sellers who had parked their pushcarts on the representative square behind the parliament – still another half a kilometre walk.

Figure 1.2   View of the monumental axis of Brasília. To the right is the parliament building by Oscar Niemeyer (1959)

Source: Photo: Panu Lehtovuori.

The third observation was that instead of operating like a city, Brasília operated like a small village. Jane Jacobs' (1961) distinction between metropolitan and small town or rural social forms is very valid: in social sense, Brasília was not a big city. Because you could not walk, it was impossible to find a free taxi, public transport was inaccessible, and, as if this is not enough, you would not know where to go or how to find anything anyway, things started to spiral around you. When you stepped out of the hotel somebody whistled, a taxi curved to you, and knew where you wanted to go. It was like magic. This was of course a tourist's experience, but it was not that different for the locals. The little nightlife was concentrated in the already mentioned retail alleys. In each retail alley there was a standard selection of services, one or two bars included. And each night, only a few of those bars in the whole city had any programme, so you really need to know what to do and where to go, always by car. There is no chance to pub-crawl, of chance meetings or to change the place. And you can be sure that your friends are in the same bar.

All this is possible only, because there are invisible externalities, so to say. Socially Brasília seemed to be a village, but this is only true for the original Plano Piloto. This unified UNESCO artefact has 243,000 inhabitants, which is only 13 per cent of the total population of the Distrito Federal (Braga and Falcão 1997). Plano Piloto is indeed surrounded by the sprawling metropolis, which I expected to see in the city centre, but the newer zones are situated so far away that you do not see them at all when in the Plano Piloto. The original Brasília still seems to be in the middle of pristine pampa, facing its romantic artificial lake. There is also heavy segregation through the very poor public transport between the centre and the rest. Only now is Brasília building a metro, for example. So the poor have difficulty getting to the city, but the rich residents of Plano Piloto and Taguatinga do visit the other, more lively districts to find the pleasures and excitement of a city.

Critiques of the Concept City

For four decades, starting when Brasília was already inaugurated, the practices of urban planning and the modernist conceptualisation of the city and urban space have been criticised both from in the profession and from outside. There has been a desire to restore urban life, marginal voices, experienced space and art to urban planning. The criticism of the rational planners' Concept City – an urban model forcefully exemplified by the grand emptiness of Brasília – has obtained its own history. However, the critiques have not been fully successful. At present planning thought could be said to be in a halfway position between the detached Enlightenment epistemology and radically new ways of representing, or non-representing, the city and urban space.

Let us briefly discuss some of the early critical writers and movements, active in both Europe and North America.

The Situationists (Situs) were a small group of avant-garde artists, led by Guy Debord. Since the late 1950s, the group criticised the power of the technocratic apparatus of planning and the demolition of Parisian quarters that had a strong spirit or atmosphere (see e.g. Sadler 1998: 47–66, Sederholm 1994). The strength of the dominant way to conceive the city and public space is well illustrated by the fact that it took several years for the Situationists to get rid of the aerial view as the representation of urban space. In the first volumes of their manifesto journal, the *International Situationist*, they used photos and maps drawn directly from Paul Chombart de Lauwe, one of the principal French adherents of aerial mapping. So, 'the Situationists are espousing, and with very similar methods, an equal if opposite vision of urbanism as totalising, and from above, as that of their enemy Le Corbusier' (Vidler 2000: 42). Only during the 1960s did the Situationists develop a critique of Chombart. The group started to avoid physical proposals. Constant, the architect who had developed the Situationists' ideas into an architectural project called 'New Babylon', was expelled from the group in 1960. Instead of physical interventions, the Situs turned to the notion of 'unitary urbanism', which could be defined as a seamless play-like urban life, including the notion of derive (drift), or an effort to explore and invent 'the terrain of experience for the social space of the cities of the future' (IS #3).

The Situationists had close links to the philosopher Henri Lefebvre. Together, for example, they studied grassroots revolutions, such as the Paris Commune of 1871 (Andreottti 1996: 13, Shields 1999: 89–91). The relationship was broken in 1968, but one of Lefebvre's most important texts on the urban, *Le droit à la ville* (1968, English transl. in Lefebvre 1996; Swedish transl. *Staden som rättighet* 1982), echoes many of the themes, which were also central for the Situs. The key point of Lefebvre is that everybody should be able to positively act to change the city and society. The city is an *oeuvre*, a collective work, and everyone should be able to participate in it, to have a stake in the political 'centrality' city represents and produces. Influenced by the events of 1968, the *IS*, and Lefebvre, architects and theorists such as Antoine Grumbach, Roland Castro and Christian de Portzamparc started to argue that the city should build on itself as a continuation of the process of transformation over centuries. They developed the theory of the 'impure' as opposed to the 'purity' of conventional modernism (cf. Vidler 2000). In the 1970s and 1980s, Lefebvre's concepts were transferred to concrete urban policies in France, of which the Banlieu 89 programme is one example. According to Kofman and Lebas, it seems that in the concrete urban politics Lefebvre's ideas were diluted and a widening gap was opened between word and deed. Lefebvre himself has ironically noted that 'his writings on space and the urban were deemed scandalous until these "truths" were proclaimed obvious and trivial …' (Kofman and Lebas 1996: 36).

Almost simultaneously with the early French criticism of the rapid modernisation, on the other side of the Atlantic a group of academics and journalists published an article series about problems of planning and virtues of urban life. The texts appeared in *Fortune* between September 1957–April 1958. Later the series was published as a book *The Exploding Metropolis*, described by the editor as 'a book by people who like cities' (Whyte 1993: 7, quoted in Schmid 2005: 125). One of the Fortune series contributors was Jane Jacobs. In 1961, she published her pamphlet *The Death and Life of Great American Cities*. Jacobs' book has become a classic, and it still exerts an effect on both the European and American planning debate. Her key point is that instead of trying to impose their detached, theoretical models upon cities, planners should realistically study what actually makes cities liveable. She underscores the importance of the complex interplay of the diverse elements in a mixed urban environment, something which can never be achieved in planners' idealistic, alienated and rigidly zoned projects, which Jacobs ironically calls the 'Radiant Garden City Beautiful'. Appreciation of the urban street, its visual continuity and detailing, the social intricacies it may sustain and its economic dynamism, are central in her argument.[9] This appreciation leads Jacobs to question the need for planning altogether. The cities might well be doing better if left totally to their own devices (Taylor 1998: 46–8, 163). If taken at face value, this suggestion radically also questions the power relations of urban space production. According to Jacobs, instead of the 'expert', it is the inhabitant and user, who should have the last word in urban questions.

Another American, Robert Venturi, also criticised modern architecture and urbanism for their reductionism. In *Complexity and Contradiction in Architecture* (1966) he claimed that by carefully limiting the problems it would solve, modern architecture produced solutions that were pure, but boring (cf. Nesbitt 1996: 72). Venturi was interested in the American everyday urbanism, and in *Learning from Las Vegas* (1972) he, together with Denise Scott Brown and Steven Izenour, did exactly what Jane Jacobs had suggested: analysed how a urban environment, in this case a very car-oriented one, actually worked. By interpreting the Strip of Las Vegas as a rich symbolic and communicative system the authors mounted a still relevant critique towards the notion of pure, 'sacred' space of modernistic architecture. They also noted the inclusive, complex or emerging order of the Strip, something that did not obey 'the rigid order of the urban renewal project or the fashionable "total design" of the megastructure. It is not an order dominated by the expert and made easy for the eye' (Venturi et al. [1972] 1997: 52–3). Already before postmodernism in architecture, Team 10, working from early 1950s until the 1980s, had criticised CIAM and utilised their observations of daily life and existing urban patterns in their designs.

Some commercial developers, notably the Austrian American Victor Gruen, studied existing cities and their public spaces, with an intention to bring their good and attractive civic qualities to housing developments and especially the new shopping malls. 'Proportion, dimension, and open space based on built precedent, as well as the inclusion of such amenities as post offices, community rooms, and facilities for events – all were part of Gruen's concerted effort to will into being the activities and tenor of Main Street' (Kaliski 1999: 92). The results, however, were not completely convincing, and step-by-step the shopping mall developed to the direction of gigantism and complete theming and simulation we are familiar today (Gottdiener 1995, 1997). Kaliski summarises the difficulty of the post-war design-led efforts to re-create urbanity by saying that '[w]hether form-oriented modernists rejecting the Athens Charter prescriptions [e.g. Team 10] or corporate architects working for market-driven developers [e.g. Gruen], twentieth-century

---

9   Jacobs' observations are mostly based on her own neighbourhood, New York City's Greenwich Village in the 1950s. Some critics point that her work is limited and parochial, leading to non-inclusive theory of place-making which devalues different urbanisms and thus fails to utilise the full spectrum of potentials (e.g. Kaliski 1999: 95).

designers have found it nearly impossible to forge approaches that empower, rather than simulate, urban spontaneity' (Kaliski 1999: 93).

To return to Europe, Michel de Certeau's ideas emphasising spatial micro-practices are part of this lengthy critical debate. He claims that everyday urban life permits the return of the 'poetic' or 'mythical' spatial experience that is excluded by planning: the city-dwellers' knowledge of urban spaces is 'blind as that of lovers in each other's arms' (de Certeau 1993: 153). De Certeau claims that the chance to see the city as a whole is a false one, and that the Icarus of planning thought will ultimately fall into the sea. 'The panorama-city is a "theoretical" (that is, visual) simulacrum, in short a picture, whose condition of possibility is an oblivion and a misunderstanding of practices' (ibid.: 153). Walking is one of those practices, eluding visual legibility. It constitutes one of the real systems whose existence makes up the city. Even though it is possible to trace the trajectories of movement and map them, these mappings miss the actual, singular experience of walking and only refer to 'the absence of what has passed by' (ibid.: 157). On a more general level, de Certeau disputes the simple distinction between 'production' and 'consumption', claiming that consumption (of television, urban space, consumer goods) is 'another production', which unfolds through ways of using the products imposed by the dominant economic order (de Certeau 1984: xii–xiii). Using 'strategies' the powerful groups and actors can generate new proper spaces and relations. The weaker groups have to resort to 'tactics', to (mis)uses and (temporary) appropriations. Spatially interesting is de Certeau's emphasis that 'the place of a tactic belongs to the other' (ibid.: xix). In the following Chapters, tactical ways of operating, using space and experimenting with design will be a recurring theme.

Towards New Epistemology

The connecting thread of these critiques is epistemological. From a multiplicity of perspectives, the critics question the central tenet of the mainstream 'planning wisdom' – the idea that there exists objective, universal knowledge about the city; that planners are in a better position than others to obtain that knowledge; and that planners therefore have the right, even duty, to exercise power in the name of the common good. After the Situs, Lefebvre, Jacobs and Venturi, the wide and deep post-colonial debate has valorised the experience and points of view of excluded groups and marginal voices (Spivak 1990, Wilson 1991, Rose 1993). Leonie Sandercock succinctly sums up that from the postmodern, feminist, and post-colonial critiques 'we can conclude that: all knowledge is embodied; it is historically situated; it is shaped by language; and it is embedded in power relations. Clearly we can no longer hold on to the idea of the expert planner knowing the public interest through rational deliberation' (Sandercock 1998: 76).

However, the long 'after-life' of the Concept City in planning practices notwithstanding, even in the field of planning theory proper the epistemological shift is slow and partial. While questioning the hierarchic status of expert knowledge, both equity planning (Krumholz and Forester 1990) and communicative or collaborative planning (Friedmann 1973, Forester 1989, Healey 1997, 2006) cling to the idea that the planner still has the lead in the practice and that she works through the state. No wonder that many planners still cling to the idea of 'public interest', as well as to the intimidating attitude that, in the end, the planners know best. Therefore, at some point of the process other actors should shut up and be happy with the experts' solution. Planners seem still to think that they know what is best 'for the city' and that they are even able to talk 'on behalf' of the city.[10]

Only radical planning would according to Sandercock offer a full alternative for the episteme of the Chicago model and its successors (Sandercock 1998: 85–104, see Friedmann 1987 for a more moderate view). In radical planning, the planner jumps onto 'another wagon', that of a community or ethnic minority group, for example, and uses her knowledge and ability to make alliances from a completely different societal position than that of the classical expert, who is loyal to the state. Examples of such 'counter-planning' abound, if we only accept them as 'planning'. Sandercock refers to the 'thousand tiny empowerments', various practices and initiatives of citizen control and radical planning across the world (Sandercock 1998: 129–). Kelbaugh (2000) discusses 'everyday urbanism' as a situated, people and practice-based mode of planning, opposed to 'new' and 'post-urbanism'. The tactical appropriation of the old railway warehouses (Makasiinit) in Helsinki will be discussed in Chapter 8 as an example of everyday urbanism. The conflict between popular uses and sentiments and the official city planning agenda also evoked forms of counter-planning.

Furthermore, the idea of radical planning might give a positive role for the planner in the Marxist theoretical frame. Gottdiener claims that there is a new division between networks and groups promoting economical growth and those opposing growth, which dynamically cuts through the Western societies. He states that 'the clash between growth and no-growth represents a basic cleavage in society, involving economic, political, and ideological practices ... Indeed, the clash of pro growth versus no growth is as fundamental to the production of space as is the struggle between capital and labor' (Gottdiener 1985: 222, 270). If we accept Gottdiener's analysis of this new societal division, planning for the 'anti-growth' instead of 'pro-growth' could be seen as a less pluralistic and a more concretely founded interpretation of Sandercock's epistemological landscape of myriad differences. If planning is in a capitalist society 'the façade of power' (ibid.: 18), taking the roles of rationalisation and marketing of profitable real-estate schemes, radical planning would represent 'cracks' in that façade. The Concept City is decaying.

---

10   And it is indeed possible to defend the argument, that as long as planning is able to control urban development and not too many citizens express their discontent with the results, the modern planning of the visible city does have a legitimacy (Häkli 1997: 50).

Chapter 2
Current Conceptualisations
of Public Urban Space

Mersey

The River Mersey undulates between its green flood protection embankments. The winter sun is dim, and the shaded slopes still have some frost. It is cool and clear. I can hear the hum of the M60 motorway. Occasionally my ear catches a sharp clap: someone's club hitting a golf ball. Frozen shouts from a distant football game hang in mid-air. I smile at Hille: a perfect Saturday for a walk.

A large flock of Canada Geese graze on our side of the river. When we approach, they hardly move. Goldeneyes, moorhens, mallards and goosanders populate the river – some of them could even be Finnish ones wintering here. A lonely cormorant is fishing.

The highway flies over the river. The river and road meet diagonally, making the bridge feel very wide. A forest of grey columns is painted with yellowish graffiti protection on their first two metres. Invisible tyres hit the tarmac above us:

Thump, thump, thu-thump.

Thump. Thu-thump.

The water is black. Last winter's flood has drawn brown marks on the columns. Suddenly we see a swan. Its slow movement and whiteness in the dark captivates us. Is it the Swan of Tuonela, mirroring itself in the dark stream? Another cormorant flies upstream, grinning like a cruel mythical creature.

Later, on the other side of the embankment we pass three old golfers, leaning on their clubs and gossiping. We smile at them, and they smile back.

Manchester 15 December 2001

***

If space in general can, with difficult reductions as discussed in the previous chapter, be conceptualised as an abstract three-dimensional continuum or a material substance, *public urban space* clearly cannot. In some way, *people* or *users* will enter the conceptualisation, and with people, the relations between them, *the social*, that is. In the most elementary terms, public urban space is both physical and social. It is part of the physical urban structure, having both a frontal 'function' and marginal uses and users (Kopomaa 1997).

In the Concept City mode of thought, these two necessary aspects of public urban space are seen as separate things or entities. Most often, the physical side is foregrounded and public urban space is conceived of as a *container* of people, a *platform* of functions, an urban *stage* or *room*. Therefore, it is possible to design a form (an image and a space-object) and put the users in brackets. Alternatively, social life and interactions may be given priority. In that case, the physical space is reduced to an invisible, neutral background, and public urban space is seen as a *meeting place*, for example. Either way, the conceptualisation of public urban space becomes one-dimensional and dry. This may explain why in books about planning, urban design and architecture, surprisingly little is written about public urban space. In the Introduction I mentioned that the concept 'space' is not rigorously treated in these disciplines. The same holds for the concept 'public urban space'. There are thick volumes filled with examples and models, documented by maps and images, but the definition or conceptualisation of public urban space is discussed little, if at all. Madanipour, for example, in his *Design of Urban Space* (1996), deals with the question 'what is public space?' very concisely, relying on dictionary definitions. He concludes that public space 'belongs to and concerns the people as a whole, is open to them, exists openly, and is provided by or concerns the government' (146). He gives the definition in the chapter on urban design process. So, even though Madanipour's book is insightful and theoretically advanced, he does not problematise the notion of public space. It is implicitly understood as an object of design, a partition of geographical space and as an official, government product. Stevens (2007: 2) notes that the discipline of urban design 'has at its heart a very vague, abstract and potentially ambiguous concept: amenity'. The concept of amenity entails both the need to balance the interests of different user groups (in the name of public interest) and the idea of function, a rather fixed and predetermined relation between form and use. Arguing for the importance of surprising and playful uses of public urban space, Stevens calls for an extended understanding the concept of amenity to mean also 'the potential which design provides for expanding people's experience and their capacities' (ibid.).

On Some Common Conceptualisations of 'Public Urban Space', with Varying Emphasis of its Physical and Social Aspects

While any conceptualisation of public urban space hints at both the physical and social aspect of space, in what follows I try to show that the Concept City mode of thought makes it difficult to keep the two aspects equally important. Different common conceptualisations stress either the physical or the social aspect, but they lack a way to bring the two together. Furthermore, crucial questions of personal experience and signification are badly sidetracked.

Public vs Private

In the paradigm of map space, the most evident way to think of public urban space is that of figure-ground. Public urban space is opposed to private space and becomes defined as all the surface not in private ownership (e.g. Lofland 1998: 8).

Public space is the ubiquitous, neutral and contingent carrier of urban functions. The notion is flat (even literally). Little is left to be said, and from lively theory the discourse is converted to finding boundaries between the two types of area or, at best, laterally collecting examples of public urban spaces. Kostof, who in *City Assembled* writes the history of physical urban form, provides a revealing example of the problems of this conceptualisation: he struggles with the problem that for him public places (squares) seem to be an 'arbitrary' subject! According to Kostof, public urban place as a subject of study cannot be easily defined, because so many areas, such as streets and harbour waterfronts, belong to public territory (Kostof 1992: 123).

Even though much used, this classificatory, map-based way to conceptualise is limited and problematic. It is Euro-centric, and can therefore with difficulty be used in other cultures and urban traditions. It contains unexpressed genderings, for example the mistaken idea that the private would somehow be the space of the woman (e.g. Wilson 1991, see also Koskela 1999, 6). Furthermore, it is unable to take into account constitutive systems and processes, which do not obey the public-private distinction. Lefebvre, for example, discusses the many technological systems, which penetrate the 'private' dwelling and firmly connect it to whatever there is beyond. Benjamin describes the 'porosity' of Naples: 'As porous as this stone is the architecture. Building and action interpenetrate in the courtyards, arcades, and stairways', so that 'the stamp of definitive is avoided', while 'each private attitude or act is permeated by streams of communal life' (Benjamin and Lacis 1979 [1924]: 169, 174).

By changing the bipolar public-private conception to a line with some shades, we get the 'semi-public' and 'semi-private' spaces. Another matrix of classification, which already offers clear links between physical and social, can be developed by distinguishing access and agency of control from the ownership of a particular space (e.g. Franck and Paxton 1989: 123). Another variation is to complement the dimension of access by the dimensions of agency and interest (Madanipour 1996: 148, referring to Benn and Gaus 1983).

I do not deny that the boundaries between public and private and especially struggles to move or question those boundaries would not be important issues and relevant objects of study. The big discourses about commercialisation, privatisation and segregation of space, for example, partly operate on this distinction. But any interesting conceptualisation in these debates certainly warrants much more aspects and more subtle distinctions.

The most important shortcoming of the public-private distinction and classificatory matrices based on it is that it only helps to describe: I can point to a space and affirm that it is public or not – it is owned by a public body or not, or access is free or limited. Both the theoretical rigour and most intricacies of lived situations are lost. The analysis is left to work on the assumed primacy of the physical space, which can be parcelled, divided, monitored and mapped. Public urban space is conceived of as a 'function' of a parcel of geographic space.

Stage

Another common way to conceptualise the public nature of urban space is to use the metaphor of a *stage*. 'Public space is the stage upon which the drama of communal life unfolds', states Carr et al. (1992: 3). Like-minded contention is that '[w]hile seldom stated explicitly, it has long been assumed that public life, just like a theatrical production, requires actors and audience, a stage and a theater' (Crowhurst, Lennard and Lennard 1984: 21). To find some focus for his above-mentioned research, Kostof, too, seizes upon the idea of a stage. He defines public place (*piazza*) as a functionally specific part of the contingent public area, 'a purpose-built stage for ritual and interaction' (Kostof 1992: 123, see also Rajanti 1999: 117–18). Urban life is played out on this imagined stage, with buildings as the 'stage setting' and fountains and street furniture as some smaller paraphernalia of the 'theatre'.

Among planners this idea is rather common, which is understandable because it reduces users to distanced 'actors' with predetermined 'roles', fitting well in the Concept City mode. The will and desires of actors are not important, they just fill the stage, hopefully in big numbers to show the 'success' of a space. People on stage can even be viewed as 'puppets'. What about the 'theatre' in the above quote? The metaphor of the stage entails a viewer or audience. Who is that viewer? The metaphor seems to postulate a distance. A stage is viewed by someone from outside,[1] and opera glasses may well be needed. I think that mostly the viewer is someone in power, maybe the planner himself on some occasions. The 'theatre' is the planning office, traffic monitoring room or the meeting room in the HQ of a big developer. In these cases, maps, video monitors and other images of the stage are the opera glasses. A stage becomes an object of thought, and the metaphor leaves us caught conceptually in the dichotomies of subject-object, material-mental and physical-social.

Crowhurst, Lennard and Lennard use Siena's Campo as their example, pointing to the theatrical quality of that *particular urban space*. Campo makes it possible for the same people to mutually 'act' and 'view'. I find this a relevant example. However, such spaces are a rather rare, very specific type of public urban space. Echoes or promises of the theatrical quality of a particular space can probably be found rather easily (e.g. Gehl 1987). In Helsinki, one thinks of the combination of grass, benches and walkways of Esplanade and the stairs of Senate Square. Urban events tend to intensify and actualise this potential, and some other specific qualities, as I will explain in Part 4. So, there is something promising in the idea of a stage, but as a way to conceptualise it is limited and tied to particular configurations. It might be called 'type' or 'proto-type' of a kind of public urban space.

---

1   The origin of this idea is probably in baroque designs (Versailles, Karlsruhe) made for the absolute king to oversee the 'scenes' of the court members or other subjects (Kostof 1992).

Room

Partly a derivative of the stage-metaphor, the idea of public urban spaces as 'outdoor rooms' is (again) gaining increasing popularity. A room is clearly a physical space. A potential/good public space is defined solely through formal comparisons. If a street is long and maybe open-ended, a plaza understood as a room is concave and enclosed. This is a normative definition, leading to the idea that a usable and sought-after public urban space needs to be defined as a physical enclosure in the urban structure.

Camillo Sitte is an important source here. He has famously emphasised the physical-visual qualities of mediaeval urban spaces (Sitte [1889] 1965). Sitte was looking for spatial characteristics (as opposed to stylistic, for example), and concluded that the success of an urban space depends on its sense of enclosure: 'The main requirement for a plaza, as for a room, is the enclosed character of its space' (Sitte 1965: 32, quoted in van de Ven 1978: 104). Sitte extended the idea of interior space to outdoor public spaces. The Campo of Siena is the central example for room-metaphorists, as it is for the theatre-metaphorists. Rob Krier's simplistic morphological taxonomy of squares, discussed below, obviously takes the outdoor room idea for granted.

Recently, the idea of rooms or 'public living rooms' of a neighbourhood has again gained currency among planners and architects. According to Doron, the British Urban Task Force report *Towards an Urban Renaissance* (1999) conceived public space as an 'Outdoor Room' (Doron 2002: 44). In Sweden, the current planning discussion also emphasises this aspect (e.g. Elmlund 2004).

For a particular space, the room metaphor seems to allow less public character than the idea of a theatre. Public urban space conceived of as a room is semi-public or even semi-private. Doron critically states that 'the spatial configuration of the term "Outdoor Room" suggests an exclusiveness, confinement, and a desire to enclose the public space' (Doron 2002: 44, also Holden and Iveson 2003). Public space becomes parochial, and the essential idea that the 'public' in public urban space can never be fully known is lost. Kostof sensed the room-character in the clan places of Italian cities, which were the centres of a well-defined group (family) instead of all citizens (Kostof 1992: 125–7). It can be concluded that the room metaphor goes against the idea of public urban space as open and political. Rendering a place a room, may justify exclusive and restrictive practices. However, a more positive interpretation is that of 'third place' (Oldenburg 1989). The notion refers to 'semi-public' meeting places, such as local pubs or barber's shops, which constitute an intermediate network of socially important arenas outside the 'first' and 'second' place, namely workplace and home. In a third place, most people know each other at least by sight.

Meeting Place

Instead of the physical, the social aspect of space can be stressed. The conception of public urban space can, for example, start from the fact that when many people occupy the same space they can meet. This leads to another planners' favourite idea, public space as the *meeting place*. However, while meeting people is important (whether it happens in the city, on the car ferry to Sweden or on a hiking trail in the wilds of Eastern Finland), meetings are not the same thing as public space, they do not ensure its existence. This is because it is the quality of the meetings that counts. Much of the space in the contemporary cities we are used to calling public (as opposed to private) should actually be termed 'the space of collective consumption'. In the consumption spaces individual (but strongly orchestrated) action is favoured, and interaction is kept minimal and superficial. This partly holds even for quintessential public arenas, such as cafés (Bauman 2001: 20–21, Uusitalo 1998).

A deep-cutting interaction may happen when strangers come together. In Richard Sennett's classic definition, a city is 'a human settlement in which strangers are likely to meet' (1992 [1974]: 39, also Lofland 1973). Facilitating the meeting of strangers, the other, is closely linked to the idea of *public sphere*. The present form of public sphere has its origin in the seventeenth and early eighteenth century practices of the emerging middle-class. In the coffee house, the mall and the theatre[2], the new, still undefined social class could meet and discuss commercial and other 'rational' interests, without a need to reveal their personal background (Sennett 1992 [1974]: 17, 49). Essential for this to happen is that the urbanites rehearse 'skills of civility', such as wearing a 'mask', which protects people from each other, yet allows them to enjoy each other's company and interact (ibid.: 264). According to Zygmunt Bauman, civility is pursued in the hope of reciprocation, so that civility, like language, cannot be private (2001: 19). Being civil – or being a proper public space – is a feature of the social setting or milieu. It is not (just) an individual habit or (just) a physical frame or location, but a social space, simultaneously a practice, a way to conceive the situation, and a meaningful lived experience. For Bauman, it means 'a city presenting itself to its residents as common good ... a form of life with a vocabulary and logic all of its own ... so that "wearing a public mask" is an act of engagement and participation rather than of noncommitment...' (ibid.). Generally, public sphere refers to the act of gathering, creating a public, and claiming to exercise critique and attain political power (Sebastiani 2001: 90). Kostof, too, acknowledges that one function of public places is to 'ensconce community and to arbitrate social conflict' (Kostof 1992: 124).

While public sphere is a political concept, its relationship to actual urban public spaces is multifaceted. In the ancient Greek city-states, *agorà* was the physical manifestation and heart of the newly achieved democracy (Arendt 1958,

---

2   The press was also important.

Rajanti 1999). The twentieth century totalitarian regimes have used monumental public spaces to orchestrate political rituals and to *destroy* the public sphere. The relationship can also be detached and indifferent, as is the case with the 'abstract' public spaces of the press, TV and the Internet.

Game and Dance

The 'play' in Siena's Campo is the crowd in the middle of the square and the 'audience' those users who sit in the cafés around the square. Another occasion of urban play is the situation in where everybody is simultaneously an actor and a member of the audience. In such a situation, the play loses its fixed spatial reference and becomes in a certain way self-referential. The physical space and measurable/mappable relations lose their defining force, and the behaviour or social situation can be described and studied alone. Physical space can be put in brackets or treated as a neutral background.

   Street sociality is such a situation. Mäenpää discusses street sociality as a reciprocal *game*, including flirting and sexual promise (Mäenpää 1993). Also the normal use of a crowded pavement can be such situation. Jane Jacobs writes about the constant *dance* (Jacobs 1961) taking place on the pavements of the Village in New York City. The same 'public space as dance' occurs on every pavement; on which street or in which geographical location is irrelevant for the notion of the dance.

***

If the physical aspect of space is thought to be primary, public urban space can be conceptualised through functional differences on a geographic map space, as a stage to be looked at or as a physically bounded outdoor room. If the social aspect of space is foregrounded, public urban space may be seen as a meeting place or as a game or dance of its users. There are also conceptualisations, which mix these aspects more successfully.

   Jan Gehl's 'ethno-spatial' analyses of people's behaviour and preferences in the urban stages of Copenhagen (1987, Gehl and Gemzoe 2001) are rather interesting in this respect. Gehl is able to take into account both flesh and masonry, both man and city, both private and public, painting a holistic picture of urban social space. A rather different notion, that of 'cyborg urbanisation' by Graham and Marvin (2001: 184–90), might be helpful, too. Graham and Marvin conceptualise the mix of technological infrastructures, urban spaces and human bodies. Both urban space and human life are seen as *socio-technical hybrids*. The 'cyborg perspective' revalorises the notion of personal place and place-experience. Even though experience is individual, idiosyncratic and difficult to share, everyone 'partakes' in technostructures that in a number of ways facilitate the experience. Echoing Latour (1986, 1996, 2005), Graham and Marvin state that '[t]he new paradoxes of connection and disconnection in contemporary cities, along with the collapse of the modern infrastructural ideal [of creating a unified and coherent city], therefore have major implications for how we think about both territoriality and temporality – the defining domains of human life' (Graham and Marvin 2001: 206). Discussing 'premium networked places', such as malls, Business Improvement Districts, skywalks, e-highways, international airports and corporate atria under CCTV surveillance, Graham and Marvin note that '[m]any practices of resistance, usually ignored by academic research in its portrayals of simple Blade Runner-style dystopias, can open such spaces to different uses and constructed meanings …' (ibid.: 398). Similarly Marc Augé claims that non-places are continuously reclaimed and remade as places.

Finally, the notions of *margin* and *non-space* refer to a rather interesting socio-spatial formulation. Studying marginal uses of space, Timo Kopomaa has typified public urban spaces using two axes. According to him, on the one hand a space can be socially open or closed; on the other it can be functionally and spatially central or marginal. Kopomaa names the spatially central types as stage and third place. Stage is central for the whole city, becoming an urban attractor, while third place is central for an area or neighbourhood, as in Oldenburg's definition. The spatially and functionally marginal types he calls 'margin' and 'non-space' (*epätila*) (Kopomaa 1997: 202). Margins are important, because they allow for negotiating the edges of the city socially and culturally. In margins reside strange and odd phenomena, people and practices, facilitating cultural innovation (cf. Goffman's front and backside). In Chapter 3, I will come back to the importance of marginality and otherness as constituents of public urban space.

While social, the notion of public space is historical. As I mentioned above, the current theory of space is rather dry, which explains the need to discuss and valorise the notion of public urban space through collections of historical examples. This mode has a peculiar problem. The historical collections always circle around clear positive examples, such as the *agorà* in classical Athens, Michelangelo's square projects, the famous *piazzas* of Siena and Venice or the prized forums of the middle-class public in eighteenth century Paris and London. This is no accident, for to be worth giving the examples need to be exceptionally good and of lasting value. But this leads to an impression that the present public urban spaces would be worse, less interesting, somehow thinner or bleaker than the fine historic cases. This way to define often leads to stories of decline and loss, Sennett's idea about the 'fall of the public man' being a prime example (Sennett 1992 [1974]).

A more nuanced analysis of varieties and differences makes clear that public space hardly is unproblematically open to all. It is not a blank canvas for all to use, but a dynamic and multilayered socio-spatial and historical construct. While privatisation of public urban space is an important theme, warranting criticism, we should not create a false imaginations about complete openness of public space, neither in some point in history (classical Athens, renaissance Siena) nor in a utopian future (new urbanist dreams). 'Open space' is actually a dubious concept (Massey 2005: 152), which may hide the fact that public space is produced in continuous negotiations and conflicts. Public space does not have any easy and pre-existing 'foundation', but is negotiated, at the same time constituted and put at risk. This aspect makes urban spaces genuinely public (ibid.: 153).

The Unhappy Marriage of Critical Urban Theory and Outdated Space-concept

The 'typomorphological' reading of cities directly addresses the conceptualisation of public urban space in architecture and urban design. Typomorphology belongs to the important critiques of the modernistic planning ethos (Rossi 1982 [1966], Vidler 1996 [1976], Moudon 1994). Developed by the Italian architects Saverio Muratori and Gianfranco Caniggia in the 1940s and 50s, it interprets city as an urban artifact, which is built and re-built over long periods of time. Focussing on the societal conditions of urban construction, the approach questions the authority of the modernist planner. The city is not a visual product or a technical project. Therefore, the simplistic notions of public urban space as object-like 'rooms' or a-historical 'meeting places' are also rejected. According to the early typomorphologists, the urban process becomes embodied in *type* (or types) as the carrier(s) of architectural knowledge (Argan [1963] 1996, Verwijnen 1997: 62). This process has its own logic and contingencies, and the city can never be reduced to a single basic idea, such as function.

However, with the increasing interest in public urban space and European urban tradition since 1960s and 1970s (e.g. Krier [1975] 1979, Broadbent 1990), a peculiar intellectual twist has occurred. In many 'postmodern' practices, which refer to typomorphology more or less directly, type is not understood as an abstract carrier of knowledge but rather as a model to be reproduced, as a 'prescription for banal and reductive convention (copying)' (Verwijnen 1996: 61). Instead of a flexible tool of thinking, the notion of type has become an excuse to superficially copy-paste historic buildings and urban spaces onto new designs. This mode of designing public urban spaces masks the radical import of typomorphology, reducing the subtle and complex approach to a simple formal question of new *vs* old, imagination *vs* imitation. The collection of historical examples is again haunting theory and practice!

This intellectual twist I call the *unhappy marriage* of critical urban theory and non-critical, outdated conception of space. As a result, in much of the recent, influential 'critical' practice of urban design the radical epistemological criticism present in typomorphology and many other above-quoted approaches is annulled by mixing it with the simple, visual idea of space, characteristic of the Concept City. This holds for the Krier brothers in the 1970s, Berlin IBA in the 1980s, and at least partly for the present debates around New Urbanism in the US and the revival of Garden Cities in Europe (Kelbaugh 1997, Hall and Ward 1998). With reference to the US situation, Robert Beauregard has pointed out that New Urbanists, who claim to represent an alternative for both high modernism and postmodernism in planning, in fact ambiguously position themselves in 'the space occupied simultaneously by postmodernism and modernism' (Beauregard 2002: 190). Their promotion of visually defined space hierarchies, 'the site plan's logic and rigor', mixed with anti-modern stylistic sentimentalism, are in the end unable to provide a real alternative.

This unfortunate union can partly be understood through an unsolved problem in the typomorphological thinking itself. The contested question is whether, in the present (super)modern situation, past built environment types can guide the production of new types. Early typomorphologists, such as Muratori, claimed that the study of traditional types would facilitate designing according to them, thus helping to resuscitate the urban tradition, which was threatened by modernistic projects. But there are other opinions. Carlo Aymonino has argued that the dialectical relationship between building typology and urban morphology has become 'reversed'. Therefore urban history would no longer guide future design decisions, but rather the independent modern types, such as Le Corbusier's *Unité* or car-oriented shopping mall, would morph the urban context. Because societal conditions have radically changed, this reversed state of the affairs should be accepted (Verwijnen 1997: 66). Aldo Rossi provides other solution. According to Colquhoun, he interprets types abstractly as mental forms of 'utmost clarity', awakening collective memory. Rossi displays type on a high level of generality. Thereby, type is 'no longer vulnerable to technological or social interference', but rather 'stands frozen in surreal timelessness' (Colquhoun 1975, cited in Nesbitt 1996: 346). Rossi's interpretation is self-centred and artistic, but it does help in linking the notion of type to artistic creativity. In their geometric, Enlightenment purity Rossi's designs clearly stand out from their context, and (even though in his later works there are decorations and classical themes) the 'rational' simplicity of plans and volumes characterises his whole *oeuvre*. For Rossi, architecture is autonomous, and its logic is the logic of Reason, superimposed by the 'analogical thought' of memory-evoking archetypes (Rossi 1996 [1976], cf. Broadbent 1990: 167).[3]

Muratori's, Aymonimo's and Rossi's solutions to the paradox of historical continuity *vs* innovation in typomorphology are different. However, all three arguments point away from freely copying past forms and transferring them to new locations.

---

3   This position may explain why Rossi admires the ultra-modernistic design of Brasília. For Rossi, Brasília is an 'extraordinary urban artifact'. Rossi claims that there exists an abstract architecture as 'structure', and the singular design of Brasília would only be understandable through its conception 'according to a architectural technic or style, according to principles and a general architectural idea' (Rossi 1982: 127). Rossi's point in my opinion mystifies 'architecture', as it becomes equated with 'the autonomous logic of compositional process and its importance' (ibid.) and disembodied from a particular city and its 'urban facts'. It is strange that Rossi admires the quintessential piece of 'naïve functionalism'. Nevertheless, the idea of 'autonomous architecture' serves some ends in urban debate and also tells about the complexity of the discourse around typomorphology.

The post-1960s interest in historical cities and public urban space as outdoor rooms warrants one further comment. In broad terms, current planning deals with land use on 2D map space and current architecture with organisation of functions in 3D geometric space.[4] This difference between the disciplines is reflected in the tools they use: planning and urban geography rely on two-dimensional GIS while architecture is primarily produced by three-dimensional CAD tools (Linder 2004). Even though the space-conception in architecture and planning is ontologically and epistemologically the same, as discussed above and in the Introduction, a theoretical question revolves around this difference. This question aggravates the problems of the unhappy marriage.

In a modernistic city plan the architecture of the buildings was rather 'free'. Many forms and styles could be built on a land use zone. Conceptually, planning and architecture were independent systems, together contributing to the production of a project or city-object. In real situations the architecture was of course tightly controlled through ideology and other means as Brasilia or Tapiola show, but nevertheless conceptually there is independence. Now, in those postmodern, New Urbanist and neo-traditional plans, in which strict, pictorial design is applied to the public urban space of a larger neighbourhood or a new town, the whole town essentially becomes an architectural object.[5] Both theoretical and practical independence of architecture and planning are lost, and the scene for the enduring duel between house-designer and city-designer is set. It can be claimed that by treating public urban spaces as visual 'rooms' planning practices that purport to be critical towards modernism have fallen in the trap of *involuntarily importing the space conception of modernistic architecture to planning*. For good reasons Rossi talks little about 'space'. This is because in typomorphology the physical form of a city is a primary data source *for studying the societal process* that produced it (Rossi 1982 [1966]: 29). Whether 2D or 3D, it is a cardinal mistake to be interested in the physical urban form itself, therefore using the form as a source *for studying form*.

Rob Krier, when discussing 'typological and morphological elements of the concept of urban space', makes the mistake. He happily states that all types of space between buildings in towns and other localities is urban space (really: 'space between buildings'), and that '[t]his space is geometrically bounded by a variety

---

4   In *Place and Placelessness* Relph states that 'architectural space, although founded on and contributing to unselfconscious spatial experiences, involves a deliberate attempt to create spaces. The space of city planning, however, is not based on experiences of space, but is concerned primarily with function in two-dimensional map space. [In planning], space is understood to be empty and undifferentiated and objectively manipulable according to the constraints of functional efficiency, economics, and the whims of planners and developers' (Relph 1976: 22–3).

5   Berlin's *Planwerk Innenstadt* is a striking city scale example. New Urbanist neighbourhoods, such as Seaside and Celebration, both in Florida, or Sankt Erikskvarteren in Stockholm are graphic illustrations, too, but less orthodoxly traditionalist comprehensive, pictorial designs, such as Katajanokka in Helsinki, follow the same logic.

of elevations' (Krier 1979 [1975]: 15). This concept of (urban) space is extremely simplistic and does not in the least differ from the arch-modernistic conception of Bruno Zevi, for example. It seems to suffer from the 'realistic illusion' Lefebvre warns about. For Krier, space is naturally simple, 'opaque', and easily defined by the built, material elevations. This naïve physicality is the complement of the illusion of 'transparency', which together sustain the belief in the validity of the Concept City (Lefebvre 1991 [1974]: 27–30). Furthermore, Krier loses the important distinction between 'type' and 'model', reducing type to what can be seen.

In all, this 'vulgar' reading of typomorphology misses the critical potential of the approach, and makes planning the most limited catalogue of past forms. This problem is illustrated by the fact that in Britain the planners' 1980s interest in aesthetic quality of cities and the quality of urban design had a direct connection to the Thatcherite New Right urban policies (Taylor 1998: 146). With or without political labels, it is clear that if the simple idea of urban space as visual space between the facades is imported to planning, the foundations of the conception of city and space in planning do not change much – certainly not for the better. Planning can only become backward-looking architecture in big scale. Problems cannot be solved by increasing the scale of design and visual control.

Excursion 2: Katajanokka

Let us take the east end of Katajanokka, situated next to the centre of Helsinki, as an example of the partially successful criticism of the Concept City and the traps of the unhappy marriage. Katajanokka is an interesting area, because it is regarded as a turning point in Finnish urban planning. In the Katajanokka ideas competition, held in 1971–1972, ideas, which took up the model of the European city, criticised the modernist open urban space and avoided *tabula rasa*, the demolition of old buildings, made a landfall in Finland. The competition was won by Vilhelm Helander, Pekka Pakkala and Mikael Sundman. Pakkala and Sundman carried on the planning of the area in the Helsinki City Planning Office in 1973–1976. The architecture is not historicising, but on the urban level the plan contains traditional urban elements, such as enclosed square and visual foci (Sundman 1991: 108–9). Pakkala recalls the process as follows: 'The relationship with the Merikasarmi complex and the location on the marine silhouette of Helsinki called for a relatively low urban fabric forming a field-like ensemble … The rhythm of the façades was underlined by making each slab stand out as a separate surface' (Pakkala 2001: 156). Although the existing buildings and environment were studied in the competition entry, the plan for the new development was nonetheless conceived and realised from above and from a distance. It can be seen as a 'field-like ensemble' by a planner with a bird's-eye perspective – but of course not by a city-dweller walking along the street.

The planners surely also considered the internal spaces of the area. It has a main street and small side streets leading to the shore. The line terminus where the tram turns around is a kind of piazza, surrounded by a gallery behind which are the advertisement-covered windowpanes of a grocery chain store. The relatively low houses of even height are clad with red brick. Despite the brick and the even height of the houses, they have many small differences, in the shapes of the windows and in the courses of the brick bonds. The façade lines are broken by numerous bay windows, withdrawn sections, balconies, overhangs and openings.

It can easily be seen that at Katajanokka an attempt was made to create urban space by means of architecture. The plan addressed a visual space by means of a bearing theme, variations and modulations, differences in elevation and changes in materials. The art of space in town planning is borrowed directly from architecture. It is an addition or ornament placed on the city seen as a jigsaw puzzle of land use (cf. Häkli 1997: 49), and if possible it will only add to the domination of the eye, the visual representation of the city. Simultaneously present are the Eye of God à la de Certeau – as if the planner had a biscuit mould taken from a map with which he cuts dough of houses into angular shapes confident that he is engaged in good works, creating good urban space – and the Renaissance perspective in which the street space and rows of houses are viewed with the ideal eye of an ideal subject capable of gaining aesthetic pleasure.

Figure 2.1   Merisotilaantori in Katajanokka

Source: Photo: Panu Lehtovuori.

The east end of Katajanokka also underscores the importance and power of the planner's own images and associations above and beyond those of other city-dwellers. Pakkala mentions that 'the zones of lawn and bushes planted between the sidewalks and the houses are to be found, for example, in my childhood environment in Väinämöisenkatu street [in Töölö]'. The example for the route meandering through the city blocks is 'Ville Helander's courtyard between Kapteeninkatu and Huvilakatu streets [in Helsinki's Kaivopuisto]' (ibid.: 159–60). Pakkala sees the features of an Italian mountain town (!) in what is perhaps the unsuccessful restless 'roof landscape'. Unwittingly, these allusions describe the methods and structure of thought of town planning – even planning that was new and critical in its day. The east end of Katajanokka is an urban object, available to visual control through the shape of city blocks, eaves lines and the rhythm of the slab block structures. Even the square (Merisotilaantori) is not a space for people, with its meaning at the core of the concepts, but the subject of an architectural discussion on the dynamics of space, in which the street 'flashes past' or whose inner corner is 'dirty'. Both of these are 'problems' that were 'solved' in the later planning stage with the aid of massing and the choice of colour.

More interesting and anticipating a profound change in the way of thinking is the approach to the old section of Katajanokka taken in the same competition entry. The entrants approached the question of revising and improving the area with small concrete measures. The relevant issues would be addressed house by house, and resident by resident. In a review of conditions carried out in stages, the preferences of individuals, the economic possibilities of owners and the means of planning involving regulations, norms, persuasion and rhetoric all merge into a complex simulation of real urban change, with the diversity and density of the city as its goals. An imagined situation involving change is described as follows: 'The courtyard wing of the building has been torn down. It contained storerooms. The structure could have remained in place as a rented space. It was quite nice, but the residents felt that a slope planted with lawns and bushes would be better. The owners agreed to this arrangement only when permission was received to use the attic space' (*Arkkitehti-lehti*, kilpailuliite 5/1972, 9).

The fact that a new house is 'nice' or that it is important that the 'owner agrees to the arrangement' refer to space as social and socially constructed instead of the visual space of the Concept City. This will be theme of the next chapter.

Conclusion of Part 1

Since 1970s, there has been an increasing interest in European urban tradition, resulting in newly 'artistic' emphasis in urban design and planning. However, the addition of visual 'spatial art' to the toolkit of planning will not produce any qualitative change in it. While this shift does affect the conceived space by adding an experiential dimension of seeing and moving to the habitual 'map space' of planning, it is not enough to reground the practice. Urban planning necessarily operates in the relational social space – whether it admits it or not. It thus needs radically new ways to conceive space. The Katajanokka competition entry by Helander, Pakkala and Sundman contained the bud of a processual and social approach distancing itself from maps and statistics, but it remained in its initial stage, and was not developed to any major degree by the urban planners of the City of Helsinki. Even though the compositions of streets and squares, viewing corridors, forced variation of façades or their forced uniformity, rows of trees, terraces and pavements – the whole set of 'architectonic means' used in planning and urban design – do enhance the Visible City (and possibly increase the planner's professional reputation), the lived space of urban-dwellers and their unique experiences are still placed in parentheses. Planning remains, as before, on the observation terrace of the 110th floor.

The question is qualitative: how to produce meaningful, sensual, strong and rich urban spaces? Or as Sandercock puts it, how to re-enchant our life spaces in cities and regions (Sandercock 1998: 82). How to change the present situation where the production of new built structures and areas actually consumes, instead of produces, experiential qualities, destroys instead of creates? In Finland, and across the developed West, the social space is changing. On both a micro and a macro scale there are increasingly 'cracks' in the façade of planning: it is not organising and mastering the change of urban space as it is supposed to do. I suggest that one important reason for the 'cracking' is that the conceptualisation of space in planning (and urban design and architecture) has remained caught in the Renaissance, in the perspectival. The structures of thought, the representations of space and city it produces and the epistemologies through which it tries to 'see' the city out there have not changed. Therefore, planning and the design of public urban spaces are becoming increasingly 'pathological'.

To change the mainstream approach of planning, the hierarchical superiority of the conceived space, the Concept City, must be challenged in a radical manner. The 'city of urban planning' or its 'space' must be understood as diverse, multifaceted, processual and open. The conceptualisation and representation of the city and the urban space need to be complex, hybrid or 'trans-discursive', crossing the line between discourse and action (Shields 1996: 234). In short, space in general and public urban space in particular must be reconceived to include *vécu*, the lived.

PART 2
Moments of Experience

Chapter 3
Social Space

Market Day

*Saturday market in the Boxhagener Platz. The pavements are lined with vendors'
stalls: bread, sausages, pastries, homemade clothes, books, Glühwein. Compared
to last night, a different crowd fills the street. While the clubs sleep, old women
and men in their worn coats, neckerchiefs, and old-fashioned caps reclaim the city.
They exchange glances, quietly celebrating. 'Guten Morgen', 'Ach so!': a moment
of Ost in the Kiez.*

*I stroll in the crowd, and decide to buy some fish. Joining the queue, I have a
look at the fishmonger's offerings. Suddenly a man starts to angrily shout at me,
telling that I had jumped the queue! I did not think so, but learned that one must
start queuing from the right. The seller looks apologetic, but there is no way to
argue. I turn away, without halibut.*

Black leather jacket and red hat is the wrong outfit for this market place.

Berlin-Friedrichshain 15 November, 2003

***

Produced Space

A lively market place with its shouting vendors, gossiping crowd, practices of
bargaining and queuing, or a theatre evening with the interplay between the actors
and the audience, are classic examples of social spaces. Social space cannot be
understood through naïve realistic conceptions, because it always has several,
qualitatively differing facets or elements. A market place has its physical form,
paved surfaces and stalls, but as important for that particular social space are the
spatial practices of the users, their locations, movements and gestures, as well as
their expectations and beliefs, which may explain why they go there, how they feel
and what becomes meaningful for them.

Many sociologists, anthropologists, geographers and architectural critics
have discussed the social aspect of space,[1] but Henri Lefebvre, in *La production
de l'espace* (1974), was probably the first to propose that all human space is

---

1   Important, 'classical' sources include texts by Durkheim, Simmel, Park and others
of the Chicago School, Foucault, Levi-Strauss, de Certeau, Goffmann, Tuan, Mumford, and
Norberg-Schulz. See Gottdiener 1985 and Strassoldo 1993 for discussion.

fundamentally social: history, society, consciousness, in a sense even nature (Lefebvre 1991 [1974]: 68). Lefebvre claims that it is simplistic and misleading to conceive of space as only an abstract mental category or a lump of matter. Rather, space is a complex *socially produced* phenomenon, where artefacts, practices and mental categories all play a role. Social space is both material and imagined (cf. Soja 1996). Space should not be understood as the neutral backdrop of social actions and relations, but rather as indelibly mixed in these relations, both produced by them and defining them. Every society, or in Marxist terms every mode of production, produces its own social space, forging its own proper space (Lefebvre 1991 [1974]: 31). Lefebvre's understanding of space is holistic and inclusive. There is no way to conceive of social space as an object, something that can be viewed from 'outside'. By stressing that we are inside, partaking in the process of production of space, Lefebvre moves the analysis of space from the synchronic discourses 'on' space (such as the sociological notion of territoriality) to the analysis of the processes by which discourses 'of' space are socially produced (ibid.: 365, Shields 1999: 146).

What is the role of architecture and planning in this production? This question is complex and central to my argumentation, so I will valorise it in all following chapters. A good platform to conceptualise different modalities of production are the distinctions between domination and appropriation on the one hand, and between creation and diversion on the other. An architectural or urban project, such as a new housing estate or urban motorway, entails spatial domination. Dominant space usually empties, closes or sterilises the previous, dominated space. Appropriation, on the contrary, resembles art. Appropriated spaces please and enchant us, but it is often hard to tell who precisely has appropriated. So, appropriation is not evident and clearly defined, like ownership for example. Domination and appropriation are often contradictory – a project destroying an established neighbourhood – but they also depend on each other (Lefebvre 1991 [1974]: 164–6).

Any new building or other work of construction is an act of creation. At some point the creation may become outdated, losing its original purpose and becoming in a sense vacant. Such spaces are susceptible to diversion (*détournement*), or finding surprising new uses (Lefebvre 1991 [1974]: 167–8). If compared to creation, which needs power to actualise, diversion is temporary and 'weak'. Therefore it can be likened to de Certeau's notion of 'tactics' (Certeau 1984). However, at present it seems that more interesting new spaces emerge through diversion than creation. Temporary uses and temporary spaces are the forefront of public space creation for example in Berlin and Amsterdam (Eberle 2002, Lehtovuori et al. 2003, Havik 2004). Makasiinit, which I will discuss in Chapter 8, is a local example of the strength of temporary diversions.

Social production is a constant process. Its 'moments' include strategic projects and tactical strokes, works of construction and works of collective art, *oeuvre* (see Lefebvre 1996 [1968]: 66, 101, 180 for discussion of *oeuvre*). Things are done and redone, while '[n]o space ever vanishes utterly, leaving no trace' (Lefebvre 1991

[1974]: 164). In this process, architecture has its established role in the service of power, building the Concept City. But in the moments of appropriation and diversion, it may also find new roles, opening up opportunities rather than closing them.

The Elements of Social Space

Spatialising Marx's terminology, Lefebvre claims that space is *concrete abstraction* (Lefebvre 1991 [1974]: 26–7, 100–101, Gottdiener 1985: 128–9, Shields 1991: 7–8). It has a binary or dual nature as an object and the condition of its creation, as physical terrain and the activity on it. In his bountiful style, Lefebvre asks that '[i]s not social space always, and simultaneously, both a *field of action* (offering its extensions to the deployment of projects and practical intentions) and a *basis of action* (a set of places whence energies derive and whither energies are directed)? Is it not at once *actual* (given) and *potential* (locus of possibilities)? Is it not at once *quantitative* (measurable by means of units of measurement) and *qualitative* (as concrete extension where unreplenished energies run out, where distance is measured in terms of fatigue or in terms of time needed for activity)? And is it not at once a collection of *materials* (objects, things) and an ensemble of *matériel* (tools – and the procedures necessary to make efficient use of tools and of things in general)?' (Lefebvre 1991 [1974]: 191, original italics).

Social space is a wide, holistic and 'unitary' notion. How to make sense of such complexity, mix and reach of scales from micro to global? What intellectual tools are there to grasp social space?

Lefebvre presents a triad or 'trinity' (*triplicité*) of concepts facilitating thinking about space. Spatial triads are a 'heuristic device' (Merrifield 2000: 173), and their various uses and versions are the recurring theme of *La production de l'espace*. According to Lefebvre, socially produced space can be viewed from the perspectives of spatial practices, representations of space and spaces of representation[2] (Lefebvre 1991 [1974]: 33). Another formulation of the trinity is that of the perceived space, the conceived space and the lived space (ibid.: 39-40). Soja (1996: 69–70) has translated a whole set of other triads from Lefebvre's later *La Présence et l'absence* (an extract translated in *Key Writings*, Lefebvre 2003b [1980]). These include Thing–Product–Work and Totality–Contradiction–Possibility. It is important to understand that Lefebvre's triads are tools of analysis and invention. The three 'spaces' do not appear separately; they are not separate spaces, realities or phenomena, but features of a single – and ever-changing – reality brought forth by analysis (Lefebvre 1991 [1974]: 352). These three 'spaces' are

---

2 Donald Nicholson-Smith has translated Lefebvre's *espaces de représentation* as 'representational spaces' but both Harvey (1989: 218) and Shields (1999: 164–5) have chosen a more accurate 'spaces of representation'. In Finnish the best translation is 'representaation tilat', ei esim. 'esittämisen tilat' (Villanen and Ilmonen 2002).

thus necessarily bound to each other. They are qualitatively different, yet unified and always present. Lefebvre's approach strongly demonstrates that analysis is not 'neutral', but it rather can create new intellectual objects and, therefore, have both practical and political significance.[3]

The *perceived space* entails the city seen by the eye, heard by the ear and touched by hand. Lefebvre associates it with the everyday spatial practices, which ensure continuity and a degree of cohesion for the social formations. Concretely, spatial practices concern the way in which people are placed and move in space. As an example of a 'modern' spatial practice (produced by a neo-capitalist society and the rationality of planning) Lefebvre cites the daily routine of a resident of a state-subsidised block of rental flats on a housing estate. This routine consists of forced movement between the home, workplace and the children's day-care centre (Lefebvre 1991 [1974]: 38).

The *conceived space* refers to explicit representations of space or the city. Lefebvre's theory is such a conceptualisation, as also the concept of space in Euclidian geometry, which Lefebvre criticises. The ideas of space in architecture and town planning, such as the stress on perspectival, visual perception or the detached 'map space', are at present among the strongest and most significant representations of space.

The meaning of a *lived space* is perhaps more difficult to understand. Here, Lefebvre goes under the skin, as it were. A physical space and professional conceptualisations can be regarded as outside of oneself, while the concept of lived space alludes to beliefs, memories, myths, hopes and fears (Lefebvre 1991 [1974]: 33, 39). At hand here is the city, abhorrence, and love lived by everyone with his or her heart and soul. As Lefebvre states:

> The user's space is *lived* – not represented (or conceived). When compared with the abstract space of the experts (architects, urbanists, planners), the space of the everyday activities of users is a concrete one, which is to say, subjective. As a space of "subjects" rather than of calculations, as a representational space,[4] it has an origin, and that origin is childhood, with its hardships, its achievements and its

---

3   In Robert M. Pirsig's brilliant novel *Zen and the Art of Motorcycle Maintenance* (1974) the main character Phaedrus discusses the university institution. The university can be analytically classified in several ways. Many of the possible classifications are correct yet uninteresting in their obviousness. Such easy analysis on an established plane includes the divisions into students, departments and administration, or into faculties. Phaedrus gives a different classification, distinguishing between 'location' and 'church', in other words, between the university as a legal corporation with its employees and buildings from the intellectual content of the university. Phaedrus's analysis of the university's 'social space' highlights its specific purpose, the preservation and continuation of the Western intellectual tradition or even analytical reason itself. At the same time, he manages to make a local administrative dispute seem trivial (Pirsig 1974: 151–4) This provides a good example of the power of unexpected analysis in creating things and having political potential.

4   See above note 2.

lacks. Lived space bears the stamp of the conflict between the inevitable, if long and difficult, maturation process and a failure to mature that leaves particular original resources and reserves untouched. It is in this space that the 'private' realm asserts itself, albeit more or less vigorously, and always in a conflictual way, against the public one. (Lefebvre 1991 [1974]: 362, original italics)

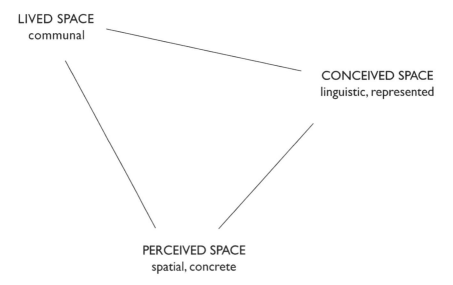

Figure 3.1   The three aspects of socially produced space

Source: after Lefebvre 1991 [1974].

Three decades later, through interpretations by Mark Gottdiener (1985), David Harvey (1989) and Ed Soja (1989, 1996), Lefebvre's ideas of social space and producing space have become rather well known (but not necessarily accepted) among urban sociologists and geographers. Recently, Stuart Elden (2004) and Christian Schmid (2005) have provided excellent constructive overviews of Lefebvre's work. To take some examples of applications, Helen Liggett (1995) has used the trinity to discuss the role of photographic evidence in spatiology, Eugene McCann (1999) has contextualised Lefebvre's concepts in the racialised North American situation and Richard Milgrom (2008) has used them to analyse Lucien Kroll's participatory design practice. In Finland, Ari Hynynen has used the trinity to conceptualise and study immigrants' process of appropriating urban space (Hynynen 2002). Harri Andersson has applied the concepts to explain the process of restructuration of the region of Turku, and especially the change and gentrification of the city centre and harbour of Turku (Andersson 1997). Timo Cantell has insightfully used the triad in assessing Helsinki's cultural transformation since 1989 (Cantell 1999: 22), providing stepping-stones for my work.

However, as I argued in Chapter 1, in architecture and planning (and many other disciplines, in fact) it is not a common way to conceptualise space.

The Relations between Physical, Social and Mental

A pertinent question is, how the many aspects of social space are related to each other. How to conceptually approach the *links* between physical, social and mental, the perceived, conceived and lived? How to tie together the qualitatively different elements or aspects? Or, more precisely, how the 'chain' of production between physical, social and mental aspects of space proceeds? Lefebvre conceptualises the relation dialectically, which I will discuss and elaborate in Chapter 5. To lay the ground for the spatial dialectics and to better understand the problematic, other approaches also warrant attention.

One idea would be to use the three 'spaces' to create a *classification*. This is problematic, however, because classification (or typology) often remains a purely descriptive exercise, having little analytical power in real situations. More fruitful would be an approach, where the classes or types are not mutually exclusive but may overlap. This would lead to a conceptualisation of social space, where various elements or 'spaces' are nested in each other, depending on or influencing each other.[5] The link may be historical or connected to the scale of the proposed spaces, for example. Strassoldo (1993) provides a clear and well worked-out matrix of social spaces, classified by scale, type, and spatial structure or schemata. Norberg-Schulz's multidimensional sequence from the pragmatic space of animals through the perceptual, existential and cognitive spaces to the abstract space of logical relations, is another example (Norberg-Schulz 1971: 11). The *structuralistic approach*[6] is based on isomorphism or one-to-one correspondence

---

5 Lefebvre provides an interesting development of the public-private classification. Referring to Japanese social space he proposes that space can be divided into 'global', 'intermediary' and 'private' (G, M, P). Each category, however, contains all the others (or has characteristics of the others) so that the spatial analysis gets nine classes Gg, Gm, Gp; Mg, Mm, Mp; Pg, Pm, Pp (Lefebvre 1991 [1974]: 155). This classification is quite subtle and allows for the study of differences and change.

6 With the term 'structuralistic' I refer to Lèvi-Strauss' anthropology, following the usage of Rajanti (1999: 9). For Lèvi-Strauss, the sources of inspiration of the structuralistic anthropology were Marxism, psychoanalysis and geology, because in all these something visible or concrete stands for or replaces something invisible, together constituting a 'system'. Language is the key metaphor for these systems. This language-based conceptualisation differs a lot from the dynamic structure-agency theory, which is a common form of 'structuralism' in social sciences and urban geography. The structure-agency relationship accounts for material process and real actors as opposed to the abstract mental structure in Lèvi-Strauss. The terms 'correspondence theory' or 'isomorphic theory' might be substituted for 'structuralistic theory', but they are little used. However, when appropriate I will use the terms 'isomorphism' and 'isomorphic' in this particular context.

between physical and social – or mental, logical, linguistic, etc. structures (Hillier and Hanson 1984, Stenros 1992, Rajanti 1999). Below I will discuss in this specific meaning the pros and cons of two structuralistic accounts on social space, space syntax and Stenros' space-theory. The *socio-semiotic approach* treats the relationship of qualitatively different elements of space as that of the signifier and signified of a sign (Gottdiener and Lagopoulos 1986, Gottdiener 1995). It provides a meta-level analytical tool that may be directly compared to Lefebvre's conceptual trinity. *Typomorphology* is a historical and contingent way to understand the evolution of urban social space. As a theory, typomorphology is less clearly articulated than space syntax and socio-semiotics, but it nevertheless provides interesting insights into the interaction between built form and the 'forces' producing it. Finally, Stefano Boeri's *eclectic atlases* are about locally deciphering the relations between the elements of social space using the visual as the cue. Like typomorphology, eclectic atlases comprise specific readings of the present form and flows, but instead of a long urban history of a site (city), the approach is concerned with events, ephemeral relations and widely differing scales. Methodically eclectic atlases are experimental (Boeri 2000, 2004).

Space Syntax – the Correspondence between Physical and Social Configurations

The idea of 'space syntax' was developed by the team of Bill Hillier at the Bartlett in London in the 1980s. From its academic origin, space syntax has evolved into a 'movement' with web sites and conferences and into a commercial consultancy. Space Syntax Limited claims to be able to aid urban design and development by 'robustly forecasting the effects of design decisions on social and economic outcomes, such as pedestrian movement flows, crime patterns and land values'. It also promises to 'overcome the often subjective nature of traditional architectural practice' and to 'provide objective, evidence-based advice' (www.spacesyntax. com).

The basic hypothesis of space syntax is that *the spatial configuration is the machine of sociality*. Originally, the idea was proposed by Hillier and Hanson in reversed form. They stated that space is 'everywhere a function of the forms of social solidarity, and these in turn a product of the structure of society'. The authors also asked whether space would determine society, and gave 'an affirmative – if conditional – answer' (Hillier and Hanson 1984: 22–3). Either way, in space syntax a deep structural similarity is assumed between the social form and the spatial configuration of a city, neighbourhood, or any other object of study. Configuration refers in this formulation to the interdependent system of visually definable urban or interior spaces. This interdependent character of configuration qualifies space syntax as a relational approach to the system of visual/physical spaces and their links to the social.

In *The Social Logic of Space*, Hillier and Hanson reject several explanations of the link between social order and space. These include territoriality (biological subject as the origin of space), cognitive mapping (cultural subject as origin), purely descriptive accounts on space and its use, as well as urban semiotics. Instead of processes of designing or interpreting spaces, the authors concentrate on existing architecture. So, the theory is substantival. Their basic, very interesting assumption is that it is a fundamental mistake to study space and society as separate things. Including the interiors of single buildings, the urban exterior space and the link between the two, *space is always already a social product*. Simultaneously, space is the 'machine' – a system of constraints and opportunities – which defines the likely pattern of social interaction. So, space is both a product and a producer. Space constitutes a form of social order in itself, and the social meaning of space is already inscribed in the spatial system or configuration (ibid.: 9).

Two social dynamics are articulated by the 'social potential of space'. Firstly, referring to Durkheim, Hillier and Hanson recognise two forms of social solidarity. The 'organic' solidarity is based on interdependence through differences, such as the division of labour, while the 'mechanistic' solidarity is based on integration through similarities, such as belief and group structure. The second dynamic is that of power, which can flow from local to global or vice versa, existing as an overarching global system over the everyday interaction. These social dynamics the authors find inscribed in urban situations with varying emphases and interactions between interior and exterior, boundary and porosity, inhabitants and strangers, spatial segregation and integration (ibid.: 18–22). Furthermore, these variations have local, interurban (intercultural) and historical aspects.

Both space and society are thought of as 'morphic languages'. The interest is in the knowability of these systems or languages. The authors claim that with respect to space, it is possible to retrieve certain rules – the syntax – limiting the underlying random process of settlement formation. With increasingly elaborate rules, more ordered and nuanced settlements emerge. Although there are bewilderingly different urban phenotypes, their genotypes are fairly simple, more easily knowable.

In the actual method of space syntax analysis, the settlement is conceived of as consisting of 'primary cells' (usually houses), the 'continuous system of open space' (usually the public urban space), and the surrounding 'carrier', which can be countryside or the rest of the city outside the study area. Socially, urban space is conceptualised as a reflection of two interaction dynamics, that of 'local' or the inhabitants' and that of 'global' or the probability of contact between inhabitants and strangers. So, ideally at least, space syntax is able to locate the sites, streets or areas, where Sennett's hope of strangers meeting each other may most likely happen. Two respective techniques address these dynamics. The 'axiality' of the spatial configuration tells about the global connectivity and probability of movement, and the 'convexity' tells about the possibilities of local interaction in a single urban space and its control (ibid.: 95–7, cf. Sennett 1992 [1974], Jacobs 1961).

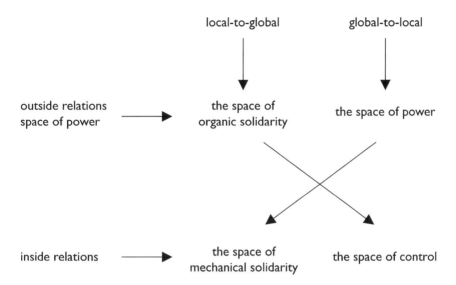

Figure 3.2   The articulation of social dynamics by the social potential of space

Source: after Hillier and Hanson 1984: 22.

Many numerical values for each space and the whole system can be calculated from these two graphical/topological analyses, but they are of no interest here. I am interested in the nature of the space-society link in the theory behind the modelling. The authors say that '[i]n setting out to exhibit the variety of spatial forms that exist as the product of an underlying system of generators we have... followed the principles of what might loosely be called the structuralistic method' (Hillier and Hanson 1984: 198–9). The structure of space[7] becomes viewed as independent and active, so that space has 'its own laws and its own logic'. The authors then discuss a resulting paradox that by giving space autonomy, the structuralistic theory runs a risk of separating space from the rest of the society – the exact opposite of its aim. However, the paradox disappears if we accept that the essence of society (its meaning) is nothing other than its structures, or in other words the 'morphic languages' and the 'patterns they constitute', a process realised and observable 'in real space and real time' (ibid.: 200).

In syntax analysis, space is viewed as a morphic language and one constitutive structure, inseparable from society and its meaning. The structural space-society connection unfolds in real space and time as settlements are built, architectural projects designed and realised and human lives lived. The central notion of this view is *configuration*. According to Hillier, 'the relation between space and social

----

7   The structure of space here means the configuration of spatial, physical elements, which are supposed to be isomorphic with the pattern (structure) of social encounters.

existence does not lie at the level of the individual space, or individual activity. It lies in the relations between configurations of people and configurations of space' (Hillier 1996: 31). Configuration refers to the relational system of all spaces (of the studied, geographically limited area) and their linkages. It is defined as 'relations taking into account other relations' (ibid.: 1). Hillier further claims that configuration is also the subconscious intermediary, linking spatial form and its cultural meaning. When we think of buildings or larger environments, we have in mind their parts, such as rooms or columns, but also their whole entity, the complex of spatial relations the building entails. '[I]t is through configuration that the raw materials of space and form are given social meaning' (ibid.: 43). Even though the built environment appears to us as collection of object artefacts, such as buildings and pavements, they are also configurational entities, in other words structures or 'abstract artefacts' (ibid.: 91–2).

Criticism of Space Syntax

What is puzzling is that space syntax entails an extremely simple concept of society. If society is 'restrictions on a random pattern of encounter between people' and spatial rules or the syntax analogically 'restrictions on a random pattern of agglomeration', there must be something missing. On the other hand, the idea of starting from small and simple to understand big and complex, of proceeding from 'genotypes' to 'phenotypes', has similarities with the constructionist thought of Berger and Luckmann. They famously conceived social forms as an 'evolution' from very simple encounters and basic human reactions towards complex and institutionalised social forms (Berger and Luckmann 1967).

However, the 'social' in space syntax seem to become reduced to the patterns of encounters. This is a very reductive, biological and individualised view. Clearly, space syntax has difficulty incorporating questions of politics, power and tactics of resistance into the theory. Space syntax sympathisers probably overestimate the explanatory power of spatial and social configurations. Cultural impulses, commercially produced lifestyles, distant friends and many other actors and factors affect both the social pattern and the meanings people attach to urban spaces far beyond any physical, urban configuration. City is not the *only* machine, we could moderate, and even though it may be conceivable that the origin of society is in differences between the meeting probabilities of individuals, these certainly do not fully explain the current, planetary social formations. The notion of 'splintering urbanism' (Graham and Marvin 2001) or Castells' idea that simultaneous global connectivity and local fragmentation would define the new urban form of the network society (Castells 1996), refer to the contradictions, not isomorphism, between the physically contiguous urban configuration and the non-local social connections beyond it.

But more interesting than fine-tuning the syntax theory, is to ask if the isomorphism of the physical and the social is a valid idea in principle. Is it really true that both space and society are – even partially or locally – 'configurations', 'restrictions in a random process' or 'morphic languages'? Or is the case rather that Hillier and Hanson have fallen into their own trap? Even though they correctly say that space is always already social, they still try to justify that by creating analogies and formal, observable links.

I suggest that the practical applications of the syntax approach might indicate both the limitations of the analogy of the configurations and the advantages of the syntax conception of space and society. The applications range from aiding the interior design of shopping malls to large-scale traffic estimation, from crime rate studies to air pollution and from crowd control to studying real-estate values (e.g. Hillier 1996, Hillier et al. 1998, Klasander 2003). In Finland, space syntax has been used in metropolitan traffic modelling (Romppanen 2002) and in finding the 'centres of gravity' on a regional scale (Joutsiniemi 2002).

With few exceptions, the space syntax applications are 'one-dimensional'. With this term I refer to studies, where one aspect of the spatial model is used to assess or predict variations of a supposedly directly dependent factor. The most typical case is to use the values of spatial integration as calculated from the axial map, which is assumed to predict traffic densities rather well, in discussing traffic-dependent issues, such as commercial potential, land value or pollution caused by car traffic. Another similar type is the converse use of linking segregated spaces with presumably sparse pedestrian traffic and the resulting lack of social control to, say, street crime or fear of it. These studies are often relatively successful and can be useful for planners and policy makers. However, it is necessary to bear in mind that this 'one-dimensional' usage is highly reductive, so the results may hold locally, but may miss adverse effects on a larger scale or with respect to other, invisibly related variables.

Nevertheless, the success of practical applications of space syntax suggests that there indeed is a grain of truth in the proposition of the interlinked nature of spatial and social configurations. This certainly is a more promising approach than concentrating directly on the visual space, leaving the social off-hand out of the picture! However, this link cannot be total or holistic, but it is present in certain, limited cases and questions. It is possible to justify and study certain specific chains of links, such as accessibility–pedestrian density–crime opportunity–crime rate–image of a street or area–its property value, or accessibility–density of car traffic–pollution–the perceived quality of space, to take two examples. These chains from physical to social and mental may be valid, but nothing guarantees that such chains link together to form a holistic understanding of urban social space. In an urban situation, there are too many different actors and causes for a single explanation to grasp all of them. So, space syntax cannot provide us with a general theory of public urban space. It is intellectually rather dry, and is at its best as a technical tool. However, while most syntax applications do not address the notion of social space in a truly interesting way, they do provide a useful stepping-stone.

Social Space as a System of Places – Stenros' Duration and Order

Anne Stenros' space theory, presented in *Kesto ja järjestys* (*Duration and Order*, 1992), is another structuralistic account or correspondence theory on social space. Instead of the interactions between many urban dwellers – the 'social logic' – it focuses on the individual experiences and the production of meaning, thus complementing space syntax.

Stenros wrote her book in the context of proliferating debates on post-modernism, complexity, and chaos theory. She states that the general perception of the world is changing from 'static' to 'dynamic', and respectively the emphasis of science from 'analytic' to 'holistic'. Because scientific theorisations in general are moving from substances and objects to the relations between them, the architectural theory of space, too, should be renewed to comply with these developments (Stenros 1992: 11–19, see also Varto 2000, Byrne 2001). In this dynamic intellectual context, Stenros sets out to create a 'cognitive theory of architecture', based on the interaction between a human being and his perceptual environment. The theory is supposed to be holistic, pluralistic and modular – to facilitate computer simulations – and its focus should be in relational systems and processes (Stenros 1992: 17, 19–25). Strikingly, though, Stenros states that 'the points of view and influences of cultural studies, sociology, environmental psychology, and behavioural science are excluded' (ibid.: 89). Interactions with other people, the possibility of social constructions, as well as the impact of cultural forms are left in the margin of the theory, and therefore, superficially, Stenros' theory does not seem to be a great account of social space. If space indeed is social, the 'spacescape' or structural level of space (cf. ibid.: 87) cannot be built on private experiences only, as Stenros suggests, but should include culture and societal processes.

Nevertheless, Stenros' space theory contains fruitful ideas. First and foremost, Stenros strongly maintains that *space and place cannot be separated* into distinct categories but are tightly connected. 'Place is like a poem, it is space in a condensed, simplified form …' (Stenros 1992: 315). This idea I consider a key point in understanding social space. Place is laden with meaning; place is the moment of signification without which social space is again just an abstract hollow core. Besides the focus on place, the theoretical extrapolations of her basic schemata, leading to notions such as 'bundle' or 'crystal' of places, 'collage of meaning' and 'spatial game' on the urban scale, are of interest concerning my effort to theorise public urban space. These notions I will develop further in the next chapter on 'weak place'. Now I just want to outline the main points of Stenros' inquiry, concerning the conceptualisation of space:

1. Stenros aims at creating a generic structural model of (architectural) space. With reference to time, structured by *dureé* and succession, she states that space has an analogous abstract structure of 'spatial duration and order', distinct from, but connected to, the actual experiential reality. This structure

has three levels: the actual, perceived landscape; the 'memoryscape', connecting past experiences, the present and future anticipations; and the 'spacescape' or the abstract structure of space.[8] The interactions of these three levels constitute our continuous, layered and laden with meaning spatial experience (ibid.: 115–16).

2. Space fundamentally consists of two kinds of element: transitional and primary spaces. Transitional spaces are linear. They connect; they are the spaces of movement. Primary spaces are the nodes, cores, endpoints or centres of the spatial system. They are the 'moments' of space, if transitional spaces are the 'durations'. On the physical level of 'landscape', transitional spaces manifest themselves as stairs, corridors, paths and streets, and primary spaces as corners, nests, rooms, houses, crossings and squares (ibid.: 153–75). It is worth noting that this idea alone would have helped Spiro Kostof in his effort to find some order to the contingent realm of public urban space (see above p. 37).

3. On the perceptual level, primary and transitional spaces link together, forming 'successions of space'. On the level of memory individual successions of space coexist as the 'system of spatial games'. On the structural level of the model Stenros discusses the sum total of many 'succession of space' as the 'collage of meanings'[9] (ibid.: 244).

The cognitive succession from perception to memory and to the abstract structure in Stenros' space theory resembles Norberg-Schulz's definition of 'existential space'. According to Norberg-Schulz, existential space is 'a relatively stable system of perceptual schemata, or "image" of the environment' (Norberg-Schulz 1971: 17). The notion of 'schemata' is derived from Jean Piaget's studies on children's' conception of the environment. Common denominators between the two cognitive space theories further include the environmental 'image', which refers to Kevin Lynch's much used studies on cognitive maps (Lynch 1960), as well as the general concern on 'orientation'. Like Stenros' abstract structure, or 'spacescape', existential space is 'a generalisation abstracted from the similarities

---

8   The Finnish '*muistimaisema*' can be translated as 'landscape of memory' and '*tilamaisema*' respectively as 'landscape of space'. However, I have chosen the neologisms 'memoryscape' and 'spacescape' because they better convey the dual meaning of the Finnish compounds as landscape made of something (like memories) and landscape in somewhere. Analogously, we can refer to 'mindscape' (cf. Tani 1995: 32) and, in a very different context, even 'scamscape' (Soja 1996: 274–8).

9   It is worth noting that the 'succession of space' (*tilasarja*) is a paradigmatic way to teach both architectural design and analysis of built spaces, at least in the Finnish, modernistic curriculum. Any building and any street can be studied as a succession of spaces, with its inviting or sometimes repelling characteristics, its managed changes of width, height, light, materials and direction. In Stenros' case analysis (1992: 277–), the succession of space is the unquestioned primary approach, which I consider problematic and limiting.

of many phenomena'. As an abstraction, it has 'object-character' (Norberg-Schulz 1971: 17). Further analogies can be found between Stenros' conceptualisation and Taina Rajanti's structuralistic theory,[10] which proposes that social space always has spatial, communal and linguistic/symbolic aspects (Rajanti 1999). For Stenros, identity, for example, is linked to memoryscape, as would be the communal identities or social bonds in Rajanti's theory (see Figure 3.3).

Space syntax focuses in understanding built urban structure, Stenros in the individual experience and meaningfulness in architectural sites and Rajanti in the 'form of community' in an abstract sense. Because the theories have these different focuses and starting points, I do not claim one-to-one correspondence, even less interchangeability, between the space concepts. I do however think that this analogy reveals interesting parallels and gaps. It points to a partial consensus about the types of 'element' of social space, entailing physical, mental, social and symbolic aspects. The interesting question is, how these three sets of concepts are linked to Lefebvre's trinity of perceived, conceived and lived space? Even though there seems to be an inviting similarity, I think that Lefebvre's terminology cannot be meaningfully compared with the structuralistic theories. This is because Lefebvre explicitly opposed stable categorisations and straightforward assumptions about structural similarities in singular, process-like phenomena. Unlike the 'levels' of the theoretical structures, the concepts in Lefebvre's trinity of space were intended as heuristic, embodied tools, fleshed out case by case in real situations (Merrifield 2000: 175). Lefebvre's theory is not a classification or a system of correspondences. Therefore, tabulation might wrongly render deeply different scientific concepts as comparable (cf. Shields 1991: 58–9).

STENROS (1992)	RAJANTI (1999)	SPACE SYNTAX (1984)	
spacescape	linguistic	the 'genotype' or rule of form	SYMBOLIC REPRESENTATIVE
	communal	social configuration pattern of encounters	SOCIAL
memoryscape			MENTAL
landscape	spatial	spatial configuration 'phenotype'	PHYSICAL

Figure 3.3   Comparison of elements of social space in some structuralistic theories of space[11]

---

10   I will discuss Rajanti's theory further in Part 3.

11   Other authors propose further trinities, but in Figure 3.3 I want to concentrate on the structuralistic accounts or 'correspondence theories'. According to Tuan, for example, '[t]hree principal types [of space], with large areas of overlap, exist – the mythical, the

Socio-semiotics – Understanding Signification as Culturally Conditioned

To complement his methodological frame needed to understand the contemporary metropolitan areas, Mark Gottdiener, with Alexandros Lagopoulos, tailored in the 1980s an own version of semiotics. The approach is called 'socio-semiotics'. It draws together ideas from Ferdinand Saussure, Algirdas Greimas, Louis Hjelmslev and Charles Peirce.

Semiotics can be used to study the articulation between physical space and its meaning. According to Gottdiener, the dominant Saussurean semiotics is problematic in this respect, though, because it is limited to the distinction between language and speech and does not address material cultures (Gottdiener 1995: 11). Lefebvre, too, scorned the post-Saussurean[12] semiotics (semiology) of his contemporaries. According to him, many structuralistic and post-structuralistic approaches to the study of social space, including Chomsky's, Barthes', Kristeva's and Derrida's, are futile. In the work of these authors, he sees a general *lack of mediation* between the mental, theoretical constructions and the lived social space. Lefebvre claims that often a 'theoretical practice' produces a mental space, which then in a circular manner becomes the locus of further theoretical practice, trying to assign priority to what is known over what is lived (Lefebvre 1991 [1974]: 6, 61). However, while social space cannot be compared to a blank page upon which someone writes messages, Lefebvre admits that space does signify. What it signifies? According to Lefebvre, space signifies 'do's and don'ts', which brings the discussion back to power: space prohibits, it 'speaks' but does not tell everything (ibid.: 142).

The foundation of all semiotics is the concept of sign. According to Saussure's well-known definition, a sign is composed of the signifier and the signified. In urban semiotics, material objects and forms of settlement space are studied as vehicles of signification. In these studies, the symbolic act always involves a physical object and social discourse on it. The objects of analysis can be streets or facades, but also planning texts or real estate advertising. As a subfield of urban semiotics, socio-semiotics focuses on the study of culturally constructed connotations, the deeper meanings or conception people attach to spaces (in distinction to denotations that work on the level of perception), or the ideological conditioning

---

pragmatic, and the abstract or theoretical' (Tuan 1977: 17). This triad resembles Lefebvre's lived, perceived and conceived (1991 [1974]: 33), even though the grounds of the conceptualisation differ a lot. Tuan and Stenros come close in their ideas about place. Tuan states that architectonic space is about 'public and material reification' of unarticulated feelings and fleeting discernments. He continues by stating that place is 'a type of object' and that places and other objects 'define space'. An example of this is familiarising oneself with a new neighbourhood, which according to Tuan requires the identification of landmarks and street corners, which become 'centres of value' in the neighbourhood space (ibid.: 17–18) – again much like in Lynch's *Image of the City* (1960).

12   Gottdiener's term.

of the individual experience. Socio-semiotics is thus explicitly linked to critical theory, avoiding the individualist bias of much of cultural studies. It can be defined as 'materialist inquiry into the role of ideology in everyday life' (Gottdiener and Lagopoulos 1986: 14). An important idea is that 'connotative codes are social products produced by groups and classes involved in urban practice' (ibid.: 13). If this is true, both social affiliations and spatial practices shape the meanings and emotions each individual invest in a particular material object. Indeed, red lights, MacDonalds' logo, or a modern glass façade are interpreted and felt differently, depending on the individuals' income, age, ethnicity, education and gender.

To circumscribe the idealist stance of post-structuralistic (post-Saussurean) semiotics, Gottdiener engages with the Peircean version of semiotics. For Peirce, sign is a vehicle conveying into the mind something from outside. Sign is not a mental thing but an articulation between object-world and the mind. 'This duality of signs as being both objects in the experiential world with consequences for our behaviour and also cognitive artefacts of consciousness is a fundamental aspect of socio-semiotics ...' (Gottdiener 1995: 10–11). Referring to Peirce's typology symbol–icon–index, Gottdiener states that icon and index, the non-intentional signs, are useful in studying spatial systems. Socio-semiotics accounts for 'the articulation of the mental and the exo-semiotic, the articulation between the material context of daily life and the signifying practices within a social context' (ibid.: 26). Like the correspondence theories, socio-semiotics is based on the principle of structural similarity. To open the semiotic inquiry, Saussure's sign is 'decomposed'. Both the 'expression' and 'content' (signifier and signified) are broken down to 'form' and 'substance'. Instead of two terms, the analysis deals with four. Data-gathering calls for both visual methods and cultural research. After good command of the subject, the relations between conditioning ideology, immediate perception, objects and their wider urban context can be richly studied. Gottdiener (1995, 1997) presents socio-semiotic analyses of environments for consumption, leisure and tourism. Socio-semiotics can also be applied to gang graffiti, visual demarcation of ethnic areas and many other elements, which together comprise the contemporary urban space.

$$\text{SIGN} \quad = \quad \frac{\text{content}}{\text{expression}} \quad = \quad \frac{\dfrac{\text{substance}}{\text{form}}}{\dfrac{\text{form}}{\text{substance}}} \quad = \quad \frac{\dfrac{\text{non-codified ideology}}{\text{codified ideology}}}{\dfrac{\text{morphological elements}}{\text{material objects, text}}}$$

Figure 3.4a   The decomposition of sign

Source: after Gottdiener 1995.

Gottdiener suggests that the 'substance of expression' (i.e. material objects or physical space) would be the mechanism of power in a society, constraining the play of signification. Material forms are understood as manipulative environments (Gottdiener 1995: 13, 30). This idea comes close to Hillier's view of the physical spatial configuration forming the constraints to social formation (see above). For an architect it is no surprise that – as Gottdiener claims – '[m]aterial forms, such as the theme park or the shopping mall, are engineered for an effect just as is Foucault's prison, clinic, and hospital' (ibid.: 30). Material forms, urban designs included, are never simply matter but always 'encoded by ideological meanings which are engineered into form' (ibid.: 28).

To study architecture, the socio-semiotic model of sign can be reformulated (Gottdiener 1995: 87) (see Figure 3.4b).

$$\text{SIGN} \; = \; \frac{\text{content}}{\text{expression}} \; = \; \frac{\dfrac{\text{substance}}{\text{form}}}{\dfrac{\text{form}}{\text{substance}}} \; = \; \frac{\dfrac{\text{social ideology}}{\text{architectural ideology}}}{\dfrac{\text{architectural paradigm}}{\text{morphological units}}}$$

Figure 3.4b   Socio-semiotic formulation of sign to study architecture

Source: after Gottdiener 1995.

Further, a socio-semiotic study of an architectural space would include both paradigmatic and syntagmatic axis. In the case of a mall, for example, the paradigm is the 'motif of the mall', a theme the mall designers apply to hide the instrumental reason of the mall (which is to make money). The syntagm concerns the articulation of the numerous design elements within the mall (ibid.: 86–94, see also Kuusamo 1991: 102). Likewise, one could envision a socio-semiotic study of an urban project or a new public urban space.

Typomorphology Revisited – Type as a Trace of Social Practices

Types structure our thinking and acting in most spheres of life. They help us to distinguish phenomena from each other, as well as to see likenesses between them. In science, typifying (classification) attempts to be exact. The types of a certain typology are mutually exclusive, and together they are supposed to cover the studied field of phenomena in its totality. The phenomena are looked at from outside, as if under the researcher's magnifying glass. In architecture, the scientific notion of type is represented by the concept of functional building type – originally proposed by J.N.L. Durand in his *Précis de lecons d'architecture données á l'École Polytechnique* (1802–1809). In *A History of Building Types* (1976) Nikolaus Pevsner, in turn, follows the function, materials and styles as the threads of the story leading to modernism.

Above on p. 43 I referred to typomorphology in the context of design practices and the 'unhappy marriage' between critical urban theory and an outdated space concept. Compared to the structuralistic accounts, typomorphology provides a different analytical approach to social space. According to Moudon, 'typomorphological studies reveal the physical and spatial structure of cities. They are typological and morphological because they describe urban form (morphology) based on detailed classifications of buildings and open spaces by type (typology). Typomorphology is the study of urban form derived from studies of typical spaces and structures' (Moudon 1994: 289). Let us discuss the characteristics, which make typomorphology a potentially interesting conceptualisation of the relationship between physical and social aspect of space.

Firstly, unlike socio-semiotics, typomorphology offers an opportunity to bridge the gap from thinking to action. In architecture and planning, type potentially has a dual use, as a tool of both analysis and design. To understand the generative moment of type, it must be distinguished from model. This distinction was originally made by Quatremère de Quincy in *Encyclopédie Méthodique* (1825). He proposed that model concerns form which can be repeated and imitated, whereas type is 'the idea of an element which ought itself to serve as a rule for the model' (Argan 1996 [1963]: 242). So, type can be defined as an abstract object built through analysis that reproduces the properties that are deemed essential by the analyst of a family of real objects (Moudon 1996: 304). Argan has also proposed a solution to the problem of continuity between existing and new types. He has identified two 'moments' in the design process: 1) the typological moment, when the rules of design and building used in the past are identified and understood, and 2) the moment of invention, when the artist answers the historical and cultural questions through a critical approach (Moudon 1994: 294, Argan 1996 [1963]: 246). Secondly, typomorphology considers all scales of the built landscape. Caniggia, for example, identifies built objects on four different scales: the building (*edificio*), the group of buildings or fabric (*tessuto*), the whole town (*città*) and the region (*territorio*) (Moudon 1994, 291). Thirdly, typomorphology characterises urban form as a dynamic and changing entity, where the built artefacts are entwined with their producers and users. In typomorphological studies, the urban form is understood 'as it is produced over time' (ibid.: 289). The approach is about dialectics over time, not about frozen city-objects, and it therefore opens up an opportunity to involve in analysis also the political and economic structures (Rossi 1982 [1966]).

In all, what is interesting concerning the analysis of social space, is that typomorphology implicitly deals with built environment as a processual whole, having formal, functional and signifying dimensions. In this view, type contains the relationship of form and use, becoming the carrier of architectural knowledge (Verwijnen 1997: 62). A type is the 'product' of long construction and wearing out. It is tied to history, changing continuously in relation to the urban context and that society in which planning, design, building and use are performed. The emphasis of process, not the synchronic, visualisable form, is important. Type can be seen as a palimpsest or a *trace* of social practices; its relation to social space is indexical.

However, as Moudon points out, typomorphologists have not *explicitly* discussed the interrelationships between the analytical approaches studying urban form as objective and material on the one hand and as subjective and perceived on the other (Moudon 1994: 304). The relationship has remained implicit, making typomorphology somewhat difficult to apply consistently (Verwijnen 1997: 63).

Eclectic Atlases

As direct criticism against the proliferation of the abstracted map-space of satellite photography and other forms of distant imaging, Stefano Boeri has proposed an alternative strategy of research and representation of space, that of 'eclectic atlases'. According to Boeri, instead of increasing our understanding of the urban process and present-day social spaces, the new images of the world's sprawling urbanised areas have produced an 'epistemological trauma'. 'The democratisation of a powerful technology for territorial observation has had the paradoxical effect of spreading a sense of impotency among the disciplines that study inhabited space', he writes (Boeri 2004: 118). The result is a 'rhetoric of chaos', with which researchers have tried to define entities they finally have been able to see, but not to explain. Boeri claims that this difficulty to make sense of the stupefying satellite images does not reflect external phenomena but is a symptom of intellectual laziness.[13]

Boeri defines eclectic atlases as

heterogeneous texts (reports, photographic surveys, geographic and literary descriptions, classifications, research reports, qualitative investigations, essays and articles, anthologies and monographs, collections of plans or projects ...) – [which] seek new logical relationships between special elements [of space], the words we use to identify them, and the mental images we project upon them. They tend to be 'eclectic' because these correspondences are based on criteria that are often multidimensional, spurious, and experimental. (Boeri 2004: 119)

Much like Lefebvre, Boeri links actual urban space and its representations. He criticises generalisations, claiming that eclectic atlases search for individual, local and multiple codes, which link the observer in each single case to the phenomena observed. He assumes a link between 'the physical city, its inhabitants, and the internal city of the observer' (ibid.: 120). This mode of research warrants the observer really entering the inhabited space he is studying. Instead of stepping back and distancing, it is about exposing oneself bodily, making lateral

---

13   See the Dutch *Archis* 2/2004 for interesting criticism of efforts to map the global social space.

connections and looking at the 'small' to see more. There are correspondences between space and society, between physical and mental, but instead of general structural connections represented as invisible layers or thematic maps, they are local, changing and elusive. Boeri thinks that physical space slowly reflects the fast changes in lifestyle. Societal changes do not immediately leave enduring traces, but rather 'more fleeting, discontinuous and shifting signs' (ibid.: 121), warranting the detective work, an effort to decipher knowledge from small (visual or material) traces with detailed fieldwork.

An example of Boeri's approach is the Uncertain States of Europe project USE (Boeri 2000). Several contributors have studied various phenomena of the changing Europe. Special interest has been self-organisation, or how new social forms and phenomena emerge in unplanned or little regulated processes. The fifty cases of USE include wild street commerce in Belgrade (Dzokic et al. 2000), the 'transnational tribes' constantly looking for new spaces for rave parties in the South of Europe (Vari 2000), professionals in the Benelux countries, who avoid metropolitan areas and rather inhabit the borders and margins of the region (Schmit 2000), and the 'autocatalytic growth' of Helsinki during the IT boom (Palmesino 2000). New socio-spatial terms, such as 'inundation', 'eruption', 'intensification' and 'clearing', respectively, describe these locally found processes. Three of the new terms seem to refer directly to public urban space. 'Inundation' is the process of the invasion of public ground by informal, mobile commerce, generating 'a form of collective space which is at once hyperfragmented and dense'. Below I will discuss how urban events 'inundate' space in Helsinki. '*Détournement*' (or diversion) is a situation where the signifier (a built form) survives the disappearance of the signified. 'Eruptions' point to temporary collective points, which are born after the collapse of traditional open and rooted public urban space. Eruptions are the other part in a 'double geography' of 'hypercoded static spaces' and 'undercoded, itinerant spaces' (Boeri 2000: 371–6). Furthermore, Boeri et al. have identified spatial types or 'metaphors', which describe self-organisatorial assemblies of individual acts and the big waves of urban and social change. If thinking new forms of public urban space, 'linear attractors', 'islands' and 'grafts' may be of interest (ibid.: 368–70).

***

Space syntax, Stenros' space theory and socio-semiotics assume structural similarities between aspects of social space. Typomorphology and eclectic atlases treat observable forms and patterns as traces (indexes) of specific, historical and contingent processes of space production. These two 'strategies' to conceptualise the relation between qualitatively different aspects may not be the only ones (classification with overlapping or nested types is a possible approach, too). However, they provide two building blocks for the dialectical, process-oriented conceptualisation, which I will develop in Part 3. The structuralistic approaches provide analytical tools and explanatory frameworks to see beyond the visible, to memories and meaning and to ideologies and economies. They are like butterflies opening their wings in the thin air, showing some aspects of social space as 'concrete abstraction'. Typomorphology and eclectic atlases, then, look back and forth in time. They open the eyes to the constant change that is occurring in space, but also to the fact that nothing is completely lost in that change. Types of built landscape and new process-concepts, such as 'eruption', can be used as generative platforms in design and planning.

Excursion 3: Two Theatres

A week ago, we went with Laura to the Apollo Theatre. The creamy building stands on a corner of a big road; Piccadilly Station is not that far. Stockport Road. In industrial Manchester it probably used to be a great street, but now the surroundings are quiet, deserted. As if the streets were looking but not seeing anything. Streets where the grey wind can blow.

Only the gig brings a moment of life to the street-corner: the audience flows in, tickets are scalped, and a man collects money for a cancer campaign. The scene is surrounded by post-war industrial sheds and a ruined warehouse, facing the fringe of a bleak suburban redevelopment. Brunswick.

Before entering the theatre, we take a short walk. Two blocks further there is a half-empty, tiny shopping centre, a time-worn church, a kindergarten and a school, surrounded by sparse rows of two-storey townhouses and a lonely council tower. Brown brick, asphalt, brown brick. Door. Door, door, door with a flowerpot. Door, door. Door with a quiet old woman standing in the doorway. Randomly in the middle of the row-houses stands an old pub like a stone in a river. Immobile, like the old woman.

When we walk back, I realise that like the pub, the theatre is a time machine, sustaining short moments of the bustling 1930s in the middle of post-1970s nausea. Brunswick is a Bakhtinian chronotope (cf. Gardner 2000, 60). Two times are juxtaposed, making a novel-like space.

Do not queue. There are more toilets upstairs and in the auditorium.

We enter the vestibule. The striking thing about the Apollo is the interior. It is dark red, all over. But more importantly, every space and room is wrapped to form a single surface. The auditorium is wrapped in a red velvet-like surface, the cramped foyer is wrapped, and so are the bar, the stairway and the ground floor vestibule. Tiny doors, no windows. It is like being in a whale's stomach.

A few weeks earlier I had visited the new Bridgewater Hall (Sven-Tüür, Sibelius, Pärt, Shostakovich). Then I saw nothing interesting in it. It is a new, modernistic concert hall with nice, precise acoustics and lofty foyers. Period. But now I am surprised at how sharp a contrast there is between the two theatres! In terms of architectural space, they seem to have nothing in common whatsoever.

Let us take the humblest element, the stairs, as an example. In the Bridgewater Hall the stairs connect open platforms, creating their own vertical space which co-exists with the horizontal spaces of the foyers. That is standard practice in any contemporary architecture. Furthermore, through full height glass walls, the stairs and the foyers alike are connected to the outside, sharing the same view. That is also standard practice. The stairs, a rather simple 'spatial element' are treated and created as a juxtaposition of at least three 'spaces', each having very different qualities and scales. In sharp contrast to those qualities, Apollo's stairs are a curving tube, separated from the foyers by doors. They are like an intestine, which connects two parts of the whale's viscera.

This difference between the treatment of space in the two theatres has various forms and intensities, but it can felt in every space, the foyer, the auditorium, the bar. Even in the toilet. Furthermore, in contemporary buildings the juxtaposed, complex and sometimes fragmented nature of spaces is amplified by the omnipresence of technological systems. Even if you wished, you would not get rid of a whole range of installations, not to mention the 'windows' of monitors and screens and the 'eyes' of surveillance cameras.

Flowing space, transparency, juxtaposition: that is the familiar language of modern architecture, spoken for 100 years. But only when you experience its opposite, you realise how common an experience it has become.

Modern, not archaic, is under our skin.

Manchester, 25 April 2001

Chapter 4
Weak Place

Arabia/Looking for Places

From home, I walk along Hämeentie road towards Arabia. I ponder the notion of place and I try to see, without prejudice, which of the things all around – bridges, roads, planted bushes, fenced-off pieces of parkland, natural rocks and icefalls on them, old depot buildings – I could call 'places'. I realise that there are very few. There is an old mansion with its park-like courtyard (now used by the Botanical Garden) while a kilometre away stands the characteristic facade of the Arabia factory; that is about it. Of course, if one were an 'artist' and searched, say, for a pictorial motif, almost anything would do, such as the crossing of a footpath and an industrial railway line, where rusty traffic signs lean against each other, with a rough fence and a clear spring sky as their background ... But would a framed picture, which becomes significant in an art exhibition, be a 'place'?

Arabia, Helsinki, 21 March 2000

***

From Space to Place

So far I have argued that in creating a new conception of public urban space, which would include *vécu*, the lived, space needs to be conceived of as socially produced. As discussed in the previous chapter, the notion of social production ties together the physical, social and mental aspects of space. In these connections, there are two different levels, which I have not yet reconciled. Socio-semiotics and space syntax address the link between physical space and wide, socially produced realms, such as economy and ideology, while Stenros' space theory deals with the link between physical space and mental representation: the realm of personal experiences, idiosyncratic interpretations, memories and unique life histories. Physical space is a starting point for both, but the linkages are built in different directions. Space syntax and Stenros' theory can be seen as complementary, but because the main space concepts in these two theories, configuration and place, are on a different level of abstraction, the personally lived and the social still remain conceptually separated.

If conceptually developed, the notion of *place* can be used as an intermediary in this space-theoretical construction. That is because the link between personal meanings and place is better established than that between meanings and space.

As I have argued, it is still not uncommon to conceptualise space in abstract terms, so that the complexity, heterogeneity and especially the personal, lived aspect of social space are lost from view. Place, in contrast, is clearly human, close to us and, therefore, *vécu*. It is in place, in the sense of place and placelessness, and in conflicts 'of' places, where the subtle voices, the strongly felt moments of significance and the 'other' environmental relationships I am looking for, surface. However, place is not an innocent concept, either, but rather needs careful reconsideration. Aristotle, in *Metaphysics,* suggested that space is the sum of all places, a dynamic field with directions and qualitative properties. This 'placial' interpretation of space was gradually undermined by Platonic and Euclidean views (Norberg-Schulz 1971: 10). The standard perspectival idea, established by Newton and Descartes, is that space is the 'upper' term, the absolute, the totality, the infinity or the container of everything there is, while place is seen as the secondary term, merely a 'part' or 'modification' of space. To avoid reproducing this perspectival misconception, the notion of place and its theoretical potentiality need to be rethought and 'rescued' (Casey 1997).

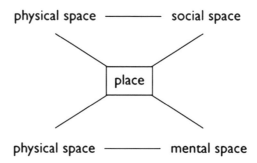

Figure 4.1   The notion of place links two distinct 'levels' of correspondence between elements of social space

In human geography, it has become established that meaning and place are inseparable. Place, topophilia, *genius loci* and sense of place belong to the central terminology of life-world in human geography (Tani 1995: 18). Place is a location in space to which people assign meanings. Pauli Tapani Karjalainen defines place as a meaningful entity of relations that we project onto our environment (Karjalainen 1997: 231). Meaning arises from intention, the striving to do something. We can ask in what way and seen from what perspective does something in a space or environment begin to mean something and be understandable. A place becomes an 'entity of means' which is relevant in relation to this intention, and therefore meaningful, facilitating the living of the place (Karjalainen 1987: 17–19). Similarly, Edward Relph (1976) emphasises the strong relationship between place and individual identity. We do not live in a place so much as we live a place or with a place. Furthermore, place (or the identity of the place) is often defined as consisting of three elements: the physical features of place, the activities that take place in it and the meanings that people project on it.

Towards Relational Understanding of Place

This definition is somewhat problematic, though. If place is defined in this manner, it 'needs' the neutral background, which all too easily appears as nothing other than the absolute Cartesian space. This neutral background, 'environment', is easily interpreted as the upper term of a dualism,[1] and the intellectual effort may fall back on the perspectival conception of space (Lehtovuori 2000). The ideas of place as a 'fusion' between objective and subjective or a 'bridge' between the two are likewise reflections of the Cartesian duality between objects and the subject. However, already Relph stated that the three aspects of physical features, activity, and projected meaning, are not quite enough to define a place. Only a special experience of being inside will distinguish places from space, and will form a place (Relph 1976: 141). Place then becomes conceived of as *the moment of signification*.

This idea is an important step towards re-conceptualising place so that it plays a role in the relational, dynamic conception of social space. But to understand place as a non-essential, ephemeral and event-like warrants considerable rethinking of the notion. As Casey says, if place is to come into its own after two millennia of foregrounding space and time in metaphysics, it must appear in very different forms than the theorisations we are familiar with. 'The shape of place, its very face, has changed dramatically from the time of Archytas and Aristotle. So much so that we may have difficulty recognising place as place …', he states (Casey 1997: 339). Place cannot be seen as the 'container' or mere location, but rather as personal, momentary, even singular. The everyday conception of place as 'something', as material, bounded and fixed, should be questioned. I will develop the new notion of place, which I call *weak place*, through discussing Stenros' place-conception, the notion of place in Castells' 'space of flows', as well as the ideas of 'non-place' proposed by Augé and the 'global sense of place' by Massey.

Residues of Essentialism in Stenros' Place-theory

Let us firstly have a closer look at the relationship between 'space' and 'place' in Stenros' theory. Stenros states that:

---

1 Michel de Certeau gives space and place different meanings than the human geographers discussed here. For de Certeau place (*lieu*) is a geometric definition, the (permanent) location of something, while space (*espace*) emerges from the movements of people and the meanings given by them (see Saarikangas 1998: 248, 266).

> The mechanistic and deterministic perception of the world [of modern science]
> has led architectural research to study space as a functional system or cognitive
> environment – not as space in itself, in other words as an experiential place.
> By and large, research views space and place as two separate and unconnected
> phenomena. Place is primarily understood as a specific, separate quality, not as a
> structural, organic part of space. (Stenros 1992: 11, transl. PL)

From the point of view of my theoretical undertaking, this passage contains both
the main interest and main difficulty of Stenros' project. We learn that space and
place are the same – space in itself is an experiential place – while simultaneously
place still is said to be 'part of space'. There is a logical contradiction. It seems that
the notions of space and place are about to collapse on each other to form a wide
understanding of the layered and time-bound 'spatial experience'. This I consider
a highly interesting idea, pointing towards place conceived of as the moment of
signification. However, on the other hand, the autonomy of individual concrete
places and their separation from 'space' is for Stenros difficult to conceptually
overcome. Why is that?

For Stenros 'space' is essentially the *meaningful* space, consisting of places.
This is because the theory from the outset rejects the absolute notion of space and
ventures into the dynamic relations between human beings and their environment.
Space is the perceived, memorised and laden with meaning space, human space,
one could say. I think that this is a fruitful way to think: we are not able to dissociate
from ourselves, we are 'insiders'. Consequently, Stenros' project is very much
about the Lefebvrean lived space, *vécu*, about myths and deeply felt meaning.

Actually, more may be at stake here. I believe that Stenros is ultimately
interested in no less than the meaning of life. Now and then she refers to emotionally
charged places of childhood, which are 'refuges of thought and heart', or talks
about intuition as the (lost) connection to the 'absolute' or 'universal' reality itself.
In my view, her theory is an effort to describe and formalise how our being in the
world, which is laden with meaning, could be related to the physical and perceptual
realm, in which architecture partakes. Because of her ultimate interest in the full
meaning of life, which for her manifests itself in god-like strokes of intuition or
deeply moving moments of emotion, beauty or understanding, Stenros views
'theory' as somehow an inferior form of intellectual activity. Theory is necessary
because after all things must be explained and communicated, but it is not the most
valuable or subtle thing. Robert Pirsig's distinction between the pre-intellectual
'quality' and formalised knowledge – be it philosophy or natural science – in *Zen
and the Art of Motorcycle Maintenance* refers to a similar idea (Pirsig 1974: 250)[2]
and so do Lefebvre's notions of 'fully lived moment' and 'total person'.

---

2   'The past exists only in our memories, the future only in our plans. The present is
our only reality. The tree that you are aware of intellectually, because of that small time
lag [between the instant of vision and the instant of awareness], is always in the past and
therefore is always unreal. *Any* intellectually conceived object is *always* in the past and

So, for Stenros 'space' seems to refer to the constantly accumulating and changing sum of individual experiences and memories, flowing from the unmediated lived moments. These moments, which actually are the only foundation and 'source' of lived space, Stenros' calls 'germs of space' (Stenros 1992: 163). But still she states that 'place is part of space'. It is as if Stenros would not fully grasp the implications of her own idea. Places, like the itineraries of walk in de Certeau, really make the space: 'they are not localised; it is rather that they spatialise' (de Certeau 1984, quoted in Harvey 1989: 217). Why does the fully lived moment not get the generative status it deserves?

The problem is a relic of the essentialist notion of place: Stenros' theory is not able to get rid of its physical fix and demarcation. While she aptly observes that a place forms at the intersections of individual, experienced 'spatial orders'[3], place incorrectly remains associated with fixed physical features or objects, because the factors distinguishing a place from its surrounding 'environment' or 'neutral space', are for Stenros the conventional means of architectonic space (cf. Stenros 1992: 148). Unintentionally the theory equates the 'birth of a place' with the physical-visual articulation of space through variations of light, changes of material, walls etc. (cf. Ching above pp. 15–17). This is unnecessary even in the cognitive frame, because the relationship between the perceiver, the perceived and the perceptions – or in other words the bodily and physical human being, built spaces and the various psycho-physical processes involved in seeing, hearing, touching, and smelling – could be discussed without including a matrix of fixed physical elements in the theory.

Stenros tries to alleviate the difficult tie between fixed locations and relational interpretation of place by introducing the element of time. According to her, depending on the structural context (spacescape), the fixed points, 'primary spaces', or 'places', can be 'active' or not. In this time-dependent system, '… a place is not only a certain fixed, geographically bound location … [but] the relationship of the preceding space with the following one gives a place its meaning' (Stenros 1992: 151). The spatial or urban experience in a given moment is a 'collage of meanings' formed by the places that happen to be activated (ibid.: 235–44). Furthermore, a strong 'sense of place' may emerge when all three levels (perceived, memorised and structural) are simultaneously 'active', so that identifying with landscape

---

therefore *unreal*. Reality is always the moment of vision *before* the intellectualisation takes place. *There is no other reality*. This pre-intellectual reality is what Phaedrus felt he had properly identified as Quality. Since all intellectually identifiable things must emerge *from* this pre-intellectual reality, Quality is the *parent*, the *source* of all subjects and objects' (Pirsig 1974: 250, original italics).

3   In my view the difficult concept of spatial order can be conceived of through the concept of the entity of means referred to above. Spatial order is a collection of spaces or places meaningful and useful for the individual. Stenros does not follow this line of thinking. For her, spatial order is mainly the 'succession of spaces', a favourite concept of architectural training and criticism.

evokes memories and sparks a momentary consciousness about 'universal structure' (ibid.: 117). All this seems to be much like the fully lived moments of Lefebvre. However, when combined with the static physical matrix of (possible) places, this seems to lead to a middle position between the absolute and relational definition of place. Stenros is forced to say, that 'place has a dualistic nature', being simultaneously generic and unique, simultaneously a physical structure and a conceptual interpretation or meaning of the structure (ibid.: 199, 245).

While Stenros' relational effort has merits, the theory of space and place should take one more step and redefine the physical side of the equation. Everyone can 'throw' meaning anywhere. Meaning is not the property of any physical location or feature by virtue of its existence (e.g. Cavallaro 2001: 3), but creating meanings is a genuinely human ability. Meaning does not 'emanate' from the physical, but the physical is invested with meaning.

Because place and meaning are inseparable, also place-creation is a genuinely human activity. Places cannot be 'found', but rather they are 'produced'. Therefore, places do not exist independently of human beings. From the primacy of physical features the theory should move to the primacy of meaning. Paraphrasing Barthes, we could say that 'meaning speaks space'. Whatever feature, even a random crack in the tarmac, is sufficient change to create a difference, to draw attention and to engender a place. It is unnecessary to include any semi-permanent matrix or lattice of physical points or places in the theory. So, for Stenros, the steps descending to the Seine, the courtyard of the Louvre with Pei's pyramid, the Eiffel Tower or the whole of Paris may all be places, or a single place. I would continue that so may any tiny shrub, patch of lawn with used needles and condoms, any nook of any metro station, any café, any nameless alley, any boulevard, park, *banlieu*… Even though Stenros does not directly state it, it is clearly so easy to find 'germs of space' that the exercise of pointing and mapping them becomes meaningless. To limit the discussion to cases of accepted high architecture, is her personal choice alone. The featureless 'neutral space' from which these 'germs' may stand out should be treated as a cognitive category of 'non-attention' but not as a physical category of homogeneity. Ultimately the whole physical environment, in the literal sense, consists of possible places, which could be called 'proto-places'. It is an unnecessary ballast of the theory to regard all these innumerable proto-places as a fixed system of localised possibilities, of which some are 'active' and some not at a given moment. The theory unnecessarily lapses into idealism, trying to imagine an existence for the 'inactive' proto-places. Furthermore, it needs to assume, again, an absolute space to locate the matrix. And how, precisely, could the infinite matrix of proto-places come together to form a finite and differentiated 'spacescape'?

The unnecessary isomorphism between physical locations and meanings given by people lessens the practical value of Stenros' theory. Even though memory, deep meanings, place and place myths are discussed, these interesting notions are unable to make any difference for the analysis of physical spaces, or their design. The canonical but obviously limited notion of the succession of spaces is the only practical element; architects know also without complicated theorising that this articulation and manipulation of space can be done more or less artfully, better if more. It is interesting to know that a change in the environment (change of light, direction, material …) is a 'germ of space', triggering attention, being memorised, and possibly growing to a place or even place myth. But this knowledge does not make much difference to the architect or urbanist in front of his computer screen.

A further question concerns imaginary places, such as places in movies, novels or dreams. For these, the material underpinning (proto-place) is even harder to specify. This is a classic problem of semiotics (what is the referent of 'unicorn') and it can be solved by thinking that the combination of printed ink spots, for example, is the material underpinning (Gottdiener 1995). This solution may be quite unsatisfactory, but is not a central consideration here, because, like Stenros, I want to refrain from discussing imaginary places. My treatise concerns lived space and practices, which have some underpinning in the material, urban space. On the other hand, films and novels can and do have importance in directing and framing the interpretations of lived situations.

Is Place Necessarily Contiguous? – Castells' Parallel Universes

If the discussion of Stenros' theory showed that the essentialist notion of place – the idea that place is a particular location in an absolute space-continuum and a corresponding 'position' in an abstract, mental 'grid' – is a burden for relational place-concept, scrutiny of Castells' dualism of 'space of flows' *vs* 'space of places' offers a way to dismantle the idea of the contiguity of place. Many believe that places are somehow suffering or fragmenting under the emerging global social space or the condition of late capitalism. It is claimed that some of the processes of contemporary society would weaken authentic lived places and erode their importance in structuring the experience of the environment. Relph in his classic study describes this as 'placelessness', referring to the destructive effects on places caused by tourism, the entertainment and experience industry, new towns and the construction of traffic routes, among other causes (Relph 1976: 117–19, also Tani 1995: 20–24, Sandin 2003: 73–5). Marc Augé, the French anthropologist, has discussed these new spatio-social forms as 'non-places' (Augé 1995). Let us study what place conception underpins these concerns.

In general terms, this 'threat' is cast in terms of dualisms. Manuel Castells states that the 'space of flows' of global media, financing and travel is structurally dominant, and therefore gradually changes or undermines the previous 'space of places', consisting of urban locales and neighbourhoods (Castells 1996: 423–8). These two spaces are on their way to becoming 'parallel universes' which can no longer meet. Therefore, '[e]xperience, by being related to places, becomes abstracted from power, and meaning is increasingly separated from knowledge' (ibid.: 428). Virtually all cities and regions are connected to global flows to some extent, but the informational economy also ushers in a new type of urban formation, the 'megacities'. These include the major 'command centres', New York, London

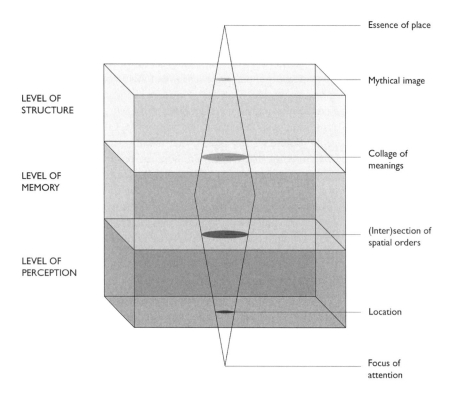

LEVEL OF
STRUCTURE

LEVEL OF
MEMORY

LEVEL OF
PERCEPTION

Essence of place

Mythical image

Collage of
meanings

(Inter)section of
spatial orders

Location

Focus of
attention

Figure 4.2   'Place crystal' according to Stenros

Note: 'Place myth', or a strong fictional content of a place, penetrates the 'levels' of
the theory, linking place understood as a significant point of the life-world to the
'essence' of place on the structural plane. In the middle, 'the collage of meanings'
(Stenros 1992: 235–45) refers to the process of signification through juxtaposition of
different logics or orders. This idea comes close to 'weak place' understood as the
coming together of qualitatively differing influences.

Source: Stenros (1992: 264).

and Tokyo, as well as cities such as Karachi, Lagos and Dacca. Megacities are all
very big, but radical social and physical duality is the distinctive feature of this
new, 'informational' urban form. The fragmentation of the local landscape results
from the intense global connections of a section of the population on the one
hand, and the fact that much of the population is redundant or 'irrelevant' in the
informational era, on the other. Megacities collect both the best and the worst, the
brightest innovation and the most abject squalor, they are 'globally connected and
locally disconnected, physically and socially ...' (ibid.: 404). Graham and Marvin
have studied the emerging urban form from the point of view of infrastructures.
Echoing Castells' thesis, they claim that cities would be 'splintering', because
the modernistic ideal of integrated infrastructures as the unifying factor of cities

no longer holds. New infrastructures, such as high-speed trains, customised IT services and networks or private highways, only serve the better off who can pay. According to Graham and Marvin, this causes both visible and invisible boundaries and partitions: some people are mobile and some places connected while others are not.

'Postmodern urbanism' proposed by Michael Dear and Steven Flusty utilises similar dual logic (Flusty and Dear 1999, Dear and Flusty 1998, 1997). Dear and Flusty argue that in urban reality, a rupture or break has occurred, and therefore the representation of the city has to be renewed. The regionally dispersed and locally fragmented change of Southern California offers itself as the new exemplar. Postmodern urbanism understands cities not as singular, self-sustained, organic realms but as being parts of global 'citistaat'. Its inhabitants are split between economic winners ('cybergeoisie') and rapidly pauperising underclass ('protosurps'), much as in Castells' analysis. The very mobile capital can produce gated communities and working islands for the elite anywhere, without relating to the surrounding (ex-)urban context. These commodified urban fragments ('commudities') float in an urban sea ('in-beyond'), occupied by cheap, migrant labour, living in abject conditions under strict police surveillance. Controlled mass-media ('disinformation superhighway'), another global leveller, keeps the populations unaware of their actual situation and produces homogeneous desires, easy to harvest commercially. The authors also develop ideas about the concrete street-level consequences of the fragmented social space and erosion of places. Discussing Los Angeles, Flusty observes that urban spaces are being developed to be unresponsive and even hostile, eroding spatial justice. 'Interdictory space' is generic term for a multitude of design features intended to discourage the access of unwanted people. Flusty's (1994: 16–18) taxonomy of interdictions include spaces that are 'stealthy' (space which cannot be found, camouflaged space), 'slippery' (space which cannot be easily reached), 'crusty' (walled-in or gated space), 'prickly' (details making use difficult), and 'jittery' (use made unpleasant by over-emphasised monitoring). These strategies can be combined, creating 'paranoid typologies'.

Saskia Sassen gives a more nuanced notion of place in the global situation. For her, global cities are 'strategic sites' for transnational economic and political operations, and both big money and officially powerless but very visible 'others' have 'new claims' concerning them (Sassen 1991). 'Global capital and the new immigrant workforce are the two major instances of transnational categories/ actors that have unifying properties across borders and find themselves in contestation with each other inside global cities' (Sassen 1998: xx). Nonetheless, her analysis also concludes that the new urban economy sets in motion 'a whole series of new dynamics of inequality' (ibid.: xxiv). In labour and housing markets, as well as in physical development, 'a new geography of centrality and marginality' emerges, similar to Castells' and Dear and Flusty's findings. 'The downtowns … receive massive investments in real estate and telecommunications while low-income city areas are starved for resources … Financial services produce superprofits while industrial services barely survive' (ibid.: xxvi–xxvii). This process can be seen in an increasing number of cities both in developed and in developing countries.

What is common to all these accounts, the 'discursive landscape of fragmentation' as I call it, is that the authors treat 'place' as physical and physically contiguous. I argue that this is a conceptual blind spot, an urban scale analogy to the essential relic of place-conception in Stenros' architectural theory. I use Castells as the main example, because he is clear and explicit in his conceptual formulations.

For Castells, '[a] place is a locale whose form, function and meaning are self-contained within the boundaries of physical contiguity' (1996: 423). Castells uses one of the Parisian *quartiers*, Belleville, as an example. He states that despite having been hit by several waves of urban renewal, messed up with 'plastic postmodernism', and inhabited by new immigrant groups, '… Belleville in 1995 is a clearly identifiable place, both from the outside and from the inside' (ibid.: 424). While this rings true, Castells' definition contains a serious logical problem. Immediately after the definition of place, he namely contends that 'it is precisely because their physical/ symbolic qualities make them *different* that they are places' (ibid.: 425, my emphasis). The idea that difference with respect to other places makes a place a place, plainly contradicts the claim that the meaning of a place would be self-contained! If difference defines the specificity of a place, some kind of 'communication' between places must be imagined. Therefore, 'place' cannot be defined without reference to the connecting 'flows', and it actually becomes rather like a 'node' in the space of flows (cf. ibid.: 413).

What is genuinely interesting in Castells' 'parallel universes', is that he articulates major societal processes, such as secularisation, de-traditionalisation or the new organisation of work *in spatial terms*. The general idea that a new social space is replacing an old one, and that the former space would have been principally made of 'places' (which may be villages, neighbourhoods, towns, cities or nations) and the emerging one would be made of 'flows', is powerful. However, because Castells' definition of space is extremely material – as opposed to Lefebvre's space (*l'espace*), which is multifaceted (cf. Gottdiener 1994 [1985]: 123) and also includes the imagined and represented aspects – his account loses the 'virtual' openness of place.[4] The approach does not do justice to the

---

4   Following the logic of structuralistic Marxism, Castells' general thesis is that: 1) there is a new technological base, especially the IT networks and the new communication opportunities; 2) that leads to big changes in the economic process, especially how companies locate and organise internally: the informational economics; 3) there must be a respective phenomenal form or space, the informational city. When defining the 'space of flows', Castells asserts: 'By space of flows I refer to the system of exchanges of information, capital, and power that structures the basic processes of societies, economies, and states between different localities, regardless of localization. *I call it "space" because it does have a spatial materiality*: the directional centres located in a few selective areas of a few, selected localities; the telecommunication system, dependent upon telecommunication

relational and laterally connected nature of place but immobilises and reifies place and acknowledges only its connections as 'depth' in time. Even though places (sustained by place-bound people living in a more or less traditional manner) indeed may be losing their physical features and symbolisms, place as a node or a point of articulation for the flows may receive a *heightened* importance in the new context. This indeed is Doreen Massey's position, which I will soon discuss. To still use Belleville as an example, what would it be without the successive waves of immigration, a factor which surely is not 'contained within the boundaries of physical contiguity'? And what would it be without the fact that it is in the middle of Paris, a 'world-city' with all its global connections and its metropolitan dynamics? Furthermore, traditions are not necessarily rooted in place. For example, the 'Islamic space', defined by the orientation of the mosques towards Mecca, their style of decoration and the characteristic voices and rhythms of prayer, is surely very traditional *and* totally global and non-contiguous (Metcalf 1996, cited in Hynynen 2002). The idea of the physical contiguity of place is naïve. It works only if we limit ourselves to strictly material aspects of space, such as built structure and street behaviour.

'Roissy, Just the Two of Us!'

Marc Augé has influentially distinguished places and 'non-places'. According to him, the supermodern space of airports, shopping malls, motorways, resort beaches and refugee camps consists of 'non-places'. In non-places the relationships of physical features, practices and attached meanings which create the identity of a place (understood as a contiguous entity) disappear. Furthermore, using non-place is covenanted. 'If place can be defined as relational, historical and concerned with identity, then a space which cannot be defined as relational, or historical, or concerned with identity will be a non-place' (Augé 1995: 77–8). In effect, non-places are the ephemeral materialisations of the 'space of flows' on the scale of the human perception. Castells notes the blandness of airports and rail terminals quite similarly with Augé, but he also senses important 'messages' in their appearance. According to Castells, '… paradoxically, the architecture that seems most charged with meaning in societies shaped by the logic of the space of flows is what I call "the architecture of nudity"'. By saying nothing, its neutral forms 'confront the experience with the solitude of the space of flows. Its message is the silence' (Castells 1996: 420).

---

facilities and services that are unevenly distributed in the space … transportation system, that makes such nodal points dependent from major airports and airlines services, from freeway systems, from high speed trains; the security systems necessary to the protection of such directional spaces, surrounded by a potentially hostile world …' (Castells 1992: 15–16, my emphasis).

So, in the context of the space of the global or the space of flows, there is societal meaning in the 'non-place', even if it does not lend its identity to its 'user'. Anonymity may actually be one of the positive or attractive qualities of non-places. Gottdiener describes his experience at the São Paulo airport. He was going to a conference in a city near São Paulo, but because his host was absent, by accident he joined another group going to another conference, which happened to be held in the same city, causing confusion. This confusion, based on the anonymity of the airport opened up an opportunity to assume a new identity, even a new life (Gottdiener 2001: 35–7). There is also eroticism and sexual promise: 'Air space is a "free area," a place where men and women who like sex with strangers, both male and female, find each other' (ibid.: 40). Also Augé, in a subordinate clause, finds excitement in the crowd and flow of an airport's non-place. He describes the feelings of his imaginary hero Pierre Dupont waiting for the departure of his plane:

> [H]e had nothing to do but wait for the sequence of events. 'Roissy, just the two of us!': these days, surely, it was in these crowded places where thousands of individual itineraries converged for a moment, unaware of one another, that there survived something of the uncertain charm of the wastelands, the yards and building sites, the station platforms and waiting rooms where travellers break step, of all the chance meeting places where fugitive feelings occur …. (Augé 1995: 2–3)

I find it extraordinary and interesting that Augé senses the same experiential quality in building sites and transit lounges. Could it be that the 'uncertain charm of the wastelands' was the essential contemporary mode of experience, the contemporary structure of feeling? If the 'city' is no longer a home for human beings, as Rajanti contends (1999: 194), maybe the 'unhomely' leftovers and spatial margins (cf. Kopomaa 1997) still are. Elizabeth Wilson in an essay titled 'Against Utopia' points in that direction. She is interested in interstitial or indeterminate spaces, '…the wrong side of the fabric of the city, a hidden and secret aspect of urban life where traces of former worlds and lives may be found' (Wilson 2001: 151). For Wilson, this 'contingent' underbelly of cities is opposed to the 'necessary' urban core and historic districts, which nowadays are often commodified and sanitised. This division of space is not far from Goffman's classic 'front' and 'back' sides. According to Wilson, contingent spaces offer 'unspecified possibilities', something in a positive sense non-utopian and non-planned. They can become 'frequented places' in the sense of de Certeau (1984), and are open for people to make them their own.

However, for Wilson Augé's non-places are the polar opposites of the indeterminate or 'interstitial' spaces she finds so potent. In wonderment Wilson refers to a cultural project on non-places, which seemed to merge the contingent urban backside and Augé's – in Wilson's reading – dystopian non-places. She states that such merging seems to require 'another narrative of urban space', and that such newly defined non-places do not yet have a language.

We are ever increasingly in transit through 'non-places'. Corners that lurk at the edge of activity. Passageways where activity occurs but the relationship between use and place remains unnamed. Places where names are incidental, meaningless because the need for communication – or the passage of time spent – is already deemed to be transient, insignificant, minimal, empty. Street corners, bus stops, shopping malls, motorways, airport lounges .... (anonymous, cit. Wilson 2001: 152)

However, as suggested above, Augé himself makes the link between non-places and their existential potential. He does not develop the idea much, though. It seems that for him the connection is in the feeling of waiting for something unexpected or letting 'fugitive feelings of continued adventure' fill your mind. It is a situation of being alone (in a crowd) and waiting for 'something'. But there is more to it.

Withington

I am taking a Sunday walk in Withington. Spreading out around me is a flat English suburb. Wide streets, neat rows of terraced houses, noonday emptiness. I hear the sound of a distant train. After a while the street ends in a modest park. I enter it and notice that there is a high railway embankment at the opposite end. I stop and listen. I am surrounded by a strange burbling and crackling sound: the wet lawn is drying in the first sunshine after many days of rain. I look at the clouds drifting in the sky. They are coming in an even grey carpet from the far-off horizon. Actually the clouds draw a ceiling and the horizon, and I suddenly sense the grandeur of the moving air space and the light flowing from between the clouds. The feeling is almost unbearable and I want to cry.

Manchester, 29 April 2001

Weak Place

The meaningful, lived place does not disappear in the emerging supermodern state: it becomes *weak* (Lehtovuori 2000). Place becomes personal, momentary, changing and even random. The kernel of this way of thinking is already present in Relph's *Place and Placelessness*. Relph quotes Alan Gussow: 'The catalyst that converts any physical location – any environment if you will – into a place, is the process of experiencing deeply. A place is a piece of the whole environment that has been claimed by feelings' (Gussow 1971: 26, cited in Relph 1976: 141–2). Relph's conclusion from this statement is that since a positive state of being within a place is not the only possible relationship with place, as one can explicitly distance oneself from a place, so that the relationship becomes one of existential outsiderness or alienation, personal interpretation will create different kinds of places (Relph 1976: 49–55, 142–3). Although this is true, it can be conceived that personal interpretation is truly able to make *anything at all* meaningful, and thereby a place. The bond between the physical traits of a place, the (shared, communal) activities taking place there and the meanings assigned to it weaken considerably, and attention must be focused on special experiences and emotions that ultimately make a place, distinguishing it from mere space.

The point of the notion of weak place is to open the physically closed and temporally fixed notion of place to many, transient interpretations, while acknowledging its contingent connection to physical space, to walls of brick and mortar, to light, to smell. Any experience of a human being cannot be 'place', but any physical feature, even a most ephemeral one such as a short spring shower or a change in light, may be enough for a momentary weak place. So, human life does not rest on a matrix of emotionally laden, localisable reference points as Stenros (1992) suggests, but is rather a constant process of signifying the flow of events; throwing meaning over sensory experiences. This always happens in some relation to physical space, but the meaning of a specific 'coming-together' is largely unpredictable.

A place is no longer something that exists self-evidently or 'strongly', like Paris, Belleville in Paris, the older inner city of Helsinki, or Suovanlahti village in Central Finland with its buildings, fields, lakes, people, their relations and histories. Rather, a place is the experience of the individual. It is momentary and arbitrary in a certain way. An experience may or may not come; a place may or may not exist. A weak place does not exist outside ourselves, but it is always done, a creation, an *oeuvre*. As Beauregard notes, in the emerging urban theoretical understanding '[s]pace exists only through action; events define place, but only momentarily' (Beauregard 2003: 1003). The architect Rem Koolhaas describes the contemporary urban experience in the following terms:

> Instead of concentration – simultaneous presence – in Generic City[5] individual 'moments' are spaced far apart to create a trance of almost unnoticeable

---

5   The Generic City expands outside the traditional urban cores, and conceptually Koolhaas' distinction is not far from Wilson's necessary and contingent spaces. For Koolhaas, architects' and planners' insistence on the centre as the core of value and meaning is destructive, because it renders everything outside it subservient and dependent. Secondly, the centre itself must be painstakingly maintained and – paradoxically – modernised to sustain it as the most important place. In this view the familiar repertoire of urban renewal and resuscitation, consisting of 'grafting more or less discreet traffic arteries', 'the routine transformation of housing into offices, warehouses into lofts, abandoned churches into nightclubs', as well as new shopping precincts, pedestrianisation and new parks is all part of a compulsive effort to sustain the centre as the most fixed and most dynamic at the same time. According to Koolhaas, this is hopeless and can only lead to the banalisation of the old centres. There simply is not enough identity for the exploding global urban realm, and the issue must be rethought. Koolhaas asks that '[w]hat are the disadvantages of identity, and conversely, what are the advantages of blankness? … The Generic City is the city liberated from the captivity of center, from the straitjacket of identity' (Koolhaas 1995c: 1248–50).

aesthetic experiences: the color variations in the fluorescent lighting of an office building just before sunset, the subtleties of the slightly different whites of an illuminated sign at night. Like Japanese food the sensations can be reconstituted and intensified in the mind, or not – they may simply be ignored. (Koolhaas 1995c: 1250)

I am questioning the physical contiguity, as well as historical and communal rootedness of place, analogously with Vattimo's questioning of the inherited metaphysical propositions. Place formation becomes a game, a choice. Place is not a pre-existing, localisable thing, lending identity, but it rather becomes a 'window of opportunity' in the contingent or generic urban environment. More than physical contiguity, weak place is about experiential nearness and caring (cf. Vadén and Hannula 2003: 17–18). Weak place links different knowledge, perceptions, feelings, beliefs, hope … This ephemeral but still (or just because of that) very emotionally moving quality characterised my above-described experience in Withington.[6] The modest little park could well have been ignored, yet at the same time it had a subtle power. I tried to analyse in retrospect the causes of my strongly felt emotion that engendered that momentary place. I had just moved there and I did not know the area yet. The contrast between the housing estate and the railway was a surprise; trains rushing from one unknown to another opened up or interrupted the boring similarity of the houses. Vehicular traffic squeezing under the line through a narrow opening in the embankment had the same effect. An important element was the southwesterly wind blowing the carpet of clouds over the landscape. It helped my thoughts leave the present, to the horizon and the sea, which I missed, having come from Helsinki. I remembered and knew that the Irish Sea lay in the direction of the wind. A few strange elements in the actual park, an extremely dismal shed and a completely dead hedge, possibly killed by the severe winter of 2000–2001, were also important. The underpass bridge in the embankment had a very industrial appearance, leading my thoughts to the industrial history of Manchester. There were, nevertheless, factors that were almost architectonic. The embankment and row of poplars at a right angle to it that bounded the park defined the *axes mundi* of the situation. The embankment was a marked boundary that also aroused mixed feelings of interest and even vague awe. What might there be on the other side, in the unknown? The sounds, the relative silence of the park and the strange gurgling of the wide expanse of lawn, were important. Ultimately, the decisive factor was most probably the general indefinite nature of the park and its emptiness. The grass was too wet to be used, and the park as a whole was very modest, hardly a park at all. It did not invite or tell anything – it just existed. One could momentarily lay claim to the space and it could be made into a place of one's own, a weak place.

---

6   See Koskela's (1999: 3) discussion about the role of emotions in the production of space.

Pensiero Debole ...

Underlying the concept of the weak place is Gianni Vattimo's concept of 'weak thinking'. Vattimo is a disciple of Heidegger, and much of his work consists of reinterpretations of Heidegger's texts. For Vattimo, Nietzsche and Heidegger were the last thinkers in the sense of producing statements on a firm metaphysical foundation: '[since Nietzsche and Heidegger] "to think" has come to mean something different from what it meant before' (Vattimo 1993: 1). The notion of 'weak thought' (*pensiero debole*) refers to the possibility of philosophical observation and thinking in a situation where no fixed metaphysical foundation for thinking can be proposed. Vattimo claims that because of the nature of the break,[7] philosophical thinking cannot hope to create or find a new metaphysical foundation. It can only 'weaken' the ideas and categories of the previous centuries, and re-think the old thoughts in new contexts (Vattimo 1988, 1993).

The notions of *Verwindung* and *Andenken* define for Vattimo the hermeneutic ontology, the fundamental post-modern mode of philosophising (Vattimo 1988: l, transl. introduction). *Andenken* refers to keeping in mind, remembering, recollecting. *Verwindung* is a mixture of overcoming and resigning.[8] Thinking becomes 'parasitical'. It cannot directly oppose the old, which continues to live in the ever more powerful technology, nor offer an equal alternative. It

---

7   The crucial dislocation is Heidegger's critical notion of Being. For Heidegger Western metaphysics and technology are parts of the same continuum. Metaphysics signifies a philosophical system of thought that is led by the question of logical truth and the use of reason. Modern technology is the most historically advanced form of metaphysics, because it represents an extreme degree of rationalisation. Through his notion of Being Heidegger aims to create a fundamental critique towards both metaphysics and the technological domination. He claims that there is an ontological difference between Being and beings. Beings (subjects and objects) *are*. Being (the self-identical 'is-ness' present in whatever exists in the world) is common to all things, but different from them. Being cannot be compared to beings; we can never speak about Being as if it were *something*. To say 'Being is X or Y' would be to lapse into tautology 'Being is a being'. According to Heidegger, Western metaphysics have systematically suppressed the difference between Being and beings. If the difference is recognised, the ontological subject-object difference dissolves and with it the whole of traditional philosophy (Vattimo 1988: xiv-xv; Rajanti 1999: 25–6). '[T]he metaphysical tradition is the tradition of "violent" thinking ... All the categories of metaphysics are violent categories: Being and its attributes, the "first" cause, man as "responsible", and even the will to power, if that is read metaphysically as an affirmation or as the assumption of power over the world. They must be "weakened" or relieved of their excess power in the sense suggested, for example, by Benjamin's talk of metropolitan man's "distracted perception"' (Vattimo 1993: 5–6).

8   The term Verwindung indicates ... a 'going-beyond that is both an acceptance [or 'resignation'] and a deepening', while also suggesting both a 'convalescence', 'cure' or 'healing' and a 'distorting' or 'twisting' (Vattimo 1988: 172). To me Verwindung brings to mind Latour's usage of the word 'translation'. It also feels to be close to the Situationists' idea of *détournement*.

can criticise by turning round, distorting and making 'oblique cuts' to the old, but its effectiveness remains unclear. 'The whole way in which *andenkend* thinking hears the metaphysical tradition has this mark of obliqueness, which in the Heideggerian texts chiefly takes the form of hermeneutical dis-location, as lostness, *Unheimlichkeit* or disorientation, which might equally be thought of in Klossowskian terms as parody' (Vattimo 1993: 134). Simultaneously with criticism, the practice of weak thought prolongs tradition's afterlife.

Drawing from Heidegger, Vattimo claims that since the early Greeks philosophical and scientific thinking has almost lost a major dimension. According to Heidegger, Being is given to thought as presencing (*Anwesen*). We are bound to this characterisation of Being, because of its unconcealment as something that can be said – or thought. This same idea forms the starting point for Gadamer's hermeneutic ontology: 'Being, which can be understood, is language' (Gadamer 1979 [1975]: 432). There is no way round this, neither is it a problem. The current problem lies in the centuries long working of first metaphysics then technology to rigidify presence to objectness only. We now tend to forget or be unable to take seriously the other nature of Being, namely occurrence, unveiling or bringing into unconcealment (*Anwesen-lassen*) (Vattimo 1993: 116). This refers to movement, becoming, change, invisibility and suspension. It refers to responding to the 'call of Being' without hastily naming and classifying it, without giving it a thought as such. Without explicating and explaining but rather taking absence as seriously as presence. That is the 'poeticizing' mode of thought of preSocratic thinkers, such as Heraclitus. Walter Benjamin's 'poetic thinking' (see below) also shares characteristics with Vattimo's idea.

Vattimo continues that we cannot revert to the position of preSocratic thinkers, though, because the entire history of metaphysics separates us from them. So, how to meditate Being without presenting it as something present? The way proposed by Heidegger is to take leave (or leap) of Being as a foundation and consider what events and possibilities are hidden 'in the unveiling occurrence of *Es gibt*' (there is). This idea has two ramifications.

Firstly, the question arises, where does the leap go? Vattimo interprets that, instead of void, it goes to *Boden*. He reinterprets Heidegger's *Boden* not as a solid ground or surface – again a new foundation for thinking, a feature he aims at escaping from – but rather as a fertile soil or humus, full of seeds of future, potential, and unexpected possibilities. *Boden* suggests depth from which something can be born, rather than causally derive (Vattimo 1993: 119). This interpretation of *Boden* closely resonates with human life. Analogously, Scott Lash in *Another Modernity, A Different Rationality* seeks the 'grounding' of the city not in logocentric thought-structures but in the 'urban materiality of place' (Lash 1999: 9) and the 'labyrinthine social space' of everyday life (ibid.: 59). These ideas seem to point to Lefebvre's work in surfacing the notion of the everyday life and defending it against dry and violent conceptualisations.

Secondly, because it is impossible to present or re-present in any way something, which is not yet born and does not yet exist, Heidegger and Vattimo turn to memory and recollection:

> *Schickung* [transmission or sending of Being, PL] lets itself be thought of only as always already having happened, as a gift from which the giving has always already withdrawn … [T]hought as memory thinks *Anwesen* as *Anwesenlassen*, as an event of disclosing … *Andenken* is the thought that lets the possible be possible, stripping it of the mask of necessity imposed on it by metaphysics, the mask which metaphysics forces on it to the highest degree in the final identification of Being with objectness. (Vattimo 1993: 121–5)

> Ein Zeichen sind Wir, deutungslos
> Schmertzlos sind Wir und haben fast
> Die Sprache in der Fremd verloren. (Hölderlin)

So, Vattimo points away from thinking in defined, object-like concepts. Rather, thinking is like waiting, suspending, feeling and wondering. It is worth noting, that for Vattimo '… truth appears precisely as an experience of art' (1988: xxvii, transl. introduction) Truth is not fixed, however, but eventual, an event. A poem is a monument in the sense that someone has written it to last and to be transmitted to someone else. In that sense there is no difference between a tombstone and a poem. But a poem, and any work of art, is simultaneously mortal, bound to time, because its truth must be interpreted by someone, remade, recollected. A work of art cannot escape from the infinite chain of reinterpretation, including a possibility of forgetting or destruction. This act of reinterpretation and recollection is the act of *Andenken*.

With reference to weak place, weak thought can firstly be seen as a *mode of conceptualisation*. What I find especially interesting in Vattimo's thought is the possibility to think the non-(yet)-existent, to think without defining the object of thought, he suggests. Thinking does not necessarily need to end in definitions, taking the form 'weak place is X' – or 'public urban space is X' – but it can discuss, distance itself from and come again closer to various possible notions and definitions. Instead of reducing, reificating and creating another 'thought-object', thinking can be wondering, musing and sounding. The epistemology of weak thought is situated (Byrne 2001: Beauregard 2003), and it opens up the possibility of an insider's or 'inspective' epistemology (Varto 2000). The mode of weak thought reveals that naming elements of space belongs to the same continuum with its design, understood as manipulation, control and construction – technology. Practical accounts on the issue, such as design guides, collections of good examples and technical norms concerning the design of public urban spaces (see Madanipour 1996 for a good review on those) or 'place making' belong to that continuum. But also thoughts, which take the form 'space/place is X', are part of the problem – however clever they may be. It does not help to re-name and re-present. Critical thinking needs to be something else, and Vattimo's 'weak thought' is, if nothing more, at least one guideline, one vector.

Secondly, the mode of weak thought can be used as an *analogy to the actual experience* of place, to the lived place, *vécu*, as an element of actual social space. This suggests an ontological analogy, a statement concerning the nature of weak place. Various elements, such as material structures, bodily movements, gestures, perceptions, memories, social ties and societal structures, which come together in experience in any moment, can be seen as both the materials and *matériel* of weak place. None of those many elements is 'basis', more necessary or more fundamental than any other. The 'truth' of the weak place is always in flux. Weak place is momentary, personal and always open to reinterpretation.

... and Other Analogies

From the nexus of ideas of *Verwindung*, recollection, oblique cut and eventual truth, several links towards architectural practice start to unfold. Essentially, all these notions refer to a mode of thinking *and* acting, which is event-like and momentary on one hand, and does change *both* ideas *and* world, but not in the sense of transcending or clearing the table for something totally different and new, but rather revalorising the existing but not yet objectified – the potential, the humus, the social space.

Eventuality, a new idea about time as singular moments, is an important element in conceptualising the weak place. Ignasi de Solà-Morales, who converted the idea of weak thought into a means of architectural criticism (Weak Architecture, 1987), claims that neither knowledge, language nor architecture can any longer be interpreted as a single system. Time is fragmenting and becoming diverse (see Gurvich's typology of social times in Harvey 1989: 224–5, also Nowotny 1994). Therefore it is difficult for architecture to organise experience within linear time, for example into controlled series, an objective the early modernists still had. Architecture becomes a singular event. The temporality of experience is a randomly produced moment that comes once and will never return (de Solà-Morales 1998 [1987]: 621–2) De Solà-Morales also reinterprets the monumental nature of architecture. For him, the idea of a monument does not reside in physical permanence or the erection of hierarchical values. A monument is like a poem that lives so long as someone remembers its words recited into the air. Important aspects are memory and the restoration of memory, Heidegger's *Andenken*. Weak architecture does the same to the elements of the modern tradition of architecture as weak thinking does to the truths of philosophy and weak place to the traditional constituents of place. Distancing and continuous re-interpretation give impressive architecture an opportunity to live. Weak architecture gains its strength specifically from its weakness – as does the weak place.

Other Vattimo analogies are the concepts of the weak urbanism (Hubacher 1999), weak social bind and weak experience (Rajanti 1999). As mentioned above, being in non-places is covenanted (Augé 1995). In Rajanti's terms one cannot begin to feel at home in them but one can be in them 'as if' at home. The skill of leading a more or less bearable life in non-places calls for avoiding absolute choices, meaningful and comprehensive relations. The experience of life becomes empty, open, opportunistic and weak; 'roots' are an impossibility. According to Rajanti, weak experience is not comprehensive and its structure is not always congruent. Rather, it touches other experiences in some points, while differing in other points (Rajanti 1999: 195). This practice or style of leading one's life may indeed be the contemporary 'Boden', a humus containing endless possibilities and seeds of the new and unexpected. It is a Boden exactly in its un-definition and ephemerality.

Global Sense of Place

To understand weak place, we need to 'non-think', to remove the still strong idea of places as spatially fixed, something that can be photographed, put on a map or sketched on a cognitive mapping questionnaire. Rather, place is fluid, open, extending from here to there and beyond.

Doreen Massey refers to this de-territorialised conception as the 'global sense of place'. In an essay of that title Massey describes her feelings and perceptions in London's Kilburn. She sounds out a possibility to feel affected to a place and recognise its character without subscribing to static, defensive, or reactionary notions of place.[9] For her, a 'global sense' emerges from the acknowledgement of the many co-existing influences. She cannot think of Kilburn High Road without bringing into play British imperial history, Indian and Muslim cultures or the intense air traffic above, heading to Heathrow (Massey [1991] 1993: 237–8). It becomes clear that rather than through boundaries and oppositions, the multiple identity of Kilburn is constructed through the links to what is beyond its physical contiguity. Anssi Paasi has made a related but different interpretation, contending that '[p]lace is not reducible to a specific locality, site or scale or specific attributes connected with these (physical or built-up environment, culture, social relations). Instead it is composed of situated episodes of life history, which unavoidably have "geographical dimensions": real, imagined or utopian. In a modern society, the episodes of one's life history will increasingly take place in several localities, which thus become constituents of one's place' (Paasi 1991: 249).

Probably the environmental perception is changing in the modern, globalising societies. If I assume a (theoretically constructed) 'space-time' constituted by

---

9   Massey's notion addresses a political debate started by David Harvey in *The Condition of Postmodernity*, where he claims that stressing places against time, eternity against change, and Being against Becoming would necessarily be reactionary and feed nationalistic or parochial sentiments.

the changing social relations, ranging from close to global, one's place is best understood as the momentary expression of these relations. The distinctiveness of the place is constituted '… not by placing boundaries around it and defining its identity through counterposition to the other which lies beyond, but precisely (in part) through the specificity of the mix of links and interconnections *to* that "beyond". Places viewed this way are open and porous' (Massey 1994: 5). This newly defined place is not fixed and closed, but open, changing and momentary. It cannot be the property of a certain group, only, and it is not necessarily attached to a historical continuum neither to spatial proximity.[10] (Massey [1991] 1993: 238–9; also 1998: 123–6) Such view is quite easy to adopt in urban settings, but Massey stresses that nature is not providing a stable foundation for places, either. Place cannot be conceptualised as location where the social and the natural meet (Massey 2005: 137). Even though the natural rhythms may be slow (circadian, monthly and annual rhythms mix with the processes of biological evolution and geological change), the natural setting nevertheless *does* change, so that place – 'here' – is best understood as 'our encounter, and what is made of it' (ibid.: 138). Place is an event, here and now!

Massey is making a political, anti-exclusionary point. But importantly for my argument, Massey views the global sense of place or place as an event as personal and singular. It is Doreen Massey seeing, feeling and thinking, which 'in no way denies a sense of wonder' (ibid.: 140). It is her personal experiences and academic knowledge, which make the reading possible and credible. I believe that the emphasis on the personal aspect is not an accident, but reflects something essential about the possibility and reality of 'place' in the present, global condition. If space syntax, socio-semiotics and the ideas of Rajanti offer 'structuralistic' theorisations on the nature of the spatial-social link in the space of the global, Doreen Massey's 'global sense of place' offers, maybe surprisingly, a 'phenomenological' account: there is keen interest and attachment to the place-experience; place entails feelings, revelations, maybe even art-like experiences. While Massey interprets Kilburn (or Lake District) from the perspective of a member of the global, cosmopolitan élite, she (indirectly at least) claims that there is some 'globality', some elements going beyond the actual setting, in everybody's experience. Even though the global aspect 'plays out' differently in different locales and for different people or social groups, the importance of it is as true for Kilburn High Road in London – the paradigmatic world city – as for a

---

10   Rob Shields refers to Deleuze and Guattari, when trying to verbally capture the complexity of place reaching beyond its physical limit. He contends that '[t]he city conceived of as a "body without organs" is both grounded and sited within a place-based spatialisation, at the same time that it is presented and offers itself as a communications node in a wider generalized space(s) of the flow of goods and information. Its hybrid quality affects its time-space character: it is always more than "mine, here and now", it is "theirs, then and there"' (Shields 1996: 243). See also Jean Hillier (2007).

small mining village somewhere in the British Midlands or the isolated island of Pitcairn in the Pacific (Massey 1993 [1991]: 238).

However, there is a possible problem in Massey's notion, which needs to be addressed. If place is a momentary articulation of relations, it may be justified to ask if the global 'net' of those relations (social, economic and cultural, including family ties, networks of trust and friendship, personal and shared beliefs etc.) should be included to achieve a sound conceptualisation. Massey's rhetorical device, *satellite* as the viewing point of the Earth, foregrounds this possible distanced and perspectival idea. I would propose not to include the totality of relations in the theory, but rather use the notion of 'translocality', proposed by Smith (1999: 127–30), in conceptualising the global links. This idea refers to *specific* points of origin and destination established by migrants, investors, political activists and socio-cultural entrepreneurs. It therefore conceptually allows the personal and unique production of the global sense of place better than the assumed global net.

Even though the scale of 'place' is rather different in the traditional architectural thought from sociology and geography, I would claim that Massey's notion is applicable to architecture and urban design, too. In social sciences, cities and even nations may be treated as 'places', while in architecture place typically denotes a room, a corner or a small, somehow defined natural site. However, the scale loses much of its meaning, as the open, flowing quality of meaning does not depend on scale. A place may be big, small or imaginary, but the place-experience never emerges from nothing. It is a gathering or coming-together of aspects of the individual life history. *Conceptually* the physical is contingent: even though we are material, bodily and situated, we do not necessarily need any fixed material system of places or set of elements to sustain our capacity to produce meaning.[11] While the moment of signifying – creating a weak place – does have its materiality (as wind, clouds, wet ground, weather, grass, voices and chill in Withington, for example), there is no way to pin down, qualify beforehand, predict or design how this materiality is connected to the meaning someone gives to it in a specific case. It is a moment of Becoming, a momentary articulation of eventual constituents, which passes by and never returns. Naming is always *a posteriori*; analysis always comes after, too late to grasp the important thing, the moment of signifying itself. Weak place is scaleless and surprising – an event. Feelings are its ephemeral reality; they can be memorised, recollected and re-projected but for the conceptualisation of weak place they always remain in the realm of absence, expectation, occurrence, unveiling, *Anwesenlassen*.

---

11   A place, a historical square for example, can be interpreted as a 'theatre of memory' (Ilmonen 1999, 2000) but such use is limited to one or a few sites. It tells more about the historical importance of such a site than about the everyday life of the person remembering.

Some Remarks on the Place in Phenomenology

Since everyone sees, knows and interprets his environment as part of a unique, individual chain of experience, the same location in a city can be a place of many kinds. Multiple seeds may take root and flower as uniquely different experiences and momentary places – at the same location. To go back to Helsinki and its Arabia district, we can imagine, for example, that for the old residents, the area becomes significant in a different way and for different reasons than for their grandchildren or for international guests visiting the University of Art and Design Helsinki. For someone the context of the place consists of memories from past decades, unpaved streets, apple trees in bloom and hard work at the Arabia porcelain factory. For someone else, the sense of a place may come from the figures and rules of Nintendo games changing into play and giving stones, bushes and stands of forest completely new content. For yet a third person, Arabia is part of the air-conditioned, hermetic chain of a 'space of flows' from the aeroplane through the arrivals hall at Helsinki-Vantaa Airport and a taxi still smelling new to the minimalist lobby of the Lume Media Centre, where an airtight conversation over cocktails may take place at a scientific congress, with the landscape panorama of Vanhankaupunginlahti Bay in view while isolated by selective glazing.

The phenomenological tradition has also recognised the diversifying meaning of space and place signified by a user or someone experiencing it. Kirsi Saarikangas quotes Merleau-Ponty, who claims that 'there are as many spaces as there are distinct spatially lived experiences' (Merleau-Ponty 1945: 337, cit. Saarikangas 1998: 248). A delimited physical space will always contain numerous lived spaces, numerous places. Moreover, the chain of personal experiences is mixed with things seen and heard from others. Sirpa Tani (1995, 1997) refers to this with the concept of 'landscapes of the mind' (cf. Porteous 1990: 17). She describes her experience of an exhibition of the Paris of film: 'I'm in Paris, I'm in a replica of stage sets for a film set in Paris, I'm in the setting of Polanski's "*Frantic*". But where am I really?' (Tani 1997: 211) Merleau-Ponty has the following to say about the imagined content of a place (environment): '… Our body and our perception always summon us to take as the centre of the world that environment with which they present us. But this environment is not necessarily that of our own life. I can be somewhere else while staying here' (M. Merleau-Ponty, *The Phenomenology of Perception*, 1962: 293, cit. Norberg-Schultz 1971: 16).

Clearly, phenomenological place can neither be understood as the static location or container of objects and people nor as a network of human activities and relations woven around a geographical location. It is an event, a unique, singular moment of reflection, bringing many elements together – 'a matter of taking place'. Casey, in the last section of *The Fate of Place*, discusses the expansiveness and connectivity of place, saying that 'place accomplishes what is begun in body: it possesses an inclusiveness that does not exclude anything but reaches out to everything, that is, to all constructed as well as natural things' (Casey 1997: 336). I would be cautious in giving place a status as subject as

Casey does. Place is always dependent on a person, and only humans can experience, reflect, and signify, create places as it is. However, the unlimited character, both spatially and qualitatively, Casey is evoking, does characterise place as we start to understand it in the supermodern era, or in the space of flows. While known phenomenologists have earlier produced some essentialist and mystifying notions of place (such as *genius loci*), the current phenomenology is admitting that place is not airtight and permanent, but multifarious, extensive and momentary – weak.

***

Or strong. Casey namely states that '[i]n a dramatic reversal of previous priorities, space is being reassimilated into place, made part of its substance and structure. The empty, metric dimensionality of sheer spatial extension no longer exercises, much less dominates, the philosophical mind ...' (ibid.: 340) But what place is Casey talking about? Whose place is it? How could place eat its big brother, space? Casey does not say it directly, but I think that with his rather generic rhetoric he tries to construct the new notion of place *in a totally different, non-perspectival conception of the world.*

I have above briefly noted some signs and interpretations, suggesting that for roughly a hundred years Western societies have been living through a slow but profound transition in their dominant conception of the world. Lefebvre had sensed that around 1910 'certain space was shattered'[12] (Lefebvre 1991 [1974]: 25). There is hardly a consensus about the contours of the new conception of the world, but at least the 'perspectival' and the 'mechanical' are seen to be in decline (see e.g. Stenros 1998). Varto claims that the perspectival has been giving way to the 'inspective' conception. The tentative inspective mode of thought dissolves the dualism between subject and the world, knower and what is known. Inspective knowledge is insider's knowledge. The world is not intelligible as a thing from an imagined position outside it, but rather from 'inside' through acting. The epistemology of the inspective mode of knowing is not yet fully established, however (Varto 2000: 40). Perspectival modes and conventions continue to

---

12   When sounding the first signs of the new, Lefebvre autobiographically writes that '[t]he fact is that around 1910 a certain space was shattered. It was the space of common sense, of knowledge (*savoir*), of social practice, of political power, a space thitherto enshrined in everyday discourse, just as in abstract thought, as the environment of and channel for communications; the space, too, of classical perspective and geometry, developed from the Renaissance onwards on the basis of the Greek tradition (Euclid, logic) and bodied forth in Western art and philosophy, as in the form of the city and town ... Euclidean and perspectivist space have disappeared as systems of reference, along with other former "commonplaces" such as the town, history, paternity, the tonal system in music, traditional morality, and so forth. This was truly a crucial moment' (Lefebvre [1974] 1991: 25). For discussion, see Harvey's Afterword to the English translation of *Production de l'espace* (ibid.: 425).

influence our thinking and doing. As Lefebvre says, a space was 'shattered' but it did not disappear. In science, the change has been especially slow, which is understandable, because the inspective conception challenges the very long Western metaphysical and scientific tradition. One of the key assumptions of that tradition is that of the separate, logically thinking subject.

Several writers have noted that first the change was visible in art. Varto refers to Cezanne and Matisse as the earliest artists, breaking the perspectival mode. Later abstract expressionists and painters such as Robert Rauschenberg and Jasper Johns have expressed the missing of distance and being inside the world – and the art-work. Pallasmaa introduces another concept, that of 'simultaneous space', stating that '[p]erspectival space leaves us as outside observers, whereas simultaneous space encloses and enfolds us in its embrace. This is the perceptual and psychological essence of Impressionist and Cubist space: we are pulled into the space and made to experience it as a fully embodied sensation' (Pallasmaa 2000: 83). James Hall, in the *World as Sculpture*, very similarly chronicles the shift towards a 'mobile, contingent, and confrontational' mode to make and experience art during the twentieth century (Hall 2000: 348). While Lefebvre used art as an example and indicator of the emerging social space (1991 [1974]: 302), for him the new pictures (and to some extent also the architecture of Bauhaus and Frank Lloyd Wright) did not so clearly show the new way to look at the world in a positive sense. In the 'violent' art and broken perspectives, he rather senses the shattering of the old and the contradictions of the proliferating 'abstract space' (see also Burgin 1996: 142–4).

Clearly, twentieth-century art indicates a conceptual shift, entailing the collapse of the (reflective) distance, of the possibility to 'put things in perspective'. In particular, the shift was a crisis in the relationship between 'subject' and the 'world'. If the developments in art are to be trusted as signposts towards the new, inspective conception of the world, the new conception of place as an event – and even as something able to assimilate space – becomes more understandable. I am not making grand ontological claims, nor am I trying to lay another metaphysical foundation. It should go without saying that I assume that material things do exist, and so does the world. I am only developing an idea about how our senses 'present the world' to us, and how the world may become significant for us. This, in my view, can only happen in direct communication with, or better 'inside', the world, through emotions claiming the momentary assemblies of qualitatively differing elements.

Excursion 4: Exchange Square

It is early Saturday afternoon, the busiest time of the busiest shopping day. There are hundreds of people sitting on the low curved walls of the Exchange Square. A brass band in traditional dress entertains the audience. I am sitting on the Sinclair's

Oyster Bar terrace, sipping bitter and observing people. The wind is cool but the autumn sun is shining brightly, making the terrace comfortable.

Reluctantly I accept the fact: the new square is popular. The number of people and its relaxed atmosphere leave no room for doubt. Pavement renovation work along the side of the Mark's & Spencer's store makes the place little bit messy, but this does not deter people from enjoying themselves. The square is a welcomed element in Manchester city centre, and certainly an improvement compared to the through traffic street which used to occupy the area. But is it a place or a non-place, in Mark Augé's (1995) sense of the word? How can the square be related to the questions of history and identity?

Firstly we can say that the square is 'historyless', quite simply because it is a new intervention. As a physical space and urban artefact, it is a result of international city centre design trends, featuring a piece of international environmental art, Martha Schwartz's 'Hanging Ditch' water feature, as its focus. There was no exchange square before this particular one, and it does not recreate any old historic phase of the city centre morphology. In its newness and rootlessness the square does not differ much from shopping malls and airports.

But it is in living city, surrounded by historic buildings, one could claim; it does not suffice to discuss the square without its surroundings and connections. Again on a purely physical level we notice that there is only one original old building on the square, the Corn Exchange. The dominant Mark's & Spencer's building is brand new and its façades do not follow historic façade lines. The Arndale side consists of a huge picture wall, depicting colourful scenes of the urban revitalisation: the city is advertising itself. Sinclair's is an old building but the current location is new. The eighteenth century *fachwerk* building was dismantled and restored in the early 1980s as part of the Arndale shopping centre development and rebuilt now on a new site and setting, forming an element of a heritage ensemble around Manchester Cathedral. The Corn Exchange itself is a shell only, the interior being heavily rebuilt as an up-market mall. Whatever history there is, is invented, synthetic or heavily recontextualised.

But more important is the social role the new square has as part of the city centre. To start the analysis from myself, I came here to have a beer, to consume and have fun, that is. I am anonymous, watching other anonymous people. The space does not lend me an identity nor assume I will take any role. It is an easy space, harmless to enter. I can just be nobody. The main attraction for me is the other people: a game of sociality (or at least a hope of it) is going on (cf. Mäenpää 1993). But again, what is the difference between watching people here and watching them in an airport lounge or shopping mall café? Not much.

Then I realise an important fact: practically everybody is carrying shopping bags. A father is waiting for his wife and boy next to a lamppost with no less than eight full bags; the boy has got a new pogo stick, the ninth item in the pile the father guards. One characteristic of the Augéan non-place is that being there is contractual, you have to earn the right to be in it. It is clear that there are two options here: to carry bags or to sit on a terrace and drink or eat. The square is

Figure 4.3   Exchange Square in Manchester

Source: Photo: Panu Lehtovuori.

'public', so this kind of selectivity of entrance can be contested. But it seldom happens, it seems. The atmosphere has something in it, which makes the poor-looking or truly aimless feel uncomfortable. It is too guarded by people and cameras, people unified in their ability to consume. The *Big Issue* vendor is almost only 'deviant' in this Saturday's crowd. But selling the *Big Issue* is a legitimate, accepted and institutionalised form of behaviour, as well.

It is clear that the Exchange Square is an integral part of the Saturday shopping round. Making the new square has been more an effort to increase the competitiveness of the city centre retail than an effort to make Manchester more 'liveable' or 'urban'. It is a monofunctional space, reminiscent of the 'plazas' and 'arcades' inside big out-of-town malls. It is reminiscent but not totally alike. The 'contract' is vague and malleable. At least in theory, the Exchange Square can be hijacked and redefined, which is not the case in malls and airports. The second difference is simply that the square is outside. Sun, rain and the night sky do make a difference. Third, a time-based or rhythm-based analysis shows a small difference. When the square is not so crowded by shoppers, it is a rather popular skating and roller-blading venue. However, as if to underline a more pessimistic view, later on during the same autumn the City installed heavy pieces of railing in the nicely curving stone railings to make skating impossible.

So, I would claim that the differences between the square and any mall plaza or airport lounge are minor *in the current social and economic moment*. Exchange Square *could* be something else, but in the present social space it falls in the same analytical category with Augé's non-places. A much more important difference than that between the square and shopping mall plazas, can be traced between the square and the un-defined or 'contingent' wastelands and forgotten pockets in the Northern Quarter and beyond, the abandoned industrial zones in Ancoats and elsewhere, the empty, wind-swept docks and canal banks around the city.

Manchester, 8 September 2001

Conclusion of Part 2

The meaningful city and lived space would appear to consist of places: urban places, places of experience. While our social space is in a deep sense place-based, it is fundamentally incorrect to think that places would be 'located' in space. It is likewise untrue that space would be a sum of places. Rather places perform the multiple links and networks, meaningful to us. The weak, relational and porous places comprise the human, meaningful space. The notion of place in human geography stresses the act of assigning meaning as the constituent of place, but incorrectly sustains the idea of abstract 'background' space, where this act may take place. Massey, among others, has advanced the geographical understanding by proposing that places are momentary articulations of relations reaching from local to global. In architectural theory, Stenros has aimed at formulating a relational theory of place. However, I argued that there are unnecessary essentialist and perspectival relics in both theories.

Weak places are the seeds of the social production of space. They are the momentary and personal condensation nuclei of the assemblies of qualitatively different elements and planes. The assembly necessarily includes a specific coming-together of material elements, too, but the materiality is not predetermined. So, the conceptualisation of weak place is relational and non-essentialistic. Weak place is the momentary, personal act of gathering knowledge, memories and feelings, and 'throwing' them over the contingent environment. This act is optional. The chance to make a weak place is like the 'window of opportunity' in space travel. You sense it, but using it is a deliberate choice. Concerning planning, urban design and architecture, an interesting result is that un-designed and bland 'urban backwoods' seem to offer more opportunities for the acts of momentary appropriation than ostensibly well-designed and carefully managed spaces. Paradoxically, wastelands are more likely to be moving and important than nice urban plazas and shiny corporate atria. Underdefined, indeterminate sites, even 'non-places' are the humus of weak place.

Clearly, if planning intends to move from conceived to lived space, from *conçu* to *vécu*, it must concentrate on places instead of space, on experiences instead of the map and other visual representations. Because of the fugitive nature of place in the societies shaped by flows, this is a challenge. Weak place is not something physical, visual and easily mappable. A place cannot be drawn.

This is not to say that the notion would be solipsistic, however. Firstly, like social space at large, weak place can be seen as a *concrete abstraction*, which makes it possible to appreciate the shared, socially produced conditions as necessary for the unique place-experience. To paraphrase Marx, people produce singular places, but in conditions they have not freely chosen. Secondly, encounters and conflicts bring place-experiences together, establishing public space. This is the theme of the next chapter.

PART 3
Conflicts Assembling Space

Chapter 5
Spatial Dialectics

Tribe

The air is heavy with smoke and sweat. The beat pounds my lungs and liver. I lean and shout without hearing; the can of 'Red Stripe' becomes immediately wet from condensation, then lukewarm after the first sips. I slowly thrust my way through the moving bodies in an orange corridor. The floor is covered with water or urine, and I cannot avoid getting my shoes wet. I force through an opening to the dance floor. It is rather dark. The music is a wall, and when in, it penetrates the mass of squeezed flesh without friction. I cannot hear it; it is me.

A drop on my head. Another. It is raining. I look up and see only the black plastic sheeting covering some dirty ducts in the ceiling. Then I realise that it is the condensed sweat, which is dripping from the ceiling back to the hot bodies and the cool concrete. A microcosm of Amazonas with the wildest tribe!

Manchester, May 2001

***

So far, I have discussed the mainstream way to conceive space in architecture and planning, as well as some approaches to space and place understood as social and relational. It has become established that both space in general and public urban space in particular are complex phenomena. They are 'mixed' and multifarious; they can be defined in many different ways (cf. Rajanti 1999) and they change in time, their rhythms ranging from glacial to momentary.

Therefore, it is clear that public urban space cannot be adequately conceptualised from the partial perspectives of mapping the physical spatial form, studying social practices or collecting historical examples. It is not enough to just look at the physical frame or what takes place in that frame. As discussed in Part 2, the conceptualisations, which rely on structural similarities between physical and social or physical and mental, are not totally convincing, either, but do provide good stepping-stones. The extended notion of weak place may bring in the lived moment and simultaneously link the two 'levels' of correspondences (physical-social and physical-material), but to view public urban space through the notion of place and as a personal experience only, is clearly unsatisfactory.

My discussion has resulted in a new, creative set of analytical divisions, but the way to synthesise is missing. Lefebvre claims that '[l]ike any reality, social space is related methodologically and theoretically to three general concepts: form, structure, function'. These entail respectively the possibility of formal, structural and functional analysis of space or a part of it. According to Lefebvre, the material realm binds the three aspects together and preserves distinctions between them, but invariably after these analyses a residue remains, calling for deeper analysis (Lefebvre 1991 [1974]: 147–8). How to proceed from analytical grids and assumed structural similarities towards deeper waters? Weak place, its singularity, socio-material mixity and event-nature, is a key conceptual tool, but the theory still needs to take a further step.

In this part, my aim is to demonstrate how to theorise and conceptualise the public aspect of urban space in such a way that it is not objectified, reified, distanced from the personal experience nor frozen in time. The analogy with 'weak thought' offered one way towards such methodology. In what follows, I will discuss certain dialectical approaches[1] to 'non-thinking', 'trans-discursive thinking' and discussing the Becoming, the not-yet-existing.

Window-shopping with Walter Benjamin

ANGELA
2nd floor, to the right. (Benjamin 1999, 40)

Walter Benjamin (1892–1940) is probably best known for his influential essay 'The Work of Art in the Age of Mechanical Reproduction' (1999) [1936]. As a thinker, Benjamin was idiosyncratic. He defined himself as a literary critic (Arendt 1999 [1970]), but he also produced autobiographical works and wrote extensively on cities, an interest culminating in the unfinished 'Arcades Project' on nineteenth-century Paris. He is considered to be one of the key theorists of modernity as a urban phenomenon (Leach 1997: 24). I am interested in his method of thinking about the past, a version of historical materialism,[2] which crystallises in the notion of *dialectical image*.

---

1   The Greek origin of 'dialectic' refers to the art of conversation. Socrates used a dialectic method based on questions, aimed at opening out what is implicitly known or exposing contradictions of an opponent's position, while Plato's dialectic meant the total process of enlightenment (*Oxford Dictionary of Philosophy*). In my work, the notion of dialectics refers to the effort of certain Marxist thinkers to rethink the fusion of Hegelian dialectic and Marx's historical materialism. Schmid (2005) gives an excellent overview, arguing that Nietzsche was the third source of Lefebvre's 'German dialectic'.

2   Benjamin's historical materialism has a strong theological and Messianic undercurrent. Contemporaries of the Frankfurt School, such as Adorno, had difficulties with Benjamin's unorthodox Marxist approach. Arendt (1999 [1970]: 18) suspects that there is nothing dialectical in Benjamin's thinking. Buck-Morss claims, however, that it is exactly the Political which holds Benjamin's work and the Arcades Project together, and that there is no contradiction between the theological and the Marxist (1989: 54, 232). She writes: 'Without theology (the axis of transcendence) Marxism falls into positivism; without Marxism (the axis of empirical history) theology falls into magic. Dialectical

Benjamin's project was to write about the modern city simultaneously in a critical and constructive way. For Benjamin, nineteenth-century Paris is the home of the phantasmagoric, the dreaming collectivity. The modern metropolis is entwined with the myth of the fetishised, fashionable commodities, and he wants to reveal this myth. Benjamin's strategy is to collect pieces and traces of the past and put them together in surprising constellations. By this, he aims at exploding the imagined, linear story we are used to think of as history and 'shock' the reader to see the unexpected in his *present* everyday. 'Benjamin's goal is reconstruction, but for this to occur, the artefact must first be liberated from the suffocation of its context' (Gilloch 1996: 112). 'False history, myth, is to be liquidated through the revelation and representation of a different past, hidden past' (ibid.: 13). Caygill interprets that Benjamin's project was to show the possibilities of different future(s), which 'lingered' in the fragments of history but had never become actual. So the Parisian arcade, the key object and symbol in Benjamin's thinking about the modern city, did not originally possess a fixed meaning. It was 'porous' and 'parasitic', opening for a moment a space where the natural constraints of weather and habitual social constraints of public and private were suspended. The 'Arcades Project' would according to Caygill describe how this open quality was lost, for example, so that in the real Paris the arcades evolved to functionally fixed department stores, or imaginary so that the idea and form of the arcade was transformed to an interior and dwelling space in Fourier's utopian phalanstery (Caygill 1998: 132–4).

The actual method of this liberation and reconstruction is *literary montage*. Benjamin wanted not to theorise nor explain, only to show by organising textual and pictorial fragments so that they illuminate each other. He believed that the historical truth is directly visible in the 'dialectical images' thus created. Benjamin's thinking in condensed, emotionally laden text-images is also called 'poetic'. According to him, '[t]he true picture of the past flits by. The past can be seized only as an image which flashes up at the instant when it can be recognized and is never seen again … For every image of the past that is not recognized by the present as one its own concerns threatens to disappear irretrievably' (Benjamin 1999d [1950]: 247). The themes of the *Arcades Project*[3] as outlined in a plan of the work, 'Paris, the Capital of the Nineteenth Century', are possible sites of dialectical images: 'Fourier or the Arcades', 'Daguerre, or the Panoramas', 'Grandville, or the World Exhibitions', 'Louis Philippe, or the Interior', 'Baudelaire or the Streets of Paris', 'Haussmann or the Barricades' (Benjamin 1999b [1935]: 3–13). The aim is to spark '[a] sudden flash, momentary illumination, and then the capturing of an image; dialectical image is a historical snapshot or, better, a frozen film image …

---

images indeed emerge at the "crossroads between magic and positivism", but at this null point, both "roads" are negated – and at the same time dialectically overcome' (ibid.: 249).

3   See http://art.derby.ac.uk/~g.peaker/arcades/Passagenwerk.html for an interesting web-based interpretation of Benjamin's unfinished project.

Just as the *Denkbild*[4] in the early cityscapes sought to provide a literary snapshot of the urban complex, so the dialectical image seeks to capture historical movement, the changing visage of the metropolis in a textual freeze-frame' (Gilloch 1996: 113–14). *One-Way Street*, too, is a good example of Benjamin's style (Benjamin 1979b).

I find the ideas of montage and dialectical image interesting, because they leave much space for the reader. Dialectical image works through the tension of absence and presence. Buck-Morss states that '[o]n their own the nineteenth-century facts collected by Benjamin are flat … It is because they are only half the text. The reader of Benjamin's generation was to provide the other half of the picture from the fleeting images of his or her lived experience' (1989: 292). This is as true for our generation. Allan Pred's Benjamin-inspired books, especially *Even in Sweden* on the Swedish cultural racism (Pred 2000, cf. Lehtovuori 2001e), show that if there is a strong point to be made, it is more efficient *not* to say it directly but rather leave it to be disclosed by the reader. In that way truth becomes an event and cuts more deeply. As Benjamin states: 'Method of this work: literary montage. I have nothing to say, only to show' (Benjamin 1982: 574; cited in Buck-Morss 1989: 73). Montage and 'picture that flits by' are somehow like the urban space itself. They allow one to go from the idea of 'reading' the city – city-as-text – to city-like textual practice – text-as-city (cf. Gilloch 1996: 94). Indeed, when reading the *Arcades Project*, the fluid, emerging social space of early-industrial Paris, its inventions, beliefs and practices, open like a landscape into which the reader is able to enter.

Excursion 5: The Display Window

While Benjamin refers to iron construction as one condition of the arcades, his main interest is in the display of industrial commodities. He comments on the arcades' social space:

> Trade and traffic are the two components of the street. Now, in the arcades the second of these has effectively died out: the traffic there is rudimentary. The arcade is a street of lascivious commerce only; it is wholly adapted to arousing desires. Because in this street the juices slow to a standstill, the commodity proliferates along the margins and enters into fantastic combinations, like the tissue in tumors. The *flâneur* sabotages the traffic. Moreover, he is no buyer. He is merchandise. (Benjamin 1999: 42)

---

4   Remember the piece wondering about the map of the Soviet Union in Moscow, pp. 23–4.

Arcades were the first commodified public urban spaces. Their most important architectural element was not the glass roof but the display window[5] (Benjamin 1999b [1935], Buck-Morss 1989).

As part of Helsinki's Olympic programme, the Glass Palace was built in 1935 (accidentally the same year when Benjamin's *Exposé* 'Paris, the Capital of the Nineteenth Century' was published). The streamlined, high-modernistic building was to signal modernity and a modern lifestyle. The glass of the Glass Palace is precisely the glass of its display windows. As the Parisian arcades a century earlier, the Glass Palace was built to display commodities, such as luxury items and exotic fruits, radiating cosmopolitanism and wealth.

In 1998 MTV3's (the Finnish commercial channel) city studio moved into the Glass Palace, repaired and refurbished to become a high-profile media centre, co-founded by the EU (Lehtovuori 1999). A television studio was equipped in a former shop. The novelty of that studio was that there was no stage setting. Cameras were directed at the display window, *from inside*. This small invention produced a chain reaction of both conceptual and palpable *détournements*.

1. The display window started to act both ways. People could look inside from the street, as before. A mechanical eye, the television camera, started to look out from inside.
2. The urban scene, captured by the camera, became a stage setting. Traditionally, the city had been considered to be the 'stage' of events; now the studio became the urban stage, and the (real) city was deprived of that role.
3. The filming of a television programme, which previously was invisible and secretive, became very visible. The event of filming was substituted for the commodities in the display window: Filming became a commodity, a product, as much as the 'real' product of the channel, the talk show or newscast.
4. Likewise, the urban scene became not only a stage setting but a commodity as well. The television channel had bought itself in the city; it had bought a right to use the urban scene for its purposes. The city became instrumental in a new televised way.

Is this a version of the Benjaminian story of a loss of aura in the period of mechanical reproduction? So it seems: 'Actors' of the urban stage – people in their everyday trajectories – become shadows, images to be cut at the producer's will to fill the broadcast flow. This resonates closely with Benjamin's discussion

---

5 One of Benjamin's ideas is that with iron construction and the possibilities of glass, architecture is outgrowing art. This concerns the problematic role of construction and classical decoration, but also the display of industrial luxury commodities. In the display windows or 'porticos' of arcades in the 1820s, industry for the first time in history was able to rival the arts in seductive power (Benjamin 1999b [1935]: 3–4).

of film actors to become shadows if compared with theatre actors in a real life act, deprived from most agencies and their acting subjected a recontextualisation on the clipboard (Benjamin 1999c [1936]). Likewise the city itself seems to be stripped of its aura as a multi-sensory experience and lived social realm, and become reduced to just a picture. Another representation, that of the TV programme, starts to dominate the lived space.

Things are not that simple, though. Firstly, why, in the first place, does a television channel want to have a foothold in the city? There is certainly a whole range of reasons, related to the evolutions of the broadcasting industry. These might include the fragmenting of television audiences and an effort to get a grip on a new, young and urban audience; a need to create new profiles for new programme types; a wish to speed up and streamline production. I will leave these media studies considerations aside. Only one point warrants a comment. Most likely, one of the reasons was a hope that the urban setting would lend programmes footed there a feeling of actuality, of being 'in the middle of events' or 'in touch with reality'. To be realised, this hope obviously presupposes the (continued) existence of the 'real' city with its events and intricacies. At least it presupposes that the television audiences imagines its existence and believes in it (see Koskela (2004) for a discussion on the usage of CCTV footage about real crimes in mass media). So, indirectly, the channel's location decision supports the existence – real and imagined – of the city as the locus of events of importance and the source of authority, and consequently the relationship of the city studio and the surrounding city is not that of stripping the aura but rather that of a parasite.

Secondly, the city studio triggers real people to do real things. Making a television programme becomes an urban event. Teenagers have gathered in hundreds, even in thousands, at the display window to watch pop stars be interviewed in a popular programme called *Jyrki*, and to be glimpsed by the cameras. Following the logic of the parasite, this is useful for the programme in two ways. The actual crowd of screaming teenagers is an advertisement in the city, and the same crowd as a stage set confirms its popularity for the audience watching TV. It is also possible to organise demonstrations *behind* the display window. This has happened a number of times, causing a remarkable debate. The TV channel claims that it should be allowed to police the street to avoid demonstrators messing up its broadcasts *as if it really owned the scene*. On the other hand, it is difficult to find a reason to force a person away from a normal, public pavement, if he or she is not causing any trouble, simply carrying a placard or banderol. This dispute was never really resolved.[6] It was managed case by case, in a grey zone between conflicting views.

---

6   MTV3's city studio, producing Jyrki was closed in 2002 (Kari Kanerva of MTV3, 12 January, 2005). The National Broadcasting Company, too, has converted its studio in the Glass Palace to a shop.

Public Urban Space as a Suspended Conflict

> Conflict is not something that befalls an originally, or potentially, harmonious urban space. Urban space is the product of conflict. (Deutsche 1996: 278, quoted in Massey 2005: 153)

I have already briefly mentioned that in her book *Kaupunki on ihmisen koti* [*The City is the Home of Man*] Taina Rajanti classifies the human states of being into the spatial, the linguistic and the communal. Rajanti views the city 'both as a metaphor of community, culture and civilization and as their material precondition and necessity' (Rajanti 1999: 12). Space and its inhabitants are one; society is 'practical' and 'mixed'. Let us study more precisely Rajanti's concept of public (urban) space, because it offers a major stepping-stone towards a relational, trans-discursive theory of public urban space.

Rajanti's idea of the city as the existential and cultural home of man has many similarities with Lefebvre's notion of social space. The Greek *polis*, the city-state, which is central to Rajanti's argument is one of the forms gained by the relationships of the perceived, conceived and lived. It is a specific social space. The same applies to the European city, living on in the heritage of the *polis*, as well as to the presently emerging 'space of the global'. Paralleling Lefebvre's idea of lived space that 'overlays physical space, making symbolic use of its objects' (Lefebvre 1991 [1974]: 39), Rajanti regards physical space as inseparable from human signification. She writes that 'the meanings assigned by people to the built environment are not secondary or superfluous, but rather its integral factors. A city without people is not perfect; but a ruin' (Rajanti 1999: 11). As I mentioned in Chapter 3, the claim that there must be mutual correspondences between the three realms, is a reflection of the structuralistic tradition[7] in which Rajanti locates her work.

For Rajanti, the Greek city-state, *polis*, is the starting point and horizon. The current 'space of the global' contradicts the social and spatial configuration of *polis*, but nevertheless cannot be understood without it. The 'invention' that produced the social space of *polis* is an unsolvable conflict. Rajanti traces its origin to *The Iliad* and the impossible cooperation of sovereign war heroes in the Trojan war. Referring to Mario Vegetti, she claims that in the ancient value system there was no way to solve conflicts between the sovereigns. Pride was a zero-sum game, so to speak. To avoid a vicious circle of mimetic violence of insults and bloody revenges, disputes could only be suspended. This conflict-ridden situation resulted in the new social and spatial form. '*Polis* is the material sett(l)ing[8] of the impossible space of the public conflict [of *The Iliad*], not its solution' (Rajanti

---

7   See note 6, p. 58 for clarification of the use of 'structuralistic'.

8   In Finnish: '*Polis on julkisen kiistan mahdottoman tilan materiaalinen asettaminen...*' I would like to use '*Verwindung*' instead of 'settling', but that would be a fairly strong interpretation of Rajanti.

1999: 61, transl. PL). City, in the sense of *polis*, is in Rajanti's analysis not less than a certain – Western – mode of Being in the world. The suspended conflict, the impossible coming together of sovereigns, is in its core, giving meaning to what we are used to calling 'public urban space'. That is why Rajanti claims that '*[a]gorà*, common and public meeting place … is primarily a coming together, an event, and only secondarily a particular space of assembly. Public space is not necessary for creating a community as such, but a community based on an unsolved dispute' (ibid.). Neither form nor function, neither squares nor vibrant commerce, can define the city-community. Instead of the material space, either as the surrounding facades or the gathered mass of people, public space is defined through 'public', understood as the potentiality or idea of the community. It is not *a* community but rather an *extension* from the actual to the potential and abstract. Especially, the potential concerns politically significant conflicts. 'The city as a public space opens up wherever there is a dispute to be resolved, where the clash of different desires hangs over and penetrates the space and connects some of the desires' (ibid.). There is tension and movement in the conceptualisation, and the physical space is just one part of the mixed totality. Rajanti's conception further evokes dialectical centrality, space as the point of assembly.

When discussing the passage from 'antique' towards 'modern' and the space of the global, Rajanti refers to Benjamin's Baudelaire study *Zentral Park*. Following Benjamin, she interprets the Parisian streets as deep abysses, which cut through the 'urban form of human life' (established as *polis*) instead of constituting its core, public space (Rajanti 1999: 167). Several ruptures or mutations occur between 'antique' and 'modern'. For the classical understanding, a city's physical structure was contingent: a city was conceived of as a political and ethical unit. In contradistinction, the modern city is a physical object and a technical project (of ordering, sanitising). Therefore Haussmann's physical 'surgery' is a powerful image of the modern. When the city is thought of as purely physical, instead of people and their relationships, it loses the quality of being a mixture of existing and non-existing, actual and potential, tiles and communal meanings. The links between space and communal meaning are broken, and everybody in a modern city, in a metropolis, becomes a stranger (cf. Simmel *The Stranger*). This, however, is not a simple development (regressive or progressive). Rajanti claims that the deep, organic community against which the modern metropolis – with its stress and loneliness but also freedom – is often posited, never existed. It is an imagination, utopia, postulated *from* the modern. *So, the modern community is built on a paradox, a suspended impossibility, as was the community of* polis.

Spatially the contemporary paradox is very different from the ancient, though. If a shared, mixed 'quasi-object', such as *agorà* (Rajanti gives several other examples), was essential in *polis*, the modern community is built in non-space, in u-topia. Therefore, being a stranger, being no-where or being outside becomes the fundamental spatial relationship of the communal Being in the world (Rajanti 1999: 150). No one has a 'home' in the space of the global, everybody, also we rich Westerners, are 'refugees' and must carve our individual, temporal places – weak places! – in the realm of identity-less and history-less non-places.[9] In my opinion, Massey's notion of the global sense of place refers to this very same condition, but with a more optimistic tone. For Massey, the carving of weak place is in its openness a genuine chance to create a more tolerant urban space.

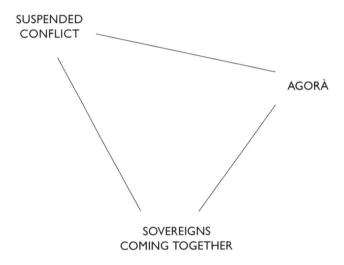

Figure 5.1   Elements of the social space of polis

Polis is without doubt a socially produced space in the wide, Lefebvrean sense. Let me hypothetically equate the act of sovereign heroes (strangers) coming together with spatial practice, physical *agorà* and the necessary routes and boundaries defining a city with representations of space, and the suspended conflict with spaces of representation.

It is difficult to imagine a similar analogy with the present 'elements' of urban social space. On the surface it seems that we indeed loose the connection between spatial and social, although the route of the loss is oblique. A human (communal) being becomes separated from its materiality; (physical) public space has no structural role to play in the modern, eventually global community. The fragmentation and loss of meaning of public urban space seem to be unavoidable. However, Rajanti is able to show that while the space has mutated from a communal

---

9   According Rajanti, quasi-object is an object without a definitive meaning and which therefore can be invested with any meaning. She refers to Michel Serres, who in his *Roma*, calls this indeterminate object 'joker', the 'white element' of a theory, story or game.

place of sustained, unsolvable conflict (*polis/agorà*) to a global placelessness, based on a lack of material space, *this is also a spatial, conflict-ridden relationship potentially laden with meaning.*

This is a fascinating, beautiful idea. Rajanti is understandably ambiguous on the physical aspect of space. She only refers to Augé's 'non-places' (highways, airports, malls, refugee camps) as the new type of place, which are a-historical and do not lend any identity to a person entering them (Rajanti 1999: 192–3, Augé 1995: 77–8). I think, however, that a dynamic, dialectical understanding of public urban space would open up a more fruitful way to involve the paradox and conflict of supermodern social space in the theory of the urban.

Dialectical Understanding of Space and its Production

> The sphere of private life ought to be enclosed, and have a finite, or finished, aspect. Public space, by contrast, ought to be an opening outwards. (Lefebvre 1991 [1974]: 147)

The way to conceive public urban space needs to be tensioned and dynamic. In this, the insightful idea of suspended conflict is central. However, public urban space constantly changes, while Rajanti's account after all 'freezes' the notion. I do not think that (a) space can stay in the same state of suspension forever. Like a stream, it never is the same again, but it always presents us with a new situation, a new configuration. Or it may be compared to atoms in a neon tube, which are charged and then emit light, electrons jumping arbitrarily. Rajanti, too, does briefly refer to change. She writes that the structures and dynamics of a community are constantly reproduced in its practices, and in those practices they may change either through wearing out or through conflicts (Rajanti 1999: 10–11). But she leaves the notion of change in the air. The reason may be that structural isomorphisms are in fact relative accounts, even though they may be complex. A 'system' is fixed, one-to-one, and its change entails 'breaks' or 'ruptures' in the chains of correspondence. Thereby, breaks fall outside the structuralistic way of conceptualisation. Public urban space, however, calls for a truly relational account, which can 'digest' ruptures and discontinuities. Its conceptualisation should be able to deal with qualitatively different aspects, with mixity and complexity, with deep-seated otherness and, most importantly, change.

At this juncture, I would like to return to Lefebvre and how his unique *dialectique de triplicité* (dialectic of the trinity) can be brought to bear on the issue of space (Elden 2004: 37). To understand what Lefebvre means, I want to discuss his notion of social production and the related contention that space is a 'concrete abstraction' in more detail. I will use Mark Gottdiener's (1985, 1993), Stuart Elden's (2004) and especially Christian Schmid's (2005) insightful interpretations of Lefebvre's dialectic. These authors also show distinct weaknesses in the work of postmodern geographers, including Edward Soja. After some fairly theoretical considerations

I will continue by specifying how Lefebvre's ideas might be applicable to public urban space, its architecture and design, instead of the totality of social space in a certain, historical society. Firstly, I suggest that physical urban artifacts can take the role of the 'other' in the dialectic of trinity. This brings distinctively architectural understanding of form, type and spatial configuration in the heart of the theory of social space. Secondly, I develop a link between Lefebvre's notion of *oeuvre* (city as art-like work) and Gernot Böhme's (1995; 1998) concept of *atmosphere*, which helps bridging the societal and historical concern of Lefebvre and architects' interest in experiential space (Lehtovuori 2008). In Part 4 on Helsinki, I reflect upon these theories in the mirror of actual experiences and sequences of events.

Lefebvre offers the notions of *production* and the *act of producing* as the unifying terms of his spatial thought (1991 [1974]: 15–16). He enlarges their meaning from the narrow industrial sense to include the production of built works, as well as spatialised meanings and other codings of the social environment (Shields 1999: 159). Space is a very peculiar product. It is simultaneously the end-result of production and the context of production, setting its conditions. This double aspect is grasped by Marx's (and Hegel's) concept of *concrete abstraction*. Like Marx's category of exchange value, which is simultaneously a material, externalised realisation of human labour and the condensation of social relations of production, space as a concrete abstraction is simultaneously a medium of social actions and a product of those actions (Gottdiener 1994 [1985]: 128–9). Hillier and Hanson's (1984) contention, discussed above, that space is both product and producer of social structure points in the same direction.

Lefebvre then asks what is the *logical form* – in distinction to 'substance' or 'reality' – of social space. He writes that in *Capital*

> Marx uncovers an (almost) pure form, that of the circulation of material goods, or *exchange*. This is a quasi-logical form similar to, and indeed bound up with, other "pure" forms (identity and difference, equivalence, consistency, reciprocity, recurrence, and repetition) … The 'pure' form here has a bipolar structure (use value *versus* exchange value), and it has functions which *Capital* sets forth. (Lefebvre 1991 [1974]: 100, original italics)

Via money, labour and their dialectics exchange reaches to the level of social practice. In an analogous manner to exchange, another concrete abstraction, which also has developed in several historical stages, governs social space. What is that form? According to Lefebvre, '[t]he form of social space is encounter, assembly, simultaneity' (ibid.: 101).

This is in my opinion one of the core ideas of *La production de l'espace*, because it opens up a way to understand Lefebvre's project of 'spatialising the dialectic' better. He continues: 'But what assembles, or what is assembled? The answer is: everything that there is *in space*, everything that is produced either by nature or by society, either through their co-operation or through their conflicts. Everything: living beings, things, objects, works, signs, and symbols' (ibid.). Also

Gottdiener stresses that 'the most important aspect of space [in Lefebvre's work] is its multifaceted nature ... Space is a physical location, a piece of real estate, and simultaneously an existential freedom and a mental expression' (Gottdiener 1994 [1985]: 123). The multiple nature of space is not (just) a description, but a precise theoretical argument, which informs Lefebvre's research strategy. If space is by necessity a multiplicity, there can be no way to conceptualise or represent it directly. There is always deep-seated *otherness* in space.[10] Space is full of 'traps' and 'secret places', making an easy comprehension of it illusory and deceptive (Lefebvre 1991 [1974]: 28–9). The only possible way to conceive is dialectical, a movement or change (cf. Gottdiener 1994 [1985]: 128). Lefebvre's genial idea, then, is to propose a *synchronic dialectic*, a dialectic of lived moments. He can be said to spatialise Marx's historical and Hegel's idealistic dialectics, both of which work with the idea of movement from one stage to the next (Lefebvre 1991 [1974]: 65–7). In Lefebvre's mature thinking, the dialectic consists of a continual movement between three terms, for example those of conceived, perceived and lived space (Elden 2004: 36). That is the discourse 'of' space, instead of scientific-representing discourse 'on' space.

The idea of spatial dialectics is both seducing and challenging. Firstly, the idea is not too clear and needs specifying case by case. According to Gottdiener, Lefebvre left his new theory on social space 'metaphorical' and did not fully develop the idea of taking account of space in Marxian concepts (Gottdiener 1994 [1985]: 132).[11] Shields even claims that '[p]aradoxically, [the idea of grounding his analysis into a broadened concept of social production] is both a significant failure and an intellectual triumph as it succeeds in interrelating most aspects

---

10   The idea of the lived as fundamentally other is also behind my effort to use place-experience, the weak place, as a site of architectural criticism, as developed in Chapter 4.

11   Gottdiener (1993) lucidly discusses how Lefebvre might have encountered the idea of spatial dialectic: 'In *Dialectical Materialism* ([1939] 1968) Lefebvre analyzed Marxian political economy at a time when he was breaking with Stalinism and the Communist Party. No doubt he was reacting to dogmatism and orthodoxy (as well as to Stalin's politics), and this reaction was reflected in a critical reading of Marx's *Capital*. Lefebvre noted that the latter work was essentially about time – the extraction and circulation of surplus value. Lefebvre believed that Marxian political economy neglected the material aspect of production: the world of commodities existed in *space* as well as time. In 1939 he announced that the dialectic was spatial as well as temporal, and that this realization put Marx's system in a new light. Lefebvre went literally to the material dimension of dialectics. In his view, the production activity of capitalism resulted in a space – that is, a materiality. Furthermore, this "space" possessed its own dialectical moment. Like the other categories of Marxian thought – money, labor power – it was a *concrete abstraction*. That is, space was both a material product of social relations (the concrete) and a manifestation of relations, a relation itself (the abstract). It was as much a part of social relations as was time. In short, by applying Marxian thought to Marx, Lefebvre arrived at insights that transcended Marxian political economy and pointed away from dogma. He needed the next 30 years to work out the implications of these early revelations.'

of spatiality while not succeeding in clarifying key points about his three-part dialectics of space …' (Shields 1999: 144). While Shields finds Lefebvre's use of non-teleological, non-linear dialectic confusing (ibid.: 150–52), Elden (2004: 37) counters this contention by claiming that *dialectique de triplicité* is 'neither a replacement of dialectical reasoning with "trialectics" [Soja] or the introduction of space into the dialectic [Shields]'. So, both Soja and Shields would have confused Lefebvre's ideas. The elements of the dialectic are in fluid, rhythmic relation to each other. The 'third' term is not the result of the dialectic, but synthesis is able to react upon the first two terms (ibid.).

When applying these ideas to the production of public urban space, the idea of simultaneity becomes very important. The notions of individual experience, moment, tension, conflict and experiment open the possibility of an analytical understanding of the provisional production of space, as well as the possibility to speculate its future. Different elements come together in a moment of production. Space features as the possibility of simultaneous existence of differences, but those differences are not necessarily on the same plane of analysis. As Massey (2005: 9) formulates, space is a 'coexisting heterogeneity'.

The notion of production in Lefebvre is broad but it is easy to mistakenly simplify and associate with manual production only. Setha M. Low, for example, distinguishes between social production and social construction. He defines production as 'the physical creation of the material setting', while social construction would refer to the 'phenomenological and symbolic experience of space as mediated by social processes', therefore becoming 'the actual transformation of space – through people's social exchanges, memories, images, and daily use of the material setting …' (Low 1999: 112). While the material definition of social production may 'make sense', the common sense appeal of Low's usage contains a trap, as it merely reintroduces the strict categorisations between physical, social and mental Lefebvre wants to question. It is a serious misinterpretation of Lefebvre to firstly focus on the construction of specific, material urban artefacts and secondly to draw an analogy between the production of an industrial artefact and the production of an urban artefact – which may be a housing estate, an office block or a waterfront redevelopment. Lefebvre's wide definition of production, so that it concerns ideas, thought-patterns and everyday practices should be taken seriously.

Secondly, it is possible to misinterpret that the core of Lefebvre's thesis is a reduction of social space to the ongoing process of its social production. However, Lefebvre constantly works against any simplistic analysis. Arguably, 'non-process elements' such as material artefacts, physical space and spatial configurations also have a role and place (sic) in his dialectic (cf. Shields 1999: 154). I will come back to this remark in Chapters 8 and 9.

Spatial dialectics is no easy theory, but a site of conflict and innovation. According to Lefebvre, '[t]he search for unitary theory in no way rules out conflicts within knowledge itself, and controversy and polemics are inevitable' (Lefebvre 1991 [1974]: 13). For Lefebvre, space is not a master term. It is not something over-arching or something that could be called 'frame' or 'point of reference' for lesser notions and applications. On the contrary, *space is always specific and unique*. In Lefebvre's Marxist thought this mainly means that a space is specific for a mode of production. This contention leads to his long history of spaces, starting from absolute space and leading through sacred and historical space to the abstract space of capitalism. But it is also possible to use Lefebvre's idea to study and shed light on more limited and ephemeral productions of space, such as the recreation of urban squares and parks and the creation of new kinds of public urban space in contemporary cities.

According to Lefebvre, the conceived space dominates the lived space in all societies; it could be said to be the 'antithesis' in the spatial dialectic. I hypothesise that lived space might be a 'window' away from the Enlightenment logic of the city of planning. Lefebvre intended the conception of space as social product to be a radical tool of change rather than a description or an academic abstraction. His theory is a call for action: '[t]he perceived-conceived-lived triad … loses all force if it is treated as an abstract "model". If it cannot grasp the concrete (as distinct from the "immediate"), then its import is severely limited, amounting to no more than that of one ideological mediation among others' (Lefebvre 1991 [1974]: 40).

The notion of lived space (*l'espace vécu*) is closely linked to another principal theme in Lefebvre's *oeuvre*, the everyday or everyday life (*le quotidien*). For Lefebvre, the everyday is *both* the alienated, colonised, repetitive and boring life under the structures of capitalism and media, *and* a rich source of surprises, alternatives and fully lived moments (Lefebvre 1991b [1947]: 228–). The first aspect is lived space dominated by representations (of those in power), while the second refers to its potential to produce creative diversions and new socio-spatial constellations. Essentially, any societal change is also a change in the spatial praxis (Gottdiener 1994 [1985]), in everyday life. To change only one or two aspects is not enough.

> Any 'social existence' aspiring or claiming to be real, but failing to produce its own space, would be a strange entity, a very peculiar kind of abstraction unable to escape from the ideological or even the 'cultural' realm. … This suggests a possible criterion for distinguishing between ideology and practice … or, otherwise stated, for distinguishing between the *lived* on the one hand and the *perceived* and the *conceived* on the other …. (Lefebvre 1991 [1974]: 53, original italics)

Based on this I maintain that the notion of 'spatial dialectics' is valid and useful. However, I do not use that notion to argue for any hierarchy between space and time or 'spatiality' and 'historicity' (cf. Soja 1996).

Interpretations of Spatial Dialectics

Before proceeding further, let us have a brief look at four developments of Lefebvre's idea about the spatial dialectics. Those are Mark Gottdiener's pioneering synthesis as presented in *The Social Production of Urban Space* (1994) [1985], Edward Soja's notion of 'thirding-as-othering' (Soja 1996), Rob Shields' diagrammatic proposal about how Lefebvre may have conceived the terms of his dialectic (Shields 1999) and Christian Schmid's thorough interpretation of Lefebvre's thinking in *Stadt, Raum und Gesellschaft* (Schmid 2005), stressing the link between thought and action.

From Class Conflict to Spatial Conflict

Gottdiener develops Lefebvre's ideas by recontextualising them and by mixing or crossbreeding them with other theoretical traditions. Firstly, he links the notion of production of space to Giddens' structuration theory (Giddens 1984). By making a distinction between structure and agency – with the implicit voluntarism of the latter – Gottdiener is able to criticise simplistic urban theories, which suppose urban changes and new urban forms to be 'natural' results of some technological or social changes, with clearly discernible causal relations (Gottdiener 1994 [1985]: 228). From the same position, Gottdiener also criticises Marxist tradition, most notably the structuralistic Marxism of early Castells.[12] Secondly, Gottdiener tries to anchor the new theory to empirically oriented urban sciences. This leads to an idea of the 'three-dimensional matrix', where urban ecology and traditional urban geography form a 'horizontal' field of analysis, and Marxist political economy its 'vertical' axis from localised places to global economic forces (ibid.: 197–8). Thirdly, he wants to shift the focus of urban research from cities to metropolitan regions, which he considers the relevant 'units' of study in the present late-capitalist situation. The core concepts of metropolitan development are 'deconcentration' and 'recentralisation', which denote a dual process of demographic shift from cities to suburban and rural areas and a simultaneous emergence of specialised new centres virtually anywhere in a metro-region (ibid.: 9, 229). In his analysis, the major structural factors are 1) the growing company size and the emergence of the global corporation with its powers to reorganise and relocate production, R&D and administration independently, 2) the omnipresent 'interventionist state'

---

12   It is rather interesting to note that even though Castells' approach in his later work, e.g. *The Informational City* (1989) and *The Rise of the Network Society* (1996) is very empirically oriented, almost the opposite to the early work, his ideas about space have not changed. The famous 'space of flows' is for Castells a purely material underpinning of the new informational economy – he refers to optic fibres, telephone lines, airports, etc. (Castells 1996; 1992) – and the new 'informational urban form' – the 'megacity' – likewise a direct, technologically determined outcome of the socio-technical process. See above pp. 81–5.

since the 1920s Great Depression, and 3) the increased importance of knowledge and technology as forces of production (ibid.: 201–5). The key agency in the production of urban space is according to Gottdiener held by the real-estate sector. It is characterised by opportunistic 'growth networks' (ibid.: 222–7, see also Dear and Häkli 1998: 61).

Compared to Lefebvre, Gottdiener is clear and systematic. However, while Gottdiener's initial project was clarifying Lefebvre's metaphors, he does lose much of Lefebvre's seductive glow. Gottdiener's modifications seemingly lead him quite far from Lefebvre's ethos of the city as a social, cultural and economic powerhouse, an experiential arena of opportunities, something to be passionately fought for, a collective *oeuvre* – an oeuvre of *people* not corporations. For Gottdiener 'city' is not a poetic source of imagination but a well-defined governmental unit with a likewise well-defined historical position in a metro-region. The differences in style and focus notwithstanding, an important driving force of both Lefebvre's and Gottdiener's thought is to show the 'softness' and malleability of space and the social relations it represents and produces. What is interesting for me is that Gottdiener is able to theorise more precisely than Lefebvre the clashes of the 'contradictory space'. According to Gottdiener, the main antagonism would now emerge between attitudes towards growth, instead of those between the traditional classes or new fractions of them (Gottdiener 1994 [1985]: 165). 'In short, the clash between growth and no growth represents a basic cleavage in society, involving economic, political, and ideological practices', he writes (ibid.: 222). The spatial dialectics becomes a struggle between abstract and social (lived) spaces, between distanced exchange values attached to space by developers and growth networks and actual use-values of individuals and communities (ibid.: 127, cf. Lehtovuori 2003b). Environmental, community and heritage preservation movements get a major societal role in this theory. Thus, it translates Lefebvre's broad historical and societal concerns to a more palpable level of projects, sites and urban conflicts. Gottdiener's ideas also interestingly link back to Taina Rajanti's contention about public space as necessarily tensioned and conflictual.

Thirding-as-Othering

Lefebvre's spatial dialectics can be seen as approximations to grasp the multiplicity of social space, the qualitatively different realms assembling and coming together. Edward Soja in *Thirdspace* is quite correct in interpreting the third element as always the 'other'. He writes that

> [w]henever faced with such binarised categories (subject-object, mental-material, natural-social, bourgeoisie-proletariat, local-global, centre-periphery, agency-structure[13]), Lefebvre persistently sought to crack them open by

---

13   It may be that Gottdiener's effort to 'operationalise' – rationalise! – Lefebvre's freely moving thought by necessity loses something essential. The structure-agency

> introducing an-Other term, a third possibility or "moment" that partakes of the
> original pairing but is not just a simple combination or an "in-between" position
> along some all-inclusive continuum … Thirding produces what might best be
> called cumulative trialectics that is radically open to additional othernesses, to a
> continuing expansion of spatial knowledge. (Soja 1996: 60–61)

Soja coins a new term, 'trialectics'. The other – or the lived space – becomes a
'strategic location', from which it is possible to understand more and, what is
more important, to criticise and change social space (ibid.: 68). According to Soja,
in Lefebvre's thinking, too, there is a strategic preference for the third term, but
'always as a transcending inclusion of the other two'. So, the third term never
stands alone (Soja 1996: 70).

   Soja then discusses at length post-colonial and feminist 'spatialisations',
such as Bell Hooks' idea of choosing political and geographical marginality or
Edward Said's critique of the Eurocentric historicism. However, he is not able
to operationalise the lucid idea of thirding-as-othering. Rather, Soja falls back
on conventional geo-historical ways to describe the present urban condition, and
the only enduring analytical strategy is his constant emphasis on 'both-and' –
both the micro and macro view are necessary; both real and imagined aspects of
urban situations need to be acknowledged (ibid.: 310). This interpretation flattens
Lefebvre's dialectic of qualitatively different terms in a very unproductive way,
losing the power of dialectical reasoning (Elden 2004: 37, Schmid 2005: 65). In
the end, 'Thirdspace' simply connotes 'everything there is': 'Thirdspace: a lived
space of radical openness and unlimited scope, where all histories and geographies,
all times and places, are immanently presented and represented, a strategic space
of power and domination, empowerment and resistance' (ibid.: 311). It is amazing
and disappointing that from the specific, situated idea of the third as always the
other, Soja moves to another Grand Theory, another static universalism. *Il y a
toujours l'Autre*, also for the totalising, Aleph-like Thirdspace!

Spatial Diagrammatics

Instead of treating Thirdspace as a master term, I would like to rescue its dynamism
and specificity. Rob Shields in *Lefebvre, Love and Struggle* (1999) has given a
diagrammatic form to the spatial dialectics, or the process of thirding-as-othering.
Figure 5.2. shows how Shields (1999: 120) interprets Lefebvre's 'terms'.

   According to Shields, both perceived and conceived are relativised by a
transcendent, deeply other moment, creative and fully lived space. So, instead
of the 'third' being the social totality or spatialisation (cf. Thirdspace), there is a

---

construction in Gottdiener, however, is more a weapon to shoot down functionalistic
theories, to argue that urban change is fundamentally contingent, than a total explanation
of the world. The real-estate sector as the main agency nevertheless leads to a somewhat
reduced picture of the production of space.

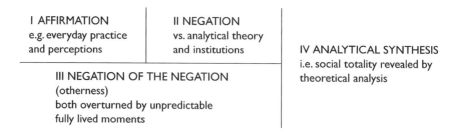

Figure 5.2   Spatial dialectics

Source: after Shields (1999: 120).

fourth, analytical term. With the reservations expressed above (p. 119), I consider this interpretation valuable, but to be epistemologically sound and practically useful it still needs one important modification.

Spatial Diagrammatics, Edition 2.0

Instead of conceiving of the fourth term as the analytical view to the totality of a social space, it would be more precise to treat the whole diagram as representing change, a movement or an *event*. If the three terms neatly sum up as a totality, open to analysis, the whole theoretical construction loses its dynamism and becomes again another master term – albeit consisting of three elements instead of one. This problem is graphically indicated in Shields' metaphor of social space as a 'pie' with three slices (Ilmonen and Lehtovuori 2002). Dialectically understood space cannot be a pie on a single plane of reality. One cannot view social space from outside, as a hungry eater. But why, exactly, can the three elements of social space not produce an intelligible totality? The reason is that as I have discussed above the 'third' or the 'other' needs to be thought of as unique, even singular. The third element of spatial dialectics is the dream, the personal revelation, the moment, the ephemeral aesthetic experience, the trigger of momentary weak place. If the diagram contains a singularity, it cannot be totality in a traditional sense. It only can 'flicker'; it is always unstable and fugitive. It may be a totality in the sense of lived, unfolding reality, confronted problems and moments experienced and lived through, but not in the sense of being totally grasped, looked at from outside as a thing. Not looked at, but may be looked past.

However, Shield's diagram works beautifully as an analytical tool to *study changes*. In this way, time indeed is part of the 'spatial dialectic'. The fourth analytical term is a view of a specific event, a specific moment of production of space. The moment or change can be about settling down or taming the 'other' (*Verwindung*), but it also can be about a big shift – the 'urban revolution' Lefebvre wrote about (*détournement*).

In final form the diagram of thirding-as-othering can be represented as shown in Figure 5.3.

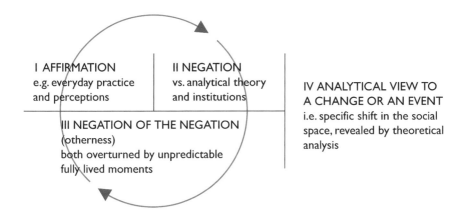

Figure 5.3   Spatial dialectics 2.0

Dialectic as a Concrete Logic: Understanding Action

Schmid (2005: 110) suggests that Lefebvre's creative synthesis of Hegel, Marx and Nietzsche – 'the German dialectic' – is a philosophical achievement without parallel. Without a deep *exposé* of Schmid's insightful and holistic interpretation (which would be impossible in the frame of this book), I would like to concentrate on two aspects that directly inform my approach in the study of public urban space.

Firstly, for Lefebvre the core of the dialectical problem of form and content is in an effort to understand action (ibid.: 98). Criticising Hegel's abstract thought, Lefebvre foregrounds social practices through Marx and individual poetic creativity through Nietzsche (ibid.: 111). The starting point of abstraction is not in thinking but in a movement between thinking and practice. A painter, for example, could not develop his skills and awareness without actually painting. Painting is not a pretext or an arbitrary manifestation of an inner, pre-existing talent, but its source.[14] Similarly, space can only be understood in its production. The terms of a spatial dialectic influence each other, co-producing space in a dialectical movement where the experiencing human being is in a central position.

Secondly, Schmid makes an interesting analysis of the sources of Lefebvre's well-known conceptual triads: perceived–conceived–lived and spatial practice-representations of space-spaces of representation. The first triad is phenomenological, with links to Bachelard and Merleau-Ponty, and the second semiotic or linguistic

---

14 'So erprobt und entdeckt sich ein Maler zunächst in seinen ersten Versuchen, worauf er seine Technik vervollkommnet und seine Gestaltungsweise abwandelt. Es wäre widersinnig anzunehmen, dass dieser Maler sein Talent entwickeln und sich bewusst machen kann, ohne tatsächlich zu malen; die Malerei ist für ihn kein Vorwand, keine gelegentliche Manifestation eines zuvor und innerlich vorhandenen Talents' (Lefebvre in *Der Dialektische Materialismus* (1966), quoted in Schmid 2005: 99).

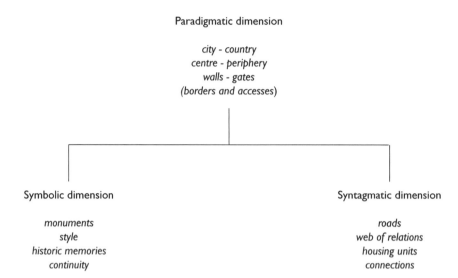

Figure 5.4   An example of linguistic interpretation of space: the three-dimensional scheme of the traditional city

Source: after Lefebvre, Le langage et la société (1966), in Schmid (2005: 237).

(Schmid 2005: 316–23) with symbolic, paradigmatic and syntagmatic dimension (Elden 2004: 148). According to Schmid, the double definition of the three dimensions or moments of the production of space valorise in a rich way the production of material environments, knowledge and meanings. Elden (ibid.) notes that Lefebvre's analysis of everyday life is situated between structuralism and phenomenology. Something can be learned from both approaches, but a new dialectical synthesis is necessary.

Chapter 6
Public Urban Space as the Event of Assembly

Lock

The sun is shining. My 'Union' is beautiful. Its black frame and moulded fittings evoke nostalgia, a yellowed image of Dutch country roads and a smell of childhood spirit. The hazy sun in the 1960s! Until now, its lock has been an innocent, simple latch. It was frail; a child's lock. Sometimes it opened by itself, and it certainly would not have stopped someone kicking it open. But today I cycled to the bike shop and bought a proper lock. Now I can leave my 'Union' in front of the university, the bookshop, the pub – anywhere.

Is it not curious that a lock can increase the freedom of movement!

Manchester 22 June 2001

Dialectical Centrality

Now I have established the main elements of a new, dynamic theory of public urban space. I view public urban space as part of the totality of socially produced space. It is not a 'fraction', though, but rather isomorphic with it. The isomorphism is not a structuralistic one-to-one correspondence of 'elements', but concerns the *logical form* of space, emerging in constant dialectic. Public urban space has a mixed character as a concrete abstraction, as a product and producer. Its logical form is that of assembly, encounter and simultaneity, like the logical form of social space (Lefebvre 1991 [1974]: 101, 149, 331). If conceived like that, public urban space does not consist of places that a function or content can 'occupy', but of points that are characterised by centrality and accumulation. These points are not simple locations, but *centres of the spatial dialects*. They are the 'gathering-together' of 'everything that can be named and enumerated' in space (Lefebvre 1991 [1974]: 331). The notion of spatial dialectics, furthermore, entails a latent contradiction or actual conflict.

An assembly with its conflicts is a process, a sequence or a *narrative*. While spatial, the dialectics are time-bound. It is no accident that storytelling is Rajanti's method of disclosing the relationship between space and society (Rajanti 1999: 19). Space, language and community are the basic dimensions of a human being. In theory (in a mental space) they are isomorphic, but to represent the production of space (in ancient Greece and Rome and in contemporary Europe) Rajanti utilises narratives. The use of narrative contains a well-founded ontological point. Rajanti wants to emphasise that public urban space is time-bound, evolving, becoming. Space *unfolds* like a story. If it is frozen it dies.

Public urban space becomes conceived of as *the event of assembly*. In public urban spaces, the experiential, particular weak places come together, suspending their potential conflicts and thereby opening a horizon of political discourse and of a community. The dialectic centrality connects punctual and global, material and abstract. As a logical form, it is general but the content, what is assembled (and 'the specificity of the mix of links' to what is beyond, as Massey puts it), makes each public urban space unique and differential.

The above diagram of spatial dialectics can, thus, be used to analyse dialectical centrality. It can analytically describe a spatial dialectic, like a suspended conflict, and to reveal the moment of its eruption, the moment of change. But it is not useful to imagine the diagram (as Shields originally proposes) as a representation of the totality of a social space. To work, the diagram must be connected to a specific case, to content that can fill its form. As form only, it is useless. (See Lefebvre 1996 [1968]: 136–8 for discussion about form and content.)

As far I understand, this way of conceiving the aspects of social space and their relationships is rather faithful to Lefebvre's own conception. Whether or not faithfulness is an aim can be questioned. What I consider important and interesting is that each of the three 'terms' are specific *mixtures* of material, mental and social. It is not so that pure categories would collide in spatial dialectics, but rather real complex practices or whole discourses of concepts, such as weak place, which entails issues discussed in Part 2. This idea resembles Lefebvre's discussion of the global, intermediary and private levels each containing aspects of the other two (see above page NN, also Schmid 2005: 323–9). I suggest that all three aspects of social space proposed by Lefebvre can have different modes of materiality and different roles in the dialectic. So, a specific planning proposal (conceived), entails both abstract conceptualisations and particular, material documents. Likewise, weak place (lived) has its singular materiality, while extending to knowledge and mental stages, too. Therefore, it becomes imaginable that the otherness, which makes the dialectic move, can be material, in some cases even 'a thing in space'. This is indeed the case with certain under-utilised and indeterminate buildings and sites.

Because of this flexibility, it is possible to 'play' with the diagram and try out different possible configurations. In some, the material is contingent, as we saw in the discussion about the 'classical' community-formation. In others, the material may be a key actant of change. The reference to Latour's actant-networks and cyborgs is pertinent, here (Latour 2005, Graham and Marvin 2001). We can ask, for example, how the personal fully lived moment could become a 'thesis' of the spatial dialectic. While the question may seem speculative, it points to a matrix of possibilities, where 'cold' thought-objects and mute artifacts may be dynamised and fully lived moments face the danger of reification.

Urban Artifacts in Spatial Dialectic – Atmosphere

If the representational space – emotions, experiences, deep symbolisms, art – is not the only mobilising 'other' in the spatial dialectic, what role material artifacts (physical space and spatial configurations) can precisely have? How we can conceptualise their active role in the dialectic?

The notion of atmosphere is a significant key (Lehtovuori 2008). As I will discuss in Chapter 8 about Makasiinit, the smell of tar, emanating from old railway sleepers in sun, the soft soundscape of old brick walls and wooden platforms, and many other elements synaesthetically produced the atmosphere of the place. One could literally 'step in' their lingering atmosphere. Gernot Böhme has developed atmosphere as a concept in aesthetics. For him, atmospheres do not exist outside (individual) perception but nevertheless they are not subjective. Atmospheres are '[s]omething *between* subject and object. They are not something relational, but the relation itself' (Böhme 2001: 54, original italics). Atmospheres are spatial and to an extent material. Böhme's notion is partly based on Hermann Schmitz's idea (1969: 343) that atmospheres are always spatial, but cannot be pinned down to positionable places (Isohanni 2006: 62). Twilight is a good example: it creeps in every nook and recess, like fog, but it also has the character of a medium, in which one is, which tones everything and mediates the relationship with things around (Böhme 1998: 19). One perceives 'through' atmosphere, but it also has some objectual materiality as a 'half-thing' (*Halbding*, Böhme 2001: 61–3).

When discussing urban places, Böhme (1998: 53–5) proposes that atmosphere of a city concerns the style and manner of its unfolding urban life.[1] Atmosphere is not primarily a question of built forms, colours or light, for example, but of citizens' activities and presence. Atmosphere has to be lived.

Centres and Margins in Dialectic

Historical data shows that social centrality is movable. Firstly, the centres of activity, like the market square or an informal red-light zone, move in the geographic space of a city. Secondly, the relative importance of cities in urban systems change. Finally, the whole notion of centrality may be reinterpreted. This is precisely the case in the present-day society, which is characterised by the tendency of centrality aspiring to be total. This centrality is political rationality or 'urban rationality' (Lefebvre 1991 [1974]: 332), information-gathering and processing and the decision-making system. Lefebvre claims that the justification of this claim to a superior rationality falls to 'the agents of technostructure – to the planners'. Lefebvre of course does not mean urban planners, only, but certainly the planners' Concept City plays a role in the totalising centrality.

---

1   'Die Atmosphäre einer Stadt ist eben die Art und Weise, wie sich das Leben in ihr vollzieht' (Böhme 1998: 55).

Figure 6.1   Calçada de Sant'Ana, an atmospheric street in Lisbon

Source: Photo: Panu Lehtovuori.

I think that this is a way to explain the recurring interpretation (or lament) that public urban spaces are in decline. The over-arching rationality, the logic of maps and statistics, erodes and evaporates difference and uniqueness, creating UFOs that violently land in rich urban situations.

While centres move, the dialectical centrality constantly unfolds through centre-periphery relations. This is the other of the axis Kopomaa used in defining four rough types of public urban space, the other being the social openness *vs.* exclusivity (see above pp. 35–6). These categories, which for Kopomaa are ideal types, can be dynamised as shown in Figure 6.2

The diagram points to the possibility of challenging the central, frontal spaces, third place which is well appropriated by a group and stage where Concept City presents itself and which is presented as the important centre. What could the non-space/utopia be? There is no general answer to this question. In the next chapter I will point to some 'utopias', for example, the local idea of the 'Europeanness' of Helsinki and its urban culture as a utopia with some power to cause real shifts. What is interesting is that marginals become constructions and events. Their 'location' is not stable or self-evident. This may have to do with the totalising efforts of political-rational centrality, which, paradoxically, *renders the whole urban realm as potential marginal* as well. Fissures, cracks, underdefined moments may open

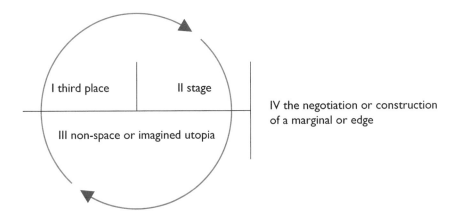

Figure 6.2   Spatial dialectics of centres and margins

as momentary marginals, which allow for new and possibly important cultural and social activity.

Assemblies and Events

According to Rajanti, *polis* is a particular, definable societal relation and spatial order, a 'mental horizon' and material humus (1999: 55). As mentioned, it is clearly a social space in the sense Lefebvre uses the word. Figure 6.3a presents the elements of the classical Greek narrative of invention of new community, *polis* (interpretation following Rajanti 1999).

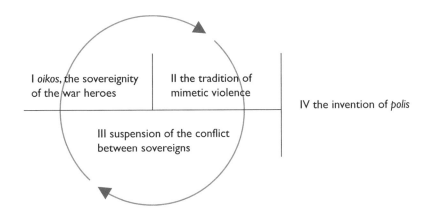

Figure 6.3a   Social space of *polis*, understood dialectically

Sennett describes the middle class publicity as it was produced in the early eighteenth century Paris and London as a special, non-personal region of sociability. In London, for example

> [p]eople thus experienced sociability in these coffeehouses without revealing much about their own feelings, personal history, or station ... The art of conversation was a convention in the same sense as the dressing to rank of the 1750s, even though its mechanism was the opposite, was the suspension of rank. Both permitted strangers to interact without having to probe into personal circumstances. (Sennett 1992 [1974]: 82)

Figure 6.3b presents the change during the *ancien regime* (the Parisian version).

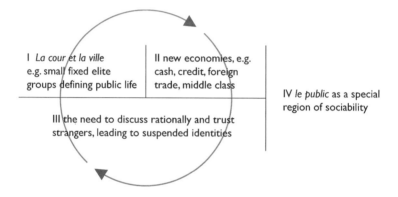

Figure 6.3b   The production of *le public*, understood dialectically

It is difficult to position any material public spaces in these diagrams. Where to put *agorà* or coffeehouse? Nowhere, because the physical 'setting' is secondary in these antique and classical forms of public space. It would be possible to write in the box IV 'the invention of *polis* with the eventual institution of *agorà*' and respectively '*le public* as a region of sociability, taking place in new public places such as a coffeehouse'. The 'public' is primary and the physical space secondary. Physical space does not constitute public urban space.

This is not the case now, in the supermodern[2] and under the new spatial paradox. Now personal lived moments, the weak place with its particular and singular material aspect, becomes the 'Other', the tension, causing change. But how to conceptualise the material and objectal reality, 'things in space', the

---

2   Here I rely on Rajanti's claim that when concerning city as a form of life, and its core, the public space, there was little change from the invention of *polis* to the advent of Modern in the eighteenth to nineteenth century. This interpretation coincides with Sennett's idea that the 'fall of public man' is a modern phenomenon.

material aspect of public urban space such as buildings, monuments and surfaces, so that they are not directly reified and can sustain social potential?

Quasi-objects

In her unfolding narrative of the production of space, Rajanti situates the invention of the socially loaded, shared object in the birth of Rome. Referring to Michel Serres' *Roma*, Rajanti tells that the patricians of Rome killed the king, Romulus (as he had killed Remus) and cut him pieces. The pieces became the constituent of the new community, *res publica*, republic. Those pieces are a 'quasi-object', something to which no-one has a relation alone. A community, thus, gets its form through the circulation of the quasi-object (Rajanti 1999: 75). If *agorà* was an empty space, the sacred sites of Rome include 'quasi-objects' or 'white objects', which can hold the community together. 'In Rome, the object that is the condition of the community becomes material, and the material foundation of the community becomes concrete, objectal … In Rome, places are objects' (ibid.: 76). I think that the spaces of the middle class publicity can still be interpreted using this idea. In this conception the coffeehouse and mall are the quasi-objects, holding the cosmopolitan community of strangers together.

In the modern city, this is no longer the case. The contemporary squares and streets are not quasi-objects in this sense; their crowd is lonely. Public urban space, if generically defined as the non-private, accessible surface (see Chapter 2), is no longer the essential ingredient of a city. Public urban space certainly has functions (traffic, shopping), which are important. Instead of quasi-object, the functional spaces form a 'skeleton' or 'veins'. Aptly they are not called space but 'infrastructures'. So the underpinning of the modern city is a complex lattice of streets, sewers, railway lines, highways, telecommunication infrastructures and 'service infrastructures'. In the modern conception, everything is material, and the public (community) has in a sense died – or is lost from view.

However, along with this change or 'loss', another radical shift has taken place, which has passed unnoticed. While it is true that public urban space in its traditional forms has lost importance, become splintered and specialised (cf. Gottdiener's notions of de- and recentralisation), simultaneously *the whole urban realm has become a quasi-object*. This is the flipside of the notion that anything in the environment, in literal sense, can be the trigger or material underpinning of a momentary weak place. In 'the space of the global', the global urban realm is the mutually shared, mixed constituent of the community. Total centrality is opposed by totalising marginality, and the horizon of 'differential space' (Lefebvre 1991 [1974]) opens up.

As an example, underused physical sites, such as old empty industrial buildings or wastelands may become the Other. Sometimes, their emptiness and 'unfit' in the dominant system of production of urban space cannot be immediately solved, and the machine of the dominant space production comes to a temporary halt. As a delay programme, a material project (temporary use) may cause a change and reopen a momentary possibility for a city as the human form of life. In those cases, the inertia, difficulty, 'stubbornness' or 'silence' (cf. Baudrillard's 'fatal strategies' in Ahlava 2002: 177–87) of the material artefact becomes the Other, gaining power. But it is just a moment, and soon the purely material otherness ceases to work as a unique spatial opportunity, needing further human appropriation.

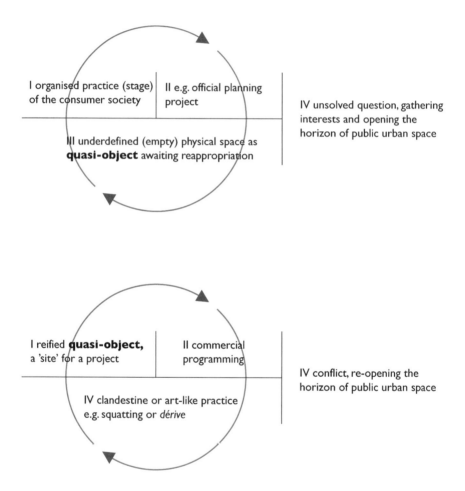

Figure 6.4   Quasi-object in spatial dialectics, two phases

If inappropriate, the momentary material 'basis', the underdefined building for example, may be defined and reified by the dominant actors, often by the workings of Concept City producers. In that case its emptiness and potentiality becomes filled in a sense, making it a new 'thesis', a ruin without either positive (appropriated) or absent (dumb) social content. Then the practical official planning questions are: How to fill it? How to reanimate or enliven the dead or empty public urban space? Such cases are commonplace. In these cases, a spatial practice (squatting or *derivé*, for example) could become the other and mover of the space, creating again another event.

It is as if there were a cycle, where the material gets reinterpreted and reappropriated, so that same stones and same configuration, essentially, can be analytically in very different positions in respect to the production of public urban space. For a planner and designer this should be a very important insight, calling for careful and detailed analysis case by case, assembly be assembly, moment by moment. On the other side of the coin is that the Other (the lived or *vecú* in Lefebvre) may also acquire surprising forms. It is not necessarily connected to a person in the sense of 'fully lived moment' but can be shared and public in the sense of a material thing as 'quasi-object'.

Heterotopias

The notion of 'heterotopia' is one way to conceptualise the spatial otherness, the insoluble differences that come together in spatial dialectics. Foucault states that heterotopias (and utopias) are linked with all other sites[3] (of city, society), while nevertheless contradicting all the other sites (1986: 24). Utopias do not have 'real place' but heterotopias do. To make a link to the Lefebvrean discussion above, I suggest to view heterotopias as assemblies. This is because in them 'real sites, all the other real sites that can be found within the culture, are simultaneously represented, contested and inverted' (ibid.). Furthermore, heterotopias house conflicts, because in them mutually incompatible sites may be assembled (ibid.: 25). Finally, change is a crucial characteristic of Foucauldian heterotopia. The 'heterotopias of crisis' concern rites of initiation and recurring states of crisis (honeymoon, menstruating); the way heterotopias function may change (the example of a cemetery, see also Bello 2004); and most often, according to Foucault, heterotopias are linked to slices in time, as breaks of traditional time or fleeting moments of festival (Foucault 1986: 26).

'New Phenomena Need New Eyes'[4]

Where to look to find the new kind of public urban spaces, assemblies, events, quasi-objects, heterotopias? The answer is: anywhere, but with new eyes.

There is much to challenge. As noted in the Introduction, the idea that in Western cities public urban space is eroding or losing importance is strong.

---

3 Foucault uses 'site' to emphasise that the discussion concerns external spaces, such as cafes and beaches, not (only) states of mind, for example.

4 Chora 2001: 74.

Jane Jacobs' observations about the alien 'projects' from the late 1950s NYC are a prized milestone (Jacobs 1961). Lofland has noted that the modern 'spatial ordering' of cities entails the segregation of social groups (Lofland 1973). More recently, Steven Flusty has talked about the erosion of spatial justice and paranoid typologies of exclusion (Flusty 1994, cf. Lehtovuori 2001c) and Sharon Zukin has pointed to the privatisation and commercialisation of urban squares (Zukin 1995). The concern is not limited to the US. Studying European examples, Zygmunt Bauman has found 'emic' and 'fagic' spaces, which either repel or ingest and where meeting the strangers is no longer part of the social code (Bauman 2001: 21–7). Furthermore, Rem Koolhaas has noted the over-consumption and emptying of historic public venues (Koolhaas 1995b), Marc Augé has coined the 'non-place' and Taina Rajanti has expanded Augé's notion to the planetary scale asserting that 'non-places, not the city, are the space of the global being-in-the-world' (Rajanti 1999: 193).

Let me rehearse *pensiero debole*, to question the dystopic view entailing an erasure of meaningful, constitutive public urban space. Counter-tendencies can also be found. There are flourishing new public urban spaces both in Europe and the US. It can be questioned how 'authentic' or 'unique' the stages of new city centres in Berlin and Manchester are, for example, but if not more, in these big scale developments public urban space is a cherished slogan and icon. Public urban space is thought to be profitable; it is a planners' and developers' tool. While it has been reified and usurped by Concept City to a large extent, its popularity may also point to some real positive issue. Why, actually, does a mall need a 'street'? Why does Printworks, a commercial leisure complex in Manchester, present itself as a NYC harbour street? Why are urban life and public space a design 'theme' (cf. Gottdiener 1995)? Why does the industrial city and its public urban space seem to have such commercial value?

The reason may be the logic of rarity: whatever becomes rare increases in price. Nevertheless, the loss of meaning and the lack of use of public urban spaces are not always true in the traditional civic sense, either. Carr et al. claim that although the North American discussion points to the apparent decline in public life, a 'public space renaissance' is also happening. The renaissance concerns new, specialised forms of public space, such as commercial spaces, community gardens and greenways (Carr et al. 1992: 1). Crowhurst, Lennard and Lennard state optimistically that while European cities have created traffic free zones and recreated 'the physical and social conditions requisite for a flourishing public life', Americans are rediscovering 'the pleasures of being in public', too (Crowhurst et al. 1984: 1). Jan Gehl's studies in Copenhagen confirm a major positive change in the use and atmosphere of Copenhagen's inner city public spaces (Gehl and Gemzoe 2001). While many of these developments could be characterised as socially parochial 'third places', or having primarily economic aspirations to boost local commerce, to compete with ex-urban malls or to attract tourists, they do also have some value as genuine, political urban spaces. The Exchange Square in Manchester (see above, Excursion 4) can be seen as an extension of the surrounding inner city malls, but it nevertheless does have a *potential* to become more actively and politically used. Obliquely it carries the memory of political public urban spaces, of riots and demonstrations. Another example: An oft-stated reason for the demise of public space in the political sense is the rise of representative democracy, combined with mass media, which have lessened the need for face-to-face contact in opinion building and demonstration. However, in new global/transnational issues, both representative democracy and media are toothless or partial, and public urban space has regained some of its significance. Anti-globalisation demonstrations in Seattle, Genoa and Gothenburg are cases in point. A different example of realised potentials of public space are playful behaviours. Quentin Stevens (2007, 2008) has found a whole range of surprising and playful uses in seemingly strongly coded places such as the Southbank Promenade in Melbourne or the Holocaust Memorial in Berlin. Clearly, the decline of public urban space is a contested notion, and there are many positive and inspiring examples of revived and new public urban spaces.

The stages of the commercial Concept City may be giving public urban space the kiss of life – or death. They may succeed, but as well they might become thoroughly ideological in the end, leaving their potentials unrealised. More important than evaluating the state of known kinds of public urban space, is realising that the interesting new ones may not look familiar. If there is deep-seated otherness in space, it may be difficult to recognise a new public urban space. Certainly, one does not find the new public urban spaces by just looking at the new uses of old squares or replicas of old squares in New Towns. If the centrality is becoming total, as Lefebvre claims, margins are also problematised. The logical form of public urban space entails a centre-periphery relation. However, the location, nature and time of emergence of the periphery are not known. In Part 4, I will discuss urban events as emerging public urban spaces. It is not accidental that a specific mix of centrality and peripherality seems to characterise Helsinki's successful event venues. The same goes for temporary uses as creators of new public urban spaces in Berlin, Amsterdam and Helsinki.

All these tendencies may, indeed, suggest that public urban space is 'weakening'. But the process may as well offer opportunities as pose further problems. What could be the new, unseen or marginal instantiations of public urban space? Instead of total loss, the process probably has modalities, producing new forms, which also keep something of the old alive. Something is erased, something new originated, then transformed, only to migrate to other areas or realms (cf. Chora 2001: 167). A logical assumption would be that public urban space weakens on one or many of its main axes, the spatial, communal and symbolic. Or its form, function or structure may become less clear. But there is no reason to attach fixed values to the new kinds of space. Furthermore, it may turn out that the weakness of new public urban space is its strength. We need new eyes and new markers of public urban space in the space of the global. Room, stage and meeting place are not good enough notions. Margins may be more important than established centres (Wilson 2001). But to find the margin and to 'see' it, takes an effort (Kopomaa

1997). Wastelands, non-commercial niches and technological experiments may open as new public urban spaces, carrying some traces of the old, strong notion and producing something new – hybrid, ephemeral or experimental.

Figure 6.5   Industrial wasteland in Ancoats, Manchester

Source: Photo: Panu Lehtovuori.

New Instantiations 1: Foregrounding the Ephemeral

> From intensification of built form to intensification of activity. (Thinkpool urbanism, cited in Lehtovuori et al. 2003)

The notion of *temporary use* opens one way to challenge the rigidities of architectural and planning thought concerning public urban space. 'Urban Catalysts', a two-year research project, focussed on the temporary uses of residual urban areas in five European cities (Bengs et al. 2002, Lehtovuori et al. 2003, Lehtovuori 2003).[5] The hypothesis of the Urban Catalysts project was that temporary uses are a neglected

---

5   The full title of the project is 'Urban Catalysts. Strategies for Temporary Uses – Potential for Development of Urban Residual Areas in European Metropolises'. This paragraph is based on the material of the research project, especially on the book *Temporary Uses – the Forgotten Resource of Urban Planning* by Panu Lehtovuori, Helka-Liisa Hentilä and Christer Bengs. The material of the Urban Catalysts initiative was collected by research

resource of urban planning and development. Instead of permanent and visible, the Urban Catalysts research foregrounded the ephemeral. It became clear that even though overlooked by the official stakeholders, temporary uses and users do have positive economic and social effects. In sustaining and renewing urban cultures, temporary uses have a key role. Even though urban events and other temporary uses of streets and squares were excluded from the Urban Catalysts research, the research groups reported that temporary uses did have direct, positive influences in creating public urban spaces.

Opening the City

Public space and a shared representation (image) of the city are closely connected. Because temporary uses often are the pioneers in using closed industrial and traffic areas, they 'open' the city and extend its public sphere. By focussing public attention on forgotten places, temporary uses literally produce new public space. Berlin's clubs in empty railyards and strange locations near the Wall zone have been such pioneers. In Amsterdam opening the city is a conscious policy: 'The Kinetic North project is in the role of pioneering the former industrial void and creating, from scratch, public space and public awareness about the north bank of the IJ. Reactions of the neighbourhood are everything from excitement to irritation about loud music' (Lehtovuori et al. 2003: 45, also Lehtovuori and Havik 2009).

Mixed Programmes

While many uses – such as residential, office, industrial, service, public, sports and leisure, commercial or storage – can be temporary, the interesting aspect is that the various types can be found on the same site, a short distance apart. The sites containing temporary uses have succeeded in fostering extremely mixed uses – a goal often set but seldom reached in urban development projects. Temporary uses produce urban density and a lively mix as a side-result of the dynamics of users' negotiating their circumstances. For example in the NDSM wharf in Amsterdam, the innovative cultural uses are a way to initiate an urban development project and create its marketing profile, but they are also expected to secure the functional diversity and urban quality of the future district (Lehtovuori et al. 2003: 47).

Fostering Political Community

Makasiinit in Helsinki (see below Chapter 8) is an important public space in the sense of dialectical centrality discussed above. The planning conflict triggered new, politically significant urban space, an arena of negotiation. Besides the conflict itself, it also facilitates debates about wider urban issues. This is the

---

groups in Naples, Vienna, Amsterdam, Berlin and Helsinki, coordinated by Philipp Oswalt and Klaus Overmeyer in TU Berlin. See www.templace.com.

classic creation of a public sphere, free citizens facing the state. A specific urban community has gathered (assembled) around the conflict and temporary project. But it is also 'weak', because for the stakeholders it is a project with a beginning and end. Furthermore, the new public space (or quasi-object) does not constitute a community in any fundamental and essential sense. A new community is constituted but it is voluntary, time and space specific. Its members are not totally dependent on the community, but rather have 'project identity' (Cantell 2001) as part of their varying identity networks.

Counter-symbol

A fantastic example of a political temporary project is the proposal to reuse the skeleton of the Palast der Republik in Berlin city centre. In 2002, the German Parliament accepted a recommendation to tear down the Palast der Republik and replace it with a new building, camouflaged behind the rebuilt historic facades of the castle demolished in 1950. However, the project has been delayed because of Berlin's economic problems. Also the programme for the new building is undecided. While this political wrangling was going on, the removal of asbestos from the Palast was finalised. The building itself could not be easily demolished, because its 'floating' foundation needed the weight of the building on it. (Dismantling took place after a long delay in 2006–2008.) In April 2002, an international expert commission proposed a temporary use for the politically sensitive ruin. The idea got support from both politicians and the press. Berlin's Urban Catalysts team contacted interested stakeholders and made a feasibility study on the temporary use of the parliamentary chamber of the GDR (Volkskammersaal). Making parts of the building accessible through the staging of cultural programmes triggered a process of saying good-bye to an important if controversial East German building with the appropriate dignity.

Spatio-temporal Island

The political role is not just limited to the community-creation. Conflicts and their (temporarily used) arenas may become 'islands' of public space in the general 'spacelessness'. This means that 'outsiders' can recognise a specific atmosphere, and are attracted to it. The new public urban space becomes spatio-temporal island or 'Medusa's ferry'.

Walks in Arabia

Arabianranta, Helsinki, 1998. I am wandering towards the shore in a state of wonderment. Tall wild grass in bloom continuing for hundreds of metres on both sides of the footpath. I breathe deep. The air bears the scent of a herb that I do not know. On the horizon are the cranes of the harbour at Sörnäinen. The orange carriages of the Helsinki metro on Kulosaari bridge move slowly like some exotic larva. Here and there from among the blades of tall grass, the reflected glimmer of a car windscreen catches my eye. The haze of a hot early summer day envelops me; it is quiet to the point of unreality. Until I hear the birds. There are many of them and they are bold, as if they had never seen people. A pair of oystercatchers is stepping along the shore, further away a lark shoots up into the sky, followed by a second one, and a third! A hawk calls out in the blue sky.

February. The sea is frozen. One side of the islands on the opposite side of the bay is white after a snowstorm. The snow is packed within the forest and it joins the bare rock and ice into a single white form. A thin layer of snow covers the grass; dry stalks, angelica and thistles pushing up through the snow. The sun is shining and the light is multiplied many times over by the snow and ice. I find buckthorn bushes and I taste the orange berries. The cold has made them sweet. The orange juice tingles on my lips and it flows on my fingers and sleeves.

New Instantiations 2: Underdefined Spaces

Underdefinition characterises spaces studied in the Urban Catalysts project. It is important as a sign of opportunity to appropriate and use temporarily, but underdefinition also has certain 'inherent', albeit relationally constructed, values.

Wastelands

The above notes from Helsinki's Arabianranta point to the emotional power of underdefined wastelands. Undeniably, they have a strong atmosphere. I believe that the atmosphere results from the *complex marginality of wastelands*. Firstly, they are the fringe of the representation of space. As Isohanni notes, wastelands are among the places that 'people have always found difficult to approach and the experience of which is aesthetically demanding'. They are 'the opposite world to all the building and development, a past Lebensraum increasingly discriminated against and weakened by the influence of man' (Isohanni 2002: 118, Böhme 1989). However, wastelands (as industrial left-overs) are not 'pure' nature, a clear opposite, but rather a mixture or juxtaposition of built and nature, or human influence and its 'innocent' absence. Therefore, secondly, wasteland can be interpreted as an interface of nature and technology. Thirdly, concerning spatial practices, wastelands have often become a kind of natural location representing a valuable 'breathing space' for many urban residents. They are 'another space', complementing the everyday routines. Finally, the properties of a wasteland can produce a feeling of a sacred place, a notion that clearly enters the realm of spaces of representation, beliefs and myths lived through. Describing the wasteland at Arabia, Isohanni notes that 'spaciousness, room, horizontality and the length of the shoreline are further underlined by the vicinity of the centre of Helsinki and the latter's denseness. Here, wasteland has the properties of a magical, sacred place'

(Isohanni 2002: 122). All in all, wastelands strangely seem a promising kind of public urban space, very able to collect and carry widely differing elements of social space.

The ideas of wasteland, retreat and leaving a situation unplanned arise from different directions. Elizabeth Wilson distinguishes between the 'contingent' and the 'necessary' city. According to her, the finished spaces built at great cost in the core areas of cities are less interesting and less significant than forgotten and unplanned marginal areas and tracts of wasteland (Wilson 2001). As noted in Chapter 4, Marc Augé in turn speaks of the 'uncertain charm' of wastelands, ports and building sites, the possibility of adventure and change (Augé 1995: 3). Unplanned wasteland is associated with indefinite states, the feeling of opportunities, deviation from the ordinary and everyday or with alterity (Isohanni 2000, Isohanni 2006, Lehtovuori 2000). Many important, recent projects spring from wastelands. The Töölönlahti Art Gardens are an interesting example in Helsinki (see Chapter 8).

Leaving Decisions Open

Thinking about the tools of planning, underdefinition is hard to achieve. Sometimes the best way to support weak places and the origination of their assembling is simply to refrain from planning, to leave things as they are. This approach can be called 'loose-fit' places (Ward Thompson 2002: 67–8). Planning retreats into the background and instead of defining takes on an enabling role. Lack of planning means freedom, the freedom to make a space one's own. The freedom to assign meanings.

I take as an example the Park van Kraal project, a plan that retreats to leave signification to future users. This future park is situated outside the city of Utrecht as part of a new town (VINEX) that was planned in a single stage. The environment of residential areas of this kind tends to become impoverished, and the architects of the project suggested an unconventional strategy for realising the park:

> All too often, park design is still seen as an architectural matter. The landscape architect is given a detailed description of the spatial, functional and ecological principles, and draws a design to fit the stated budget … It would be a missed opportunity to construct Park van Kraal in the same way. For centuries, the time factor has been the landscape architect's most important instrument. During the design phase – which usually involved creating an impression of the most desirable target scenario – a management plan was drawn up that gave a description of the measures whereby that target scenario might be attained. Sufficient scope was thereby left for changes of a natural, social, cultural, or economic nature … Although contemporary management structures now make it difficult to accommodate such a process, we nonetheless propose a design strategy … that makes it possible, even during construction, for the park to respond to the ways in which people use it. The construction process is thus

part of the design … It will be adventurous, exciting, unpredictable, and always challenging. (Karres and Brands 2000: 57, Lehtovuori 2002)

Another example is the planning of a city park in Berlin's former military airfield Adlershof (Isohanni 2002).

As in temporary uses, time, the process of change and events play an important role (see also de Solà-Morales above). It appears that one way to challenge the Concept City of 'strong' urban planning is to take seriously the process of producing the actual space, a partly unpredictable, multidimensional situation of interaction unravelling in time, lived reality. Open planning is achieved only by leaving things truly open, for users.

New Instantiations 3: Technological Hybrids

Cyborg Space

It is also worthwhile to look at totally new ingredients that might assemble and partake in the production of dialectical centrality. New technologies may prove important in that respect. Graham and Marvin in *Splintering Urbanism* discuss the notion of 'cyborg urbanisation', claiming that if the *a priori* distinction between 'social' and 'technological' is abandoned, 'contemporary life is seen to be made up of complex and heterogeneous assemblies of both social and technological actors …' (Graham and Marvin 2001: 185). Infrastructures, such as telecommunications and water, are clear examples of the technological reliance and provide increasing examples of differentiating social construction (through alternate pricing and unequal access) of the socio-technical complex. To me it is clear that public urban space may also increasingly be an assembly of technologies, among other constituents. Ward Thompson, for example, discusses technologically enhanced 'responsive landscapes' (2002: 66–7). In Finland, heated pavements are a seemingly simple example, nevertheless leading to rather complex symbolic and economic changes (Lehtovuori 2003c). Another case of the use of 'old' technologies in new ways is the intentional lack of lighting. In London's Docklands, there is a large ecological park, totally *without* lighting. This move has produced a park with unusually strong atmosphere, while providing space for species that suffer from artificial light.

Location-based Media

In the field of new media, there are several test projects and initiatives to mix physical space and virtual technologies. In Helsinki, a key actor is an organisation called M-cult, aiming to establish a new kind of hybrid 'media centre'. The public urban space can be seen as an interface or an enhanced reality. 'Locative media' is one neologism, trying to grasp the idea of juxtaposing virtual and material, globally interlinked and concretely localised.[6] One definition of the emerging field states that 'locative media uses portable, networked, location aware computing devices for user-led mapping and artistic interventions in which geographical space becomes its canvas' (Hemment 2004).

Location-based (locative) media and other technological hybrids may increase the contingence of physical places, strengthening the rootless experience in the 'space of the global'. Following Rajanti, in it 'it is not important in which particular "here" one is, but it is important to be in some particular here. It is not important to be home, but as if at home' (Rajanti 1999: 199). However, the example of the 'Blinkenlight' project in Berlin points in the opposite direction. A technological solution to show animations and play the 'Pong' game with mobile phones, shown in an urban scale in the windows of an empty office tower in Berlin's Alexanderplatz, became a most situated event, gathering crowds in the physical space and redefining the meanings of the square. The project was active in Alexanderplatz from 12 September 2001 to 23 February 2002, but it continues as an open-source programming initiative and thus a 'virtual' community. A webcam was also used (http://www.blinkenlights.de/).

New Instantiations 4: Urban Events

This brief list of potential new instantiations of public urban space is not exhaustive. I am only suggesting that situations and spaces that are ephemeral, indeterminate and technologically hybrid may be sources of new kinds of public urban space. As noted in the Introduction, urban events are an important way to produce momentary public urban spaces. The Reclaim the Streets movement and Berlin's Love Parade are examples of complex and politically significant events.

Especially interesting urban event, regarding experimental production of public urban space, is the Zinneke Parade in Brussels. Organised every second year since 2000, it is an artistic event, built by the residents of the different, multi-ethnic neighbourhoods of Brussels. It is produced in special 'Zinnopoles', or artistic workshops, in close cooperation with local network of associations, organisations and schools, engaged artists acting as drivers. The year-long preparation results in a parade in the public space, where the teams from different Zinnopoles unite and expose their creations (Stoffen 2004: 108).

Clearly, the Parade provides an opportunity for the residents to reclaim the city. This appropriation happens in a hybrid cultural context, where ethnic boundaries and differences in socio-economic status can be negotiated. While the aim is to fight racism and exclusion based on identity, the initiators of the Parade do not wish to avoid conflict. According to Myriam Stoffen, the leader of the Zinneke organisation, '[t]he idea is to consider conflicts as quintessential for a confrontation between different opinions, values, perceptions, interpretation schemes and habits.

---

6   See, e.g., http://locative.net/; http://www.pixelache.ac/locative/ for further information.

Figure 6.6   Video-based public art gathers crowds in Chicago

Source: Photo: Hille Koskela.

From this point of view, confrontations and conflicts become portals that allow us to question ourselves, our references, and our society in a critical manner' (ibid.: 110). The experimental juxtapositions and a temporary open space, created by the parade, help the participants to deepen their ideas about urban life and society. Through physical re-appropriation of urban space, a space of encounter and mental appropriation is achieved. The event becomes a common experience, that the participants can return to other residents and their own neighbourhoods. Key challenge of Zinneke Parade is how to retain its experimental character. There is always the danger that such an event becomes pure attraction, a folkloristic spectacle. So far, the event has found new energies and tackled new tensions in the urban field of Brussels in such a way that the radical social content has remained.

In the next chapter, I will elaborate further on the role of events in producing space.

Conclusion of Part 3

As I have argued throughout the preceding chapters, predominantly, architects and planners tend to define their art in terms of articulating space. Time-related ideas of process, change, chance and event have certainly interested architects, but it has remained difficult to incorporate time in the core of architectural ideas. Even humble and temporary structures, not to mention public space projects, are valued in terms of both aesthetic and conceptual permanence, reducing time to a rigid horizon of the eternal – distant past or distant future. Furthermore, this conceptual finality concerns not only the physical frame but also the programmes. Architectural and planning education, the judicial system of land-use regulation, as well as the common map-based representations of city plans, direct the programmatic imagination to a few well-established categories, such as 'housing', 'offices', 'commerce' or 'public buildings'. Open areas get comparable treatment and are designated as a 'market square', 'car parking area', 'pedestrian surface' or 'nature precinct'. These categories are black-boxed, and in turn taken as stable and ever lasting (Lehtovuori 2003).

In this mode of thought, public urban space is seen to be in decline, losing its importance as the core of urban community and carrier of deep meanings. However, if public urban space is reconceptualised, using spatial dialectics, this 'weakening' can be seen as an opportunity. In the 'shattered space' of the global, public urban spaces are not necessarily in decline, but they are taking new forms. It is not a question of on-off, but rather a question of new directions and modalities. Public space is a means to produce difference and social order (cf. Sibley 1999), but those processes may be potential instead of actual, temporary instead of long lasting or concerning rather small groups only instead of the whole city.

The notions of weak place, conflict and quasi-object are the indispensable elements of the dialectical production of public urban space. Public urban space is best understood as a suspended conflict, constantly unfolding in time. In the formation of new points of dialectical centrality, new technologies, idiosyncratic interpretations or professional representations alike may be important constituents, each taking surprising 'roles' in the game-like production of space. Even the inertia of material space and spatial configuration, may momentarily play an active role as 'dynamist' or the Other of the dialectic, thus becoming quasi-object, the 'joker' waiting for a new definition.

PART 4
Hi-jacking Helsinki

Chapter 7
Urban Events Producing Space

Figure 7.1   Plasticiens Volants in Makasiinit, 2000

Source: Photo: Ossi Kajas.

Urban events are an important form of new instantiations of public urban spaces. In this Chapter, I will discuss in some detail how events have produced public urban space in the City of Helsinki. A medium-sized European city, Helsinki is interesting case especially because it has witnessed a remarkable urban cultural change since the late 1980s, a process that culminated in the European Capital of Culture celebrations in 2000.[1] Urban events have played important role in that change, providing a graphical illustration of Lefebvrean spatial dialectics. In events the 'otherness' appears momentarily in the middle of everyday spatial practices. Unlike many unusual and strange social spaces that one might imagine to be 'other' spaces or 'heterotopias' (Foucault 1986) – such as exotic tourist destinations, ethnic neighbourhoods or imaginary spaces of films and fairytales – Helsinki's urban events have taken place in the city centre's squares, streets and parks (Cantell 1999, Lehtovuori 2000b, 2001, 2005). In urban events, the otherness cannot be thought of as belonging to something else, to someone else's life or to another city, country or time. It comes near to the often-visited places and can be felt by any participant in an event. Thereby urban events clearly show the complexity and richness of social space.

In the last two decades, events have recurringly produced moments of change. They underline the softness, malleability and potentiality of ostensibly fixed urban space. For many, they show that space is not 'natural', opaque and immobile but fluid and changeable. It is not translucent and easily intelligible, but may contain surprises. Events point to the hidden and clandestine aspects of space, providing channels for the Other to appear and influence the production of space.

Because of events, the fixed and taken-for-granted understanding of Helsinki's central spaces has shattered. Events have detoured meanings, even hi-jacked aspects of space, and the production of public urban space has taken adventurous, game-like forms. A specific juxtaposition of both configurational and symbolic centrality and peripherality partly explains the 'event potential' of Helsinki's urban spaces (Lehtovuori 2001).

The Idea of 'Dead Public Space'

As mentioned, Helsinki has witnessed an important urban cultural change during the late 1980s and 1990s (Mäenpää 2005, 2000, Eskola and Ruoppila 1999, Cantell 1999, 1999b, 1992). After the culmination in the intensive and innovative European Capital of Culture programme in 2000, a certain maturation has occurred, characterised by a slower change and an increasing commercialisation of the new urban cultural forms. A sign of full institutionalisation of the event-scene is that the City of Helsinki is preparing an official 'events strategy'. The strategy, supposed to be published later in 2009, is based on the recognition that large commercial events, such as the Eurovision Song Contest (in Helsinki 2008),

---

1   Helsinki got the ECoC 2000 nomination with eight other European cities.

stadium concerts, cultural festivals, sports events and fairs, are an important element in city's economic development and international appeal.[2]

In two decades, urban events have moved from fringes to political focus, from experimental tests on what urban space allows to grand spectacles. But how to describe Helsinki's urban space and its use-culture *before* that change? How big was the change and what precisely did it concern? Cantell argues that during the 1970s and 1980s the urban culture of Helsinki was something in between the models of socialist Eastern European cities and capitalist Western European cities. While life was safe and Helsinki did not have many of the urban problems Western cities usually struggled with, 'Helsinki's "structure of feeling" featured a rather dull, uninspiring, even severe urban appearance, a city that could not be described as an exciting urban hub' (Cantell 1999: 88). 'Urbanism as a way of life' was relatively underdeveloped, and Helsinki lacked sophisticated urban characteristics, such as the *civitas* of public places, crowds, cafés and informal street-life (ibid.). Historically, Helsinki has not been a city for its citizens, but first and foremost a city built to represent power – first the power of the Russian Czars then that of the independent Finnish nation state. This inherited role as a showpiece and stage for power characterised Helsinki's urban space still in the 1980s. The meanings of public urban space were given from above, practices were regulated and the urban atmosphere was lacking fun, spontaneity and vibrancy. Even official actors recognised the dullness. An example is The General Master Plan of 1992. Its Development Scenario, a pseudo-strategic official document, regards the lack of urban culture as a particular weakness of the city. 'Compared to major European cities, Helsinki has been found to be boring and inactive, as well as green, clean, and safe. The image of Helsinki has been construed on the basis of the historical centre, administrative and cultural institutions and dense inner city' (Helsingin yleiskaava 1992: 72). In the early 1990s, Landry and Kelly found that the outsiders' image of Helsinki was still rather 'stereotyped'. Helsinki was 'cold', 'distant', 'unknown' and 'mysterious' (Landry and Kelly 1994: 65).

When discussing Senate Square, the focal point of the valuable administrative and representative centre, Cantell refers to Sennett's concept, claiming that '[a]s a square it can be characterized as a "dead public space"' (Cantell 1999: 202, cf. Sennett 1992 [1974]: 12–16). While Cantell's use of Sennett's concept is not quite accurate[3], the words 'dead public space' capture well the idea that before the 1990s Helsinki's central public urban spaces were 'grey', too controlled and too little used. This reading, based on more or less well-founded European comparisons,

---

2   Personal communication with Helsinki's culture director Pekka Timonen and researcher Sampo Ruoppila.

3   With the notion of 'dead public space', Sennett does not refer to the limited use of historic squares (the reason for limitations in Senate Square being the imagined need to guard against 'improper' uses of the symbol-laden place of power), but a general tendency towards the meaninglessness of the public domain, which according to him results from an imbalance between public and personal life in Western societies.

is widespread among researchers and academic commentators (e.g. Ruoppila and Cantell 2000: 35). Some films also reflect and reproduce the idea. Jim Jarmusch, in *Night on Earth* (1992), presented Helsinki as cold, dark and desolate. He pictured Senate Square as totally empty, and let a lonely taxi make its way through snow and sleet, circling the sinister statue of Alexander II (cf. Ilmonen 1999). A decade earlier, in Warren Beatty's *Reds* (1981), Senate Square and some other locations were used to re-enact the Russian Revolution (see also Tani 1995). Aki Kaurismäki, the famous Finnish *auteur*, has pictured the quiet and empty scenes of Helsinki in several films, for example *Kauas pilvet karkaavat* (1996) and *Mies vailla menneisyyttä* (2002).

Both researchers and artists characterise the city centre of Helsinki as an architectural stage-set to represent power, which has partly become obsolete (Stenros 1998). Its public urban spaces are seen to be empty, lacking use and present-day purpose. The editors of *Quaderns*, the Catalan journal, went as far as to claim that instead of spaces Helsinki's city centre would consist of 'voids', too large expanses of useless and meaningless public surface (Keskuskatu 1995).

I have to note, however, that the idea of emptiness only holds to the actual use, the spatial practice. If viewed as a repository of historical events – as mental space or 'space of representation' – Senate Square and many other of Helsinki's public urban spaces are not dead but most alive. Public space as 'a theatre of memory' (Ilmonen 2000, cf. Crang and Travlou 2001) may be highly significant, both personally and communally. Below I will show, that symbolic richness is an important factor of *event potential*, contributing to the formation and change of public urban spaces. This importance is invisible, though. It barely concerns the present public interaction, but rather refers to personal meditation. To 'see' and 'experience' the past requires knowledge and will. In a contemplative mode, one needs to dive through the layers of memory.

So, by and large, researchers and artists viewed Helsinki's public urban spaces as a hollow core waiting to be reappropriated, reused, reinvigorated. Their symbolic layers were acknowledged, but only as a question of personal mnemotechnique, possibly leading to discoveries about the city or oneself.

While the idea of emptiness may have been exaggerated, producing a rhetorical background for the discourse of the new and livelier post-1989 urban culture, I do believe that it contains more than a seed of truth. In the early 1990s, a dialectical process of change was already going on. New forms of public urban space were produced. The change concerned both spatial practices, representations of space and spaces of representation, both perceived, conceived and lived. Because of the complex nature of the change, it would miss the point to ask how empty the city centre really was or how little it actually was used at a particular moment. The idea that space is dead is in fact a 'hard' fact. The citizens of Helsinki expected something else, a new space and culture. The notion or discourse of dead public space can be seen as an element of a new space of representation, a hope, belief or anticipation. The belief that there is something wrong about Helsinki's public urban spaces was the 'dynamist', causing action and making way for changes and innovations not only in privately held perceptions but also in public 'image', rules, practices, programmes, rhythms of use, aesthetics and urban artefacts.

It is possible to argue that the changes of Helsinki's public urban space were produced by wider structural shifts, outside or 'above' the realm of the city and its urban spaces. Those shifts would include new real-estate investment patterns, new planning ideas and doctrines, economic growth, the related commercialisation of the everyday life, increasing importance of entertainment and enjoyment as urban programmes, as well as new and newly visible professional, youth and (other) subcultures. An important aspect is that the change concerned and was produced by the lifestyles and preferences of the children of the rural-urban migrants of the 1960s and 1970s. Because of this, the cultural change has been described as the 'second wave' of urbanisation, the enhancement of Helsinki urban culture and thus a maturing process (Eskola and Ruoppila 1999: 126, Cantell 1999, Tapaninen 1994). The arenas of this change – of this social production of space – have been urban printed media (*City-lehti*), local, commercial radio (Radio City), bar, café and club culture (e.g. Lepakko, Bar 9, Soda), as well as new public institutions (most notably Kiasma, the museum of contemporary art, which opened in 1998).

These commercial and public forums and institutions constitute the readily visible and mappable part of the cultural change (as products of it). However, I consider the re-appropriation of Helsinki's central public urban spaces the most intriguing field and result of the change, especially because the political impacts of certain spatial struggles suggest new ideas about good city life more generally. Urban events have played different 'roles' in this production of public urban space.

The Role of Urban Events in Official Policies to Reinvigorate Public Urban Spaces

Helsinki's post-1989 urban cultural change has many origins, multiple actors and surprising outcomes, some of which I will discuss below. However, it would be mistaken to believe that it was only a grassroots phenomenon or 'blind', contingent process. On the contrary, already before the current 'events strategy' it was to an extent a planned initiative, the urban policies of the City of Helsinki consciously fostering the changes. An important factor is the early 1990s economic recession and the changed financial position of the city as more susceptible to risks (Eräsaari 1999, Helin 1999, Cantell 1993). The above-mentioned 1992 General Master Plan, for example, was compiled and approved while the recession was rapidly deepening and unemployment started to seriously dent the municipal tax base and increase welfare expenditure. The authorities realised the need to increase Helsinki's 'competitiveness' *vis-à-vis* other cities in Finland and abroad, most notably Stockholm and Copenhagen. Helsinki started to actively market itself, polish its image and create links to financial and cultural exchange networks. Among other initiatives, Helsinki established the Helsinki Metropolitan Development Corporation, marketing the city as a node of Eastern and Western trade, it became a member of the Eurocities network, and it applied successfully for the status of European Cultural Capital (Mäkelä 1996, Landry and Kelly 1994, 2000.hel.fi, Heikkinen 2000).

The historical public space – the face of the city – has been for Helsinki a traditional marketing asset. That can be verified, for example, by checking how postcards on sale abound in images of the Empire centre of Helsinki (Tani 2000). Yet these spaces must also be changed in order for them to meet the expectations of users regarded as 'global'. Along with relaxed licencing policies, pedestrianisation, beautification of streets and squares and indirectly subsidising inner city shopping through traffic infrastructures, urban events were promoted to address the perceived lack of vibrancy of Helsinki and to boost its image as a nice, lively urban place. Organised urban events were an important part of the city's post-recession urban policies. As part of the culture-led change[4], events acted in at least two different ways.

Image

Firstly, events foster the image of a vibrant city, which is important because vibrancy is generally associated with the strength and success of a city (Mommaas 1999: 178). From an international point of view Helsinki in the early 1990s was lacking any image or the image was weak and connected to general views about Finland (Helsingin imago Lontoossa). It needed to put itself on the European map, and events were one of the chosen tools. According to the General Master Plan of 1992, 'the city will harbour a more active policy towards commercial activities inherent in urban culture, street life, and events … In order to reinforce the public image of Helsinki and create a highlight of culture and leisure services providing diversity in city life a project should be initiated to attract international interest' (Helsingin yleiskaava 1992: xxx–xxxi). Image-wise only big events were seen as efficient, and eventually, the event policy culminated in the successful application to be the European Cultural Capital in 2000. During the application process, Laura Mäkelä, a researcher at the City of Helsinki Urban Facts, wrote that '[a]n image of an active city where there's always something going on is at least partially created by culture' (Mäkelä 1996: 9). 'The application process for the City of Culture in 2000 can be seen as a project through which the city is developed in a desired direction. The project provides a chance to raise the city's cultural and financial profile in the European context' (ibid.: 13).

---

4   The entire year of 2000 is regarded as a single big event (Cantell 1999). A critical view on events is justified as well. Sharon Zukin (1995: 28) discusses 'pacification by cappuccino' (also Atkinson 2001); in the German discourse appears the notion of *Politik der Festivalisierung* (Dangschat 1996).

Street Sociality

Secondly, events concretely attract people to city streets. This helps to improve
and reinvigorate the negative 'dead public space'. It is about crowd, hustle and
bustle, but maybe more importantly about a certain 'urban' attitude and behaviour.
The researcher Pasi Mäenpää (1993) has conceptualised the social aspect of street
culture as games with autonomous meaning. According to him, situations with
lots of people organise themselves through the four forms of games characterised
by Roger Caillois: *agôn* (competition), *alea* (coincidence), *mimicry* (imitation)
and *ilinx* (vertigo) (also Stevens 2006: 36–46). The game of coincidence is
particularly central to street culture: it is also encompassed by Sennett's above-
mentioned classical definition of a city as a human settlement where one is likely
to meet strangers (Mäenpää 1993: 1–2, Sennett 1992 [1974]: 39). Coincidence
characterises both a wish to bump into someone we know in the middle of a crowd
– or to make a new, interesting acquaintance – and, in the realm of commerce,
the shopper's wish to find something enjoyable and significant in the shopping
arcade or flea market. Urban events attract people, create crowds and increase the
possibility of coincidence, thus contributing to the creation of an active, enjoyable,
game-like and maybe indeed 'European' street culture. To some extent the change
can be felt; Helsinki has changed. To take an anecdotal example, in summer 2004
one foreign student commented upon the special feeling of Helsinki city centre
around 3 or 4 a.m. Bars were closing, but people continued the night in the streets,
dancing around street musicians. White summer nights (at least) can be quite
festive and relaxed, citizens producing a shared urban space.

Unexpected Outcomes of Event Policies

The image someone has about Helsinki concerns representations of space; the
games of street sociality concern spatial practices. To be well known and vibrant:
there is nothing particularly new about the aims and results of the city's event policy.
However, there is more to events than their ability to attract people and possibly
affect the image of the city held by transient tourists and faceless investors. Events
can indeed produce public urban space; they can challenge established meanings
and use patterns. From the Night of the Arts (since 1989) to the Human Wall
demonstration in Makasiinit (2000), events have brought forward something new.
For very many citizens, the way to relate to the city centre has changed (Mäenpää
2000). The change concerns a new mind-set and, as a result, a new use-culture.
Further, the change has had direct political ramifications.

Urban events have opened up opportunities for a new reading of space, a new
use or a novel vision of the future. Charles Landry, a consultant who analysed the
'urban creativity' of Helsinki in a project spanning several years, names five urban
events or event-like projects in his list of innovative projects: the City of Culture
project, the Total Balalaika show, the Night of the Arts, the Forces of Light and

the Huvila tent of the Helsinki Festival (Landry 1998: 65–79). In none of these projects can the innovation be restricted to a pre-conceived shift of 'image' or a gathering of a crowd. Rather, the innovations nest in the non-linear and surprising processes of re-appropriation of public urban spaces. At their best, urban events are agents, which unearth new, forgotten, emerging and possibly incompatible layers of urban potential while happening, taking place, becoming actual, *being experienced*.

The unexpected, innovative outcomes of events include the creation of momentary but annually recurring 'liminal space' in the first Night of the Arts (1989–1992), which according to Cantell helped in changing the public perception of Helsinki and in moulding 'a utopia of a European city' (Cantell 1999: 189). In the Total Balalaika Show (1993) the innovation concerned the chance to publicly renegotiate political traumas between Finland and Russia (Landry 1998, Cantell 1999: 194, 206), while the artist-led urban lighting works and experiments of Forces of Light have opened up opportunities for local participation and fostered appropriation of public spaces during the darkest and least inviting season. Since the events discussed by Cantell and Landry, at least one has had the characteristics of a real urban innovation. That is the constitutive conflict around the fate of Makasiinit (1998–2002), culminating in the Human Wall demonstration in autumn 2000. The Makasiinit conflict I consider a sign of another – political – maturing process of the post-1989 urban culture. It opened up a chance to publicly show affection towards the city. It was about new, public caring about Helsinki and the way it is developed. The official project of urban construction was opposed, but the novelty was that the Makasiinit movement could demonstrate a positive alternative, a new kind of urban cultural venue, scene and process (see more below, Chapter 8).

The moments of events constitute an oblique path of diversions and tactical moves *vis-à-vis* the official event policy. Events may have enhanced the image held by outsiders and they may have increased the number of people on streets. But besides those calculated outcomes, events have changed citizens' thoughts and expectations about city life. Events have become weak places; they have shown the malleability of space and its political potentiality. My central argument is that by adopting the wide, social and process-oriented understanding of space developed in the preceding chapters, events can be appreciated as the 'other', the third term, or the destabilising element in the spatial dialectics of public urban space. In some cases events have literally 'hi-jacked' the established understanding and use pattern of a space. The Total Balalaika Show in the Senate Square in 1993 for example ranks as such a hi-jacking, a *détournement* of space (see Plant 1992 and Sadler 1998 for the Situationist's idea of *détournement*). Below, when presenting the notion of 'event potential', I will further discuss the facets of the influence of events on public space, including the personal, experiential aspect of change (timeplace and space of exploration), as well as the physical forms and configurations of event spaces (centrality, edge quality and labyrinthine character).

In the game of appropriation/domination of the production of public urban space, events have had a double role. Firstly they have been spectacles, a programmed pastime for the 'masses'. But they have also been moments of grassroots appropriation of space, undermining or shifting official policies (cf. Debord 1994 [1967]).

Excursion 6: Turning Helsinki's Senate Square into a New Kind of Event Venue

Senate Square was created in the early nineteenth century as a showcase of political and spiritual power by the Czar of Russia and the architect, Carl Ludwig Engel. The square is imported architecture, much like St Petersburg. It is bounded by the stylistically coherent facades of the main building of the University of Helsinki and the Palace of the Council of State, dominated by the Cathedral with its monumental stairs. The Supreme Court also used to be situated here.

In its aesthetic purity and unusually clear status as a space built to represent power, Senate Square nevertheless is ambivalent. The originally imposed, foreign and dominant square has been in a sense appropriated during its history. It is a traditional setting for military parades and various national and religious rituals. At present, the most visible of these uses are the torch procession of students on Independence Day, December 6, which starts from the Hietaniemi war hero graveyard and ends in the Senate Square, and the festivities related to St Lucia Day on December 13. The square is also a traditional stage for political demonstrations: the workers' and leftist parties' May Day march has traditionally started from the 'red' Hakaniemi Square and ended in the 'white' Senate Square. During recent years, peace organisations have arranged candlelight demonstrations on UN Day, October 24. These national and political uses have resulted in a mixed symbolic landscape. Cantell claims that the distinctive characteristic of Senate Square is its juxtaposition of 'the most un-Finnish place of all' and 'the most important single place that the Finnish people identify themselves with' (1999: 202).

The square also has local and communal uses. The traditional New Year's Eve gathering with the Mayor's speech to the citizens of Helsinki (see Mäenpää 1999 for the shifting symbolism of the event) is an example of these. According to Pauline von Bonsdorff (1998: 179–83), in both national and local events the group appropriating the square not only manifests its own values and message, but also that of one of the surrounding institutions, or the event is otherwise related to the historical strata of signification (such as the marching of White troops in the square in 1918). One of the many meanings of the square is given priority, as the square is for a while claimed for the use of one group, without actually interfering with the existing meanings. While traditional events do not change public perceptions, in my opinion they have an important 'function' in reproducing the ambivalent, multilayered and rich symbolisms and reference points of the square. It is about valorising the 'extraterritoriality' (Cantell 1999: 202), the shifting identities

(Finnish/Russian/European or local/national) embodied in Senate Square, as well as its flickering spatial centrality and marginality.

In addition to political demonstrations and local interests, Senate Square also has carnival-like uses, such as the university students' traditional Akateeminen Vartti running competition. Von Bonsdorff illustrates these uses as follows:

> [Carnivalesque use] presents something which is not normally there, but it does not present this as an additional element but as a total atmosphere. The carnival does not enter the space but conquers and transforms it. Even if this transformation is only temporary, it will stay on as a memory of the possibility of a different state, of the impossible and the improper. (von Bonsdorff 1998: 182)

Carnival shortcuts and reframes the negotiation over 'proper uses' of the square, which are based on the existing layers of meaning.

Although what has been said above may give the impression that Senate Square is a lively place, the opposite is true. Until the early 1990s the square was little used and indeed felt dead and museal – at least compared to the adjacent commercial streets, the Esplanade Park or the Market Square crowded with tourists and local trade. The rock concert Total Balalaika Show in June 1993 marked a radical change, a true carnival-like innovation. The square was hi-jacked. Charles Landry gives an enthusiastic account of the event:

> This is the famous combined Leningrad Cowboys and Red Army Choir concert in Helsinki's Senate Square in 1993 which attracted 80,000 people, and thus used a 'special' square in a new way rather than as traditionally for military parades. It was based on a bizarre combination of performers and marked the transformation of an era that resonated with meaning for the Finns and helped create a new phase of Fenno-Russian relations … Total Balalaika is a prime catalytic event that happens very rarely, after it 'nothing could be the same again'. It shows that an isolated event can have deep-seated impacts. Innovation matrix rating: Innovation veering on a paradigm shift – this is a very high rating (Landry 1998: 66–7).

Figure 7.2   Ethnic food event 'Makujen piazza' on Senate Square during the Night of the Arts 2000

Source: Photo: Mikko Mälkki.

Figure 7.3   Total Balalaika Show 1993

The Total Balalaika Show really 'opened' the Senate Square: it revealed its commercial and attraction potential to event organisers and its attraction to the public. The Balalaika Show had been preceded by the Cinema Night included in the first Night of the Arts. Yet this event was still carried out in a respectful atmosphere: the symbolic meanings were not tampered with, instead this was 'a quiet promotion of urban culture. Residents were trying to establish a relationship with the most important public space in the country, turning it into a liminal space escaping definitions' (Cantell 1992: 48). Since the Balalaika Show, the Senate Square has established itself as a truly popular stage for events. The square has gained new 'local' uses as von Bonsdorff categorises them, such as the Snow Church, a miniature replica of the oldest church on the square, erected at the initiative of Helsinki's master builders in 1998 and 1999 or the fairly popular dramatised Via Crucis Easter procession. At the other extreme, there are the purely carnival-like uses, such as the extravagant Samba Carnival included in the festivities of Helsinki Day, which 'turned Helsinki into Rio for one night' (*Helsingin Sanomat*, 13 June 1999). In the mid-1990s, tents for ethnic food filled the square annually during the Night of the Arts, as do tents and stages of the 'Regional Days', an event that brings one of the country's regions to show its products and culture in the capital. In 2004 and again in 2009 Estonia had a show instead of a Finnish region.

In March 2001, the Red Bull City Flight, a commercial snowboarding night, set a new standard for the size of temporary construction on the square. The jumping tower was dozens of metres high, with imported snow covering much of the square. The Red Bull City Flight again sparked the old discussion about the 'proper' use of Senate Square. A conservative view won this time. VodkaBull and a Lutheran shrine did not fit in the same space, and City Flight was forced to move to the nearby Market Square in 2002.

Once in a while, the spirit or memory of Total Balalaika show is expressed. The culmination of summer 1999 was Festadi, a sneak preview of the City of Culture programme: in a postmodern spirit, it imported 'Finnish' tango and traditional dance floors into the administration square of the country to mark the start of Finland's EU Presidency. My interpretation is that Festadi was an attempt to marry the innovative spirit or cultural radicalism of Total Balalaika to a mature, bourgeois and correct urban celebration. Moreover, it was openly a PR event marketing Helsinki and Finland. The tango floor of the event attracted some 15,000 dancers and onlookers (*Helsingin Sanomat*, 2 July 1999). In August 2003 the square hosted the 10th anniversary of the Total Balalaika Show, the Global Balalaika Show. The Helsinki Festival programme announced that '[t]he Lord Mayor's Popular Concert is here again! It's ten years since the Leningrad Cowboys first joined forces with the Red Army Choir for a concert in Helsinki's Senate Square. To celebrate the decade, there will be a totally new show complete with international guests' (www.helsinkifestival.fi).

Global Balalaika Show (23 August 2003) was a tribute, recreating the memory of the first event, the unique moment which changed popular perception and use of the square. But it also had new tones. The setting was more hierarchical than in the Total Balalaika Show and, if possible, more consciously commercial. The differences are difficult to pin down, but I believe that Global Balalaika was less a people's carnival and more a spectacle staged for them than the 1993 event. Somehow it was 'Roman', not 'Grecian', more 'colosseum' than *'agorà'*. Bo Karsten of Aurora Ravintolat describes the experience of Global Balalaika as follows:[5]

> Saturday's concert was promotion for Makasiinit … Cowboys did indeed surprise. They had terrific international guests.[6] I did enjoy the music. It is the wet dream of a Christian democrat politician [refers to Mayor Eva-Riitta Siitonen, who spoke at the event]: the people, a huge mass, on your feet. Fredi [Mayor's husband, *schlager* singer] smirks. The VIP terrace took half of the Cathedral's staircase. There, far away above the mass of people, those who were defined important could enjoy the hum … It was global; there was a feeling that anything crazy and strange can happen.

Quite interestingly, the statue of Alexander II, Czar of Russia and ruler of Finland 1855–1881, has become central for the symbolic *détournements* of Senate

---

5   Interview 26 August 2003

6   The guests included Angelique Kidjo (Benin), 'Coto' Antomarchi Padilla Juan de la Gruz (Cuba), Wild Magnolias, Big Chief 'Bo' Dollis (New Orleans, USA), Johanna Rusanen (Finnish opera star), Tulikansa, Yamar Thiam and Galaxy Drums (Senegal/Finland), Kirsi Tykkyläinen and Figurantes de Cuba.

Figure 7.4   Festadi's ad in *Helsingin Sanomat*

Square. In 1999, the big newspaper advertisement of Festadi featured the statue with Leningrad Cowboys style sunglasses. In the Global Balalaika event in 2003, the stage was extended from the University facade over half of the square to the czar's statue. The stage was built to look like a huge wedding cake, so that the statue took the position of the kitsch plastic figurine, featuring the wedding pair on top of the cake. In 1993, the statue was not important, but the whole event worked around Fenno-Russian tensions (Cantell 1999). Since then, the statue seems to have started to most pointedly represent the Russian aspect of Senate Square.

The Notion of Event Potential

One way to analyse the success of Senate Square as an event venue is to refer to Kopomaa's typology of public urban spaces. He proposes four ideal types of public urban space: stage, third place, margin and non-space. These are based on two classificatory axes, from socially open to closed and from spatially central to marginal (Kopomaa 1997: 202, see above pp. 35–6, 130). Interestingly, Senate Square does not fit neatly into one type, but can momentarily belong to any of the four types. It can be radically open and inclusive, as in some of the successful big events, or parochially appropriated by a group, as in a Workers' Day demo. Configurationally, the square is central but simultaneously it is characterised by a certain functional marginality, quietness and emptiness. This ambivalence or indefinitive character seems important. Despite its symbolic richness, Senate Square is open to redefinitions. It can become a 'quasi-object' for countless communities. Cantell, when discussing the carnivalistic elements of the Night of the Arts event (taking place in Senate Square among other city centre spaces), uses another social-spatial typology, based on the axis from rational to non-rational and from public to private (Cantell 1999: 175). He concludes that during the early successful years the event operated in the space that is left in between the well-defined polarities so that 'carnivals bring about ambivalence, features outside of conventional definitions and spaces of in-betweenness' (ibid.).

Both a successful event venue and an event in that venue are characterised by ambivalence or 'in-betweenness'. Not a single factor or feature explains the prominence of Senate Square, but many qualitatively different aspects together may explain its success. I tentatively suggest that the *event potential of an urban space*, the likelihood that event organisers prefer a space and that the urban public finds it good and interesting, concerns all three aspects of Lefebvrean spatial dialectics. It is a relational concept, as many of the important factors cannot be found in the space itself but are brought in (produced) by people using the space, participating in events. The Lefebvrean scheme (Figure 7.5, also Lehtovuori 2001: 71) provides a conceptual umbrella.

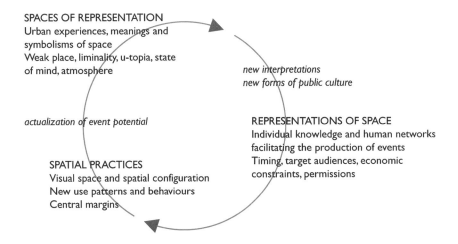

Figure 7.5   A framework to analyse the production of public urban space in events

While many of the important aspects in the scheme of event potential are beyond objective research, two aspects clearly can be studied, leading to what I call an *extended spatial analysis*. It concerns the social/symbolic and configurational properties of space. The former is a careful study of the historical process of domination and appropriation of a space, discussing important events, shifts of identity, uses and disuses. It concerns the symbolic layers that can be found and un-earthed (see Isohanni 2006 for an excellent description of the methodology for such layered 'archaeology'). The latter is a present-day spatial analysis. One of the tools is space syntax modelling, through which it is possible to explore more precisely the centrality and marginality of spaces and learn more about spatial practices and their configurational underpinning. The extended spatial analysis is a combination of diachronic and synchronic understanding of the spatio-temporal processes producing space (also Gottdiener 1994 [1985]).

The event potential of a space is an inclusive and temporal concept that is not easy to quantify. Like space, it dialectically unfolds. Event potential is not a property, but a leap. It is constantly produced in a game-like societal process with its tactics and strategies. However, the humus of that leap can be studied to some extent. The richness of symbolic layers and social meanings combined with a flickering, ambivalent juxtaposition of configurational and functional centrality and marginality are the hallmarks of a potentially successful event venue.

Social and Symbolic Aspects of the Event Potential of Helsinki's Urban Spaces

Most of the urban events organised in 1997 and 1998 took place either in Senate Square, Esplanade Park, Kaivopuisto Park, Railway Station Square or Töölönlahti

Bay area.[7] Of these, the Senate Square was the most popular venue. It has become so popular that in the late 1990s the rent charged by the city varied from FIM 10,000 to 100,000 (€1,700–17,000), depending on the expected audience and commerciality of the event. The lower end of this scale was also applied to strictly non-profit and non-commercial events. The only place with a similar policy was Kaivopuisto Park.[8]

All the above-mentioned new event spaces are central in a number of ways. They take place in downtown Helsinki constructed in the nineteenth century, including Kaivopuisto Park, and within walking distance of each other and public transport terminals. Secondly, except for Kaivopuisto, all are situated at the very edge of the commercial centre. It seems therefore that urban events are centre-oriented, adding a new element to the Helsinki marketing slogan, 'a pocket-size metropolis'. Thirdly, all these spaces are historical and inherently central from the point of view of urban culture, deeply anchored in people's mental landscape (Tani 1995: 33, cf. Porteous 1990, cf. von Bonsdorff 1998: 109–19). The Senate Square's density of meaning is paramount. Makasiinit, the area comprising the old warehouses and field by Töölönlahti Bay, is also part of a complex, symbol-laden landscape of political and media power, characterised by Hakaniemi workers' castles, Linnunlaulu middle-class villas and monuments of State and Culture. The Esplanade and Kaivopuisto Parks are among the oldest in Helsinki, and the Railway Station Square is memorable particularly for its monuments, the Atheneum, the National Theatre and the Railway Station designed by Eliel Saarinen.

There are no counter-examples, no new, 'historyless' event spaces. This is understandable: where else than in a place laden with meaning could an event fundamentally based on changing meanings be situated? – In Turku, the Down by the Laituri festival one year tried to extend to an inner city suburb from the downtown area, but the experiment failed. The problems related to the long process of creating a new event field, which would replace Kaivopuisto Park, also underline the importance of the strata of meanings. Antti Lilja, marketing

---

7   My data is based on permits granted by the Real Estate Department and the magazine Helsinki Happens; I have excluded very small, culturally insignificant events and events aimed at an individual neighbourhood only. Some of the neighbourhood events, especially in Käpylä and Kumpula, are urban culturally important as they define positive 'village' identities (Keinänen 1992).

8   Heino Piispa of the Helsinki City Real Estate Department in an interview 16 June 1999. I checked the data in 2005. It turned out that in spring 2003, the rent and permits decisions of the event use of streets, squares and parks were moved to the Public Works Department. In 1 September 2004, a new unit [*alueidenkäyttö*] was founded to take care of the activity. The pricing policy has, in practice, not changed so far. In February 2005, the new unit will publish its new policy, which according to the Head Risto Ollila will not radically change. However, 'there is a need to apply special rules to all the most central urban spaces' (Jouni Paasonen and Risto Ollila of the Public Works Department, 12 January 2005).

Note: white dots represent events in 1997, black dots in 1998. Dotted lines are marches and
    processions.

Figure 7.6   The distribution of events in 1997 and 1998

secretary of the Helsinki City Youth Office commented in an interview[9] that only a very well equipped new place might work: '… if Kaivopuisto is out of question, there should be a corresponding new place somewhere … It could be built in Rastila [Eastern suburbs] or somewhere, something really cool, with fixed stages and state-of-the-art systems.' However, it is unclear if such a new, 'cool' venue would work.

Why, however, are only some of the downtown squares and parks used by events? Why, for example, is Kasarmintori Square not in use; it is centrally located and has symbolic meaning deriving from the presence of army offices? Or Fredrikintori Square or the Iso-Roobertinkatu pedestrian street?

This question approaches the nucleus of Helsinki's event potential. The popular event spaces in Helsinki are characterised by a special edge quality, or a juxtaposition of centrality and marginality. Sometimes this is overt and visual: the Market Square and Kaivopuisto Park are located by the sea and open toward the horizon; they exist simultaneously in the city and the seascape. Kaivopuisto has a marina, with its connotations of leisure and freedom, and fishermen bring the countryside to the Market Square with their boats during the annual Herring Market in October. The peripherality of Töölönlahti Bay is more complex. It is the vacuum between well-to-do Töölö and working-class Kallio; due to water and the railway, it is a physical hindrance; it is a traditional 'cemetery' of urban plans; and finally, it is also a landscape, 'natural' surroundings external to the city, Alvar Aalto's 'forest pond' which the Finlandia Hall, the National Opera, the Helsinki City Theatre and the new glazed surface of the Sanoma Oy publishing company's 'media square' faithfully look at. Töölönlahti Bay is simultaneously at the edges of visual space and spaces of representation, of meanings. What about the Senate Square then? Although the square is a closed architectural composition, the topography does provide it with a connection to landscape, for from the upper landing of the cathedral stairs one can see the sea and the funnels of ships. The Railway Station Square is situated within the city, but it also integrates into Kaisaniemi Park, right behind the National Theatre. Owing to its size, it is a void rather than a controlled square.

Configurational Aspects of Event Potential

Above (pp. 59–62) I discussed the theoretical foundations of the space syntax approach to urban social space. Centrality and marginality, or integration and segregation, belong to the key concepts of space syntax. With this in mind, I set out to test if the experienced qualities of event venues would feature in the modelling. The basic idea is to juxtapose the location of events and the axial map of the Helsinki peninsula.

---

9   Helsinki City Youth Office, 23 June 1999.

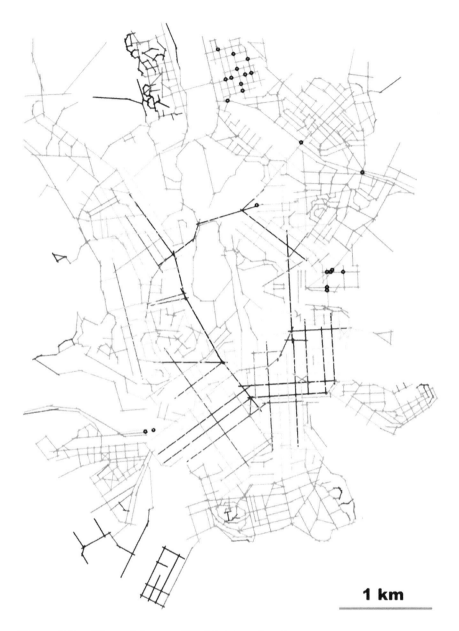

1 km

Figure 7.7   The axial map of Helsinki peninsula

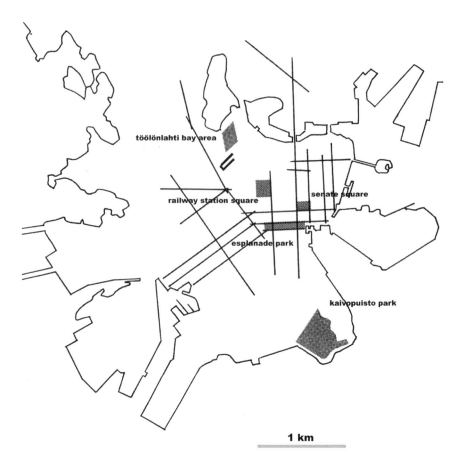

Figure 7.8   Most frequented event spaces and 20 most integrated lines of the axial map

I have compiled the modelling of the Helsinki peninsula with Roope Rissanen. The modelled area is roughly 10 km², covering the continuously built, rather easily walkable pre-1960s urban area. In the axial map (Figure 7.7) an individual element consists of each space perceivable at a single glance – an open street space, for example. The model based on the map and personal observations is fed to the computer, which calculates the numerical distance – steps from one element to all other elements, all modelled space, that is. The element within the shortest distance to the others is called the most 'integrated' and the one with the longest distance, the most 'segregated'. Furthermore, the counting can be done for all the lines of the axial map, resulting in the 'global model'. Another possibility is to count only some 'steps' from any given line, for example four. This is how a 'local model' is produced. The value of such modelling is that it manages to cover some features of the entire spatial system of the city, the interaction of several spaces. In the space syntax terminology, this is called 'configuration'. As discussed above, such a relational model has many applications. For example, integrated lines are likely to have lively traffic and commercial potential, while segregated lines may be prone to street violence.

The close relationship of centrality and peripherality of Helsinki's event spaces is evident in the space syntax modelling, as well. Figure 7.8 shows the 20 most integrated lines in the entire area we studied, thus the most central and easily accessible ones, and the most important event spaces. The main streets in the commercial centre and Unioninkatu street passing the Senate Square are among these, as one would expect, and all event spaces, including Kaivopuisto, are situated not more than one step off these integrated lines. Figure 7.7 shows the entire axial map. The segregated nature of the entire Töölönlahti Bay area is apparent. Despite its location in the middle of the modelled area and the fact that it is surrounded by the most integrated lines of the global model, there are some extremely segregated lines within the area. The void, the black hole of Töölönlahti area is thus also visible in modelling. A similar proximity of integrated and relatively segregated lines is manifest in the Market Square and Kaivopuisto, where quay lines and the routes touching the shoreline are quite segregated.

Correspondingly, the degree of integration of lines tangential to spaces within even the city block structure is fairly similar. For example Fredrikintori Square with no events is situated in such area. In everyday experience this lack of edge quality or otherness – homogeneous blocks and steady integration – may for instance be present as the difficulty in remembering the exact location of a given shop or the order of streets in the grid.

The combination of centrality and edge quality as the indicator of event potential can be compared, for example, to the combination of easy access and cheap rent as the indicator of spaces suitable for temporary uses. Jerker Söderlind in a paper on 'urban mine canaries' has presented this combination of two, semi-independent factors in a diagrammatic way (Söderlind 1999, Figure 7.9). What is unique about the finding concerning Helsinki's event venues is that the proximity of centrality and marginality is the property of a single field or 'factor', the city's spatial structure or spatial configuration. I would hypothesise that the nearness of segregated lines, of another ambience, makes a space feel more interesting and 'softer', more malleable. The otherness or 'alterity', the possibility of change is nearer the surface, and an event organiser senses that in such a space it is possible to *do* something, to influence the city and its social space. So event potential goes side by side with the Lefebvrean notion of city as an *oeuvre*, a collective work.

The Heterotopias of Events

In actual events, the mappable aspects of event potential get local, momentary instantiations. In a truly successful event the coming together of qualitatively different elements create a 'heterotopia'.

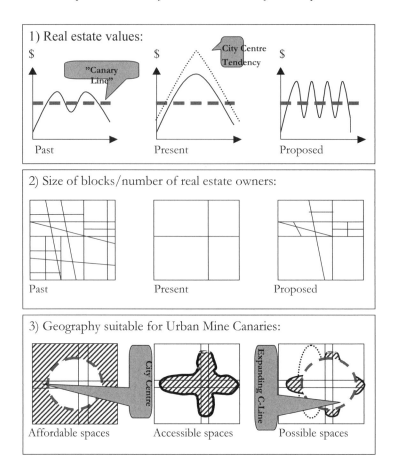

Figure 7.9   A proposal to promote the city's 'soft infrastructures': real estate value, configuration and location

Source: after Söderlind 1999.

Timeplace

Events have their physical and practical aspect but they are as much mental, changing people's understanding of their city, of their places. The special, festive feeling, surprise effect or carnival-like atmosphere of an event may provide a chance to see one's surroundings in a new light, to break the everyday. For a short while the participant may be somewhere else, or no-where. Frequented places seem to abound with unforeseen opportunities, and habitual routes become spaces of exploration. Events momentarily actualise something new and create a volatile, liminal situation. Even though the change is temporary and the everyday comes back, an echo, a memory or a trace about the alterity of the everyday may survive.

An event is a 'timeplace', a moment in which the change of the meaning of a place is condensed (Lehtovuori 2000b: 106–7). As an experience, such a moment is very near that of the weak place.

Space of Exploration

One reason why events are attractive is human curiosity. Richard Sennett, who has studied the relationship between urban form and lively street-life, claims that it is possible in an attractive space to find something yourself and be surprised. From a historical point of view, he compares the Renaissance space, based on a fixed viewpoint perspective to the Baroque space, which cannot be seen at once, but warrants movement. An example is the reorganisation of routes to the holy sites of Rome by Pope Sixtus V. An obelisk at the end of the view line attracted the pilgrims' gaze, directing movement and suggesting a place of interest to be explored nearby (Sennett 1990: 152–8).

In Helsinki, events that occupy larger areas in the city, such as Night of Arts and Forces of Light, may create a 'dispersed space', which resembles the Baroque example in some respects. Event venues become points of attraction. Momentarily they add new elements that motivate movement and facilitate feelings of curiosity and discovery. Furthermore, the visual fields (isovists) of frequent event venues overlap, which means that from a venue it is possible to partly see to the next.

The new events scene also has its 'obelisk'. The moving high-intensity light beam by the artist Ekku Peltomäki has become a much-used (maybe over-used) marker for events. When the light sweeps the clouds over Helsinki, one can spot the event. The light feature has become a cliché and a simple symbol, but the moving light spots nevertheless manage to signal that there is something going on in the city, something to be explored and found.

Labyrinths

The physical structures made for events, such as selling booths, stages, rows of temporary toilets and fences, reduce the scale of the public spaces they occupy. During an event, the open and rational, even over-sized, squares of Helsinki often acquire bazaar-like and labyrinthine characteristics. This is another form of the 'space of exploration' – labyrinth could be said to be the form of exploring, the form of being lost and being able to discover something new. Spatial clarity and simplicity is replaced by opaqueness and complexity.

In configurational terms, the temporary labyrinths add marginal spaces (lines) in the very central spaces they are built in. This is one way to intensify the nearness or juxtaposition of central and marginal spaces. In the spatial aspect comparable small-scale construction took place in post-communist cities in the early 1990s. In cities like Tallinn and St Petersburg, new commercial spaces appeared as 'sieves', 'lines' or ephemeral 'squares' made of small, cheap kiosks. 'Inundation' is one term used to describe such change and creation of other spaces (Dzokic 2000).

Inundation can be seen as a 'tactic', trying to shift the overarching 'strategy' of rationally organised urban space. It provides a functional platform for activities that are alien or new for the existing spatial order.

City as a Loft

Urban events clearly have influenced the popular perception of Helsinki's public urban spaces. Now they are viewed in a new way, as a 'platform' for the extraordinary. The city has become a loft, filled with new programmes. Or a 'shell' or '*casco*' of social projects and experiments.[10] If not all events and venues, at least the most successful of them have established a game of change, a game of re-appropriation. There are more differences in Helsinki, more chances to be surprised, while of course not all events are innovative.

Part of the game is that it is difficult to hijack again and again, as the comparison of Total Balalaika and Global Balalaika showed. That is also Cantell's result concerning the Night of the Arts; the first years were the most innovative. Commercial 'spectacle' (Debord 1992) and fully lived moments alternate and compete in the production of new public space in events. Events very easily seem to become annual, part of the 'event calendar'. This results in 'infiltration' of the event by 'standard' cultures, most notably the abusive drinking culture of teenagers (cf. First of May). In that sense the European City of Culture 2000 was a success. Because it was only once, events of the year retained their uniqueness.

Structure and Agency in Event Production

In addition to layered meanings and the configurational aspect, there are many other explanations for the event potential of a space. *The size of the venue* is an apparent factor. The organisers of an event have a target audience size in mind. Kaivopuisto is clearly the largest park in the inner city, allowing up to 60,000 visitors. Its diversity and the natural seating provided by the hillsides contribute to its usability. The Aurora field by Töölönlahti Bay and Kaisaniemi Park, where the Maailma kylässä ethnic festival and other concerts have been organised, offer alternatives, but these areas can only take 15,000 people. The planned new 'event field' that is part of the official Töölönlahti park design has the same limitation. During the Total Balalaika Show, there were 80,000 people in the Senate Square, but much fewer can be accommodated there comfortably. In comparison, the Olympic Stadium seats 40,000.

---

10   In Amsterdam, the squatting activists, organised around 'Gilde van werkgebouwen aan het IJ' have proposed to conceptually treat the whole city as an open, freely usable platform or 'casco' for social projects. They call this approach 'casco philosophy' (Stadt als casco). Kees Christiaanse, the architect, has coined the notion of the city as a loft (www. templace.com).

Another apparent physical factor is *access to utilities*. Electricity and technology in general often present extra problems for event organisers. The use of Makasiinit, for example, has not been so easy because of the need for long temporary cabling (Antti Lilja).

Thirdly, *the city's policies* of permits, prizing and marketing play a role. Permit policy does influence the locations, even though both the city and the police will try to oblige provided that the practical problems caused by the event (for traffic for example) are not insurmountable. Politicians have clearly understood the image value of events arranged in the Senate Square, for all permits concerning the use of the square are directly under the authority of the Real Estate Committee consisting of members of the City Council, while normally permits are granted by an anonymous Real Estate Department employee. The permit procedure has not become any simpler in other respects either, quite contrary to the impression given by the city's strategy talk and Charles Landry's mid-1990s' analyses, for example. Owing to the expanding number of events, the permit process for minor events has, nevertheless, been simplified. Organisers also know better how to get through the system. Furthermore, during the 1990s, the police have become more willing to close streets to traffic,[11] which has facilitated the use of the Esplanade Park, for example. For the DTM Race in Sörnäinen the city rented several kilometres of a central exit road, which caused heavy traffic congestion both times the race was arranged.

This complexity of factors behind the event potential of public urban spaces may seem to reduce the power of historical analysis and configurational modelling as the main tools in establishing if a certain space might be suitable and interesting for events. Nevertheless, historical and configurational analyses are clearly valuable as heuristic tools. They explain the event potential for a great deal, and for example city's policies rather follow where event organisers and audiences go than proactively direct their choices. For example the above-mentioned high rents of the Senate Square and Kaivopuisto could be said to reflect their popularity. The strict regulations on temporary constructions in Kaivopuisto belong to an attempt to reduce its attractiveness to save the delicate vegetation of the park, as well as to please the conservative neighbourhood.

However, to avoid understanding event potential as an inherent 'property' of a site, a spatial configuration or a shared collection of memories, thereby falling into the trap of essentialism, it is worthwhile to think of other ways to conceptualise the workings of event potential. As noted above, an interesting way to express the relationship between potential and actual is the Giddensian structure-agency scheme (Giddens 1984, Gottdiener 1994 [1985]; Dear and Häkli 1998). Mark Gottdiener, especially, has introduced the notions of structure and voluntarist agency to make Lefebvre's idea of the social production of space more concrete on the one hand, and to fight the simplified determinism of certain economist approaches on the

---

11   Seppo Mäntylä and Tapio Bröms of Helsinki City Police in an interview 25 March, 1999.

other. Using a similar approach, the production of public urban space in events can be seen as unique, contingent processes with structural and voluntarist aspects. In this scheme, structures would mainly refer to the potentialities behind successful event venues but, importantly, agencies would both add to the event potential and make its actualisation real. The structure-agency scheme is not another simple, dualistic analysis of the field, but a way to approach the dialectics of production of public urban space. Who or what has the agency in that case? What are the structures?

I suggest that the socio-economic and cultural issues discussed above make up the important structures of the production of public space in post-1989 Helsinki. While many of these points most likely can be generalised to other Western cities, local variation always need to be observed. Let me sum up the discussion by proposing a list of structures of the production of public urban space in events.

1. Helsinki's vulnerable post-recession fiscal position (Eräsaari 1999) led to an effort to find new ideas of urban development and eventually new sources of income. This situation has not changed even though the national economy has recovered during the latter part of the 1990s. The effects of the global financial crisis add on to the picture. Likely, it will remain in the foreseeable future as the state continues to 'streamline' and 'lighten' its actions, pushing tasks and fiscal burdens onto cities (Helin 1999). Helsinki therefore needs to restructure its organisations, find new income and market itself. In cultural policy this is gradually translating to economically 'efficient' ways to promote the city and produce cultural programmes. There is less emphasis in constructing new buildings and venues and more in directly supporting activities. Events are well suited to this kind of 'cultural policy lite'.[12]

2. Secondly, tourism and the leisure-oriented lifestyle of some Western populations (cf. the 'second generation' of rural-urban migrants) are important factors. Tourism, along with new technologies and media, is seen as the growing economic sector, thus able to help in the fiscal problems. In the Finnish context, new media, cultural tourism and event production are the three economically most significant areas of the cultural industries (e.g. Sotarauta 2004). While the relative size of cultural industries is debated (e.g. O'Connor 1999), it is clear that cities increasingly are tourist destinations and event platforms. Their urban space is modelled to meet the 'gaze' of those leisure and experience-oriented consumer groups. The city's and citizens' increasing acceptance of the private use of public urban space is part of that logic.

---

12   Marianne Kajantie of the Cultural Office of City of Helsinki in the 'Kulttuuritalojen muuttuvat mallit' seminar, Annantalo Helsinki, 24 March, 2004, anticipating the current 'event strategy'.

3. Thirdly, reorganisation of industrial production[13] leaves not only buildings, but also larger urban areas, such as railyards and industrial complexes, empty. The reuse of these areas tends to be commercially defined. Expensive new housing and a well-organised retail/office/education programme in the preserved buildings characterises the Sinebrychoff area, Arabianranta and the current plans for Pasila Engineering Works, for example. This formula to develop these 'soft locations' leaves few opportunities for emergent public spaces. However, temporary public spaces provide counter-examples, sites that have become attractive, new public urban spaces (Lehtovuori, Hentilä and Bengs 2003: 44–8). These opportunities can further be seen in the context of regional deconcentration, which in the Helsinki area has led to three main specialised centres, the Aviapolis around the airport in Vantaa, the IT led 'Golden Ring' in Espoo and Western Helsinki, and the old city centre. The old centre is finding its uniqueness (not surprisingly) in leisure and culture, as well as in traditionally urban values, including politically central and significant public urban space, the value of public appropriation and a stake in the urban process. Attractive industrial conversions, such as Cable Factory and in a certain way Makasiinit, are an important part of the development of the old centre.

4. Fourthly, to take the discussion to a very general level, some researchers have noted a new cultural sensibility that values non-material and event-like more than stable and strongly defined. In urban cultures, Mäenpää has noted that citizens value a feeling that something is happening, things change and the city is 'in movement' more than final, eternal stages and big architectural projects (Mäenpää 2000, 2000b). If looked at from the perspective of creating architecture Gromark has found out that more than walls, currently the most interesting architecture consists of construction situations. According to him, Lacaton and Vassal's Palais de Tokyo project in Paris is clarifying: 'superficially an architectural achievement next to nothing, but groundbreaking in so many other respects' (Gromark 2004). Kelbaugh's notion of 'everyday urbanism' points in the same direction. Because of complex cultural reasons, built objects seemingly can convey less meaning than before. The emphasis has moved to moments, emergence, the contingent mess of everyday life.

The discussion of structural factors is not exhaustive. I hope, though, that I have been able to show that a set of socio-economic, spatial, historical and cultural factors is creating a shifting urban cultural landscape that increasingly provides opportunities for ephemeral projects and events as new forms of public urban

---

13   To some extent, Helsinki is suffering from deindustrialisation, but I call the process rather a reorganisation of industrial production, as many vacant industrial sites in the inner city of Helsinki have resulted from regional plant relocation and corporate mergers rather than closures.

space. Partly the same forces cause problems for genuine, authentic situations, since commercial interests tend to be very strong.

The question of key agency is a more concrete one, but it nevertheless has its complexity. To state that event organisers have the agency would seem clear, if not obvious. It would be Leningrad Cowboys, PopZoo Productions, Helsinki International Production Office, Diiva Produktio and the like – creative people in small organisations – who have utilised the event potential and actualised new, momentary urban spaces. This is true, but the assertion is limited, as the social production of space is a collective process. A slightly wider idea would be to state that the city's cultural sector has the key agency. Helsinki's Cultural Office and Youth Office, as well as Helsinki Festival, act concretely as event producers (Helsinki Day in June and Mayor's Popular Concert among many other events), but they also provide financial and other support systems, influence politicians and the decision-making system and have a role in building favourable discourse (with the city's urban researchers) through informal networks, seminars and publications.

This multiple role in shaping both actions and beliefs leads to the idea that *agency is part of the event potential*, the context or roots of the new urban culture. The mixity of agency becomes clear with the third proposition, namely that the audiences also have a key agency. The citizens' novel attitude towards the city and new ways to use its public urban space are in my opinion one of the most important urban cultural shifts in the period studied 1993–2003. Without the anticipating attitude the event scene would be poorer; without people there would be no event. Event is a moment of combined consumption and production. The participants' fully lived moments of signification, weak places, are the seeds of change. Change entails tensions and questioning of established ideas and practices. Sometimes, urban conflict and the tensioned community it gathers makes the singular moments shared and tangible. Those shifts demonstrate the power of the 'silent' or 'faceless' public. In Makasiinit, which I will discuss next, the new attitude and use-culture had its first actualisation as a semi-permanent public urban space.

Events are produced by a set of agencies. When discussing the production of public urban space in events, the main point is that the agency of the Giddensian scheme is not 'owned' by someone. As Figure 7.9 aims at summarising, agency involves people and their actions, but it cannot be limited to certain kinds of people or organisations. Neither is it limited to one economic sector as in Gottdiener's analysis about the production of urban space. Rather, agency is simultaneously part of the event potential and its actualisation. Agency itself is a product and condition of production.

Chapter 8
Makasiinit – a Lost Opportunity

Figure 8.1   Töölön tavara-aseman makasiinit (the warehouses of Töölö goods station) in 1928

Source: Photo: Helsinki City Museum.

Makasiinit, more officially known as the State Railway's warehouses[1], were located in the Töölönlahti Bay area in the heart of Helsinki. Since 1987, when the railway-related uses were moved elsewhere, until their demolition in 2006, Makasiinit were appropriated by citizens and used in novel ways. Makasiinit gradually became one of Helsinki's most popular event venues, hosting a versatile array of events and some semi-permanent uses. The variety of their programme and the easy-going, lowbrow character of the historic buildings made Makasiinit well known and frequented by many kinds of visitors. Their uniquely central location,

---

1   In Finnish, its old official name is Töölön tavara-aseman makasiinit (the warehouses of Töölö goods station). The nickname Makasiinit comes from this. During the 1990s, a popular name was Tsaarin Tallit (Czar's stables), but it must be considered a historical and cultural mistake.

literally on the footsteps of the Finnish Parliament, underlined their image as an alternative space for grassroots phenomena.

The current round of official planning concerning the Töölönlahti Bay and Kamppi areas started in the mid-1980s. Despite their increasing popularity during 1990s, Makasiinit were not considered in that process before its very end. So, in comparison to Helsinki's other popular event venues, Makasiinit were unique because of their endangered status. A citizens' protest movement, active roughly from 1998 to 2002, finally put Makasiinit on the official agenda. The Makasiinit conflict became one of the most intense and influential planning conflicts in Helsinki's recent history. Opponents' argumentation and critical alternative plans forced planners to take the uses and popular meanings of Makasiinit seriously. Planners studied the urban cultural potential of Makasiinit and drafted plan versions to keep parts of the buildings (Makasiinityöryhmä 2001, Manninen and Villanen 2001). In 2000, Makasiinit became an influential municipal election theme, helping the Green party to a victory in Helsinki (Haukkala 2003).

Besides affecting planning and political decision-making about the Töölönlahti Bay area, the Makasiinit conflict touched wider issues, too, such as desirable city and urban life (Mäenpää 2000b, also Sundman 2000). Essentially, the struggle to save the Makasiinit buildings and its organically emerged use fostered a project-like political community (Cantell 2001). In actions around Makasiinit, the citizens of Helsinki showed they *cared* about the city and its urban way of life. Makasiinit gathered people, interests, opinions; it made certain structural forces concrete and fostered new kinds of agency on urban space and planning. Essentially, Makasiinit became a point of dialectical centrality, a new public urban space in a fundamental sense of the concept.

I took part in the Pro Makasiinit movement, which was one of the many actors in the conflict.[2] Here I am interested neither in reiterating the arguments for keeping the buildings nor in writing a history of the movement. I have other concerns. Firstly, the Makasiinit conflict provides a valuable case to understand how new forms of genuine public urban space may emerge. The dialectics of domination and appropriation are important, as are the conflicts between spatial practices, representations of space and spaces of representation. The very different rhythms of planning and decision-making, on the one hand, and rapidly unfolding urban cultural innovations, on the other, also play a role. There is a discrepancy of *Planungszeit* and *Eigenzeit*, so to say, which opens up opportunities for unplanned phenomena, but causes friction, too (Lehtovuori, Hentilä and Bengs 2003, cf. Novotny 1994). Secondly, I want to show how important a part of Helsinki's new urban cultural

---

2   Pro Makasiinit was a loosely organised group of young activists and professionals. Other vocal opponents of the official Töölönlahti Bay plan were Kaupunkisuunnittelun seura, neighbourhood associations of Töölö, Kamppi and Kruununhaka and several independent architects, planners, journalists and politicians. These actors had differing reasons for objecting to the plan. The official city plan was most clearly supported by the two biggest groups of the municipal parliament and Pro Musiikkitalo association.

sensitivity Makasiinit became – the memory of a differential space still exerting power. For a moment, Makasiinit were indispensable as they provided the one and only semi-permanent manifestation/instantiation of the *political ramifications* of the post-1989 urban culture. The uses of Makasiinit and the conflict their fate sparked showed that the new urban culture is not only about leisure, self-presentation and personal enjoyment through consumption (cf. Mäenpää 2005: 35–6, 221–6), but also about politically challenging urban agenda setting.

Note: Sanoma HQ under construction, Kiasma and Makasiinit in the middle. The circular form North of Makasiinit is the so called Korpisen nurmikko [Vice mayor's grassland].

Figure 8.2   Aerial view of the Töölönlahti Bay area in the late 1990s

---

Kamppi and Töölönlahti Bay Area: Planning History since 1985

General ideas competition 1985–1986
   – three projects share the first prize

Agreement between the city and the state concerning the land policy of the competition area 1986
   – the city gets 62 and the state 38 per cent of the total future building right

Component master plan 1991
  – diluted mix of the three winners

New general master plan 1992
  – strategies for competition and culture
  – leisure-oriented city centre → a shifting view about the Töölönlahti Bay area

Competition for the museum of contemporary art 1992–1993
  – Holl's 'Chiasma' as a veiled critique towards the component master plan
  – the new museum could integrate with Makasiinit

Sanoma Ltd buys a lot for its new headquarters

Draft of the detailed town plan 1996

International landscape architecture competition 1997
  – a 'rendering' of the component master plan wins, no integration of Makasiinit

Kiasma opens 1998

Sanoma headquarters completed 1999

Music hall competition 1999
  – the brief provided no real choices, and a design destroying Makasiinit wins
  – funding shared between the Ministry of Education (50 per cent), National Broadcasting Company (25 per cent) and City of Helsinki (25 per cent)

The new Landuse and Building Act 2000
  – more stress on public participation, but does not apply in retrospect

Helsinki is the European Capital of Culture 2000
  – draft of the park design realised (Art Garden partly continued to 2003)

City planning office's first study about the importance of Makasiinit 2000–2001

The detailed town plan for Töölönlahti approved by the City Council on 27 February, 2002
  – the Music Hall planned on the site of Makasiinit
  – small fragments of Makasiinit suggested to be kept as part of a park

The last complaints about the plan rejected by the courts 2004

The National Broadcasting Company decides to participate in the funding of the Music Hall in 16 November, 2004

The foundation work of the Music Hall starts in summer 2006

Pekka Niska, a private entrepreneur, approaches the City asking for lot for a Dance Pavilion, replacing the Makasiinit ruin, October 2006
- floor area bigger than that of the Makasiinit fragments and new pavilions of the detail plan
- January 2007 the lot is conditionally given by the City

The new mayor Jussi Pajunen decides to start planning the new Central Library in the Töölönlahti Bay area, 30 May 2007
- a u-turn in programming, plans to re-zone some lots from offices to culture

UPM, the global paper company, expresses its intention to move its headquarters to Töölönlahti Bay area, 25 June 2007. The City responds very positively.

Agreement signed with SRV, chosen as the main contractor of the Music Hall project, 24 June 2008
- the realisation of the project is secured

After several design options the City accepts the Dance Pavilion, supporting the needed exemption from the detail plan, August 2008–February 2009
- the exemption from the detail plan rejected by the regulatory body Uudenmaan ympäristökeskus, 23 March, 2009
- the developer and the City Planning Office will continue to work with the problem

Invited architectural competition of the UPM headquarters 2008–2009

The City start negotiations with the State about the Central Library, February 2009
- aim to get the building ready 2017 for 100th anniversary of the Finnish independence

Music Hall opening planned in 2011

Makasiinit: History of Temporary Use

The last railway functions (Transpoint terminal) moved away in 1987

Two artists' collectives install themselves in Makasiinit
- Muutospuisto, Finland's first environmental art project 1990
- artists' collective MUU ry makes an alternative use plan of Makasiinit with City's Building Department, plan handed to vice-mayor Korpinen in April 1992

Art gallery Jangva 1990–2001

Small scale commerce: Ruohonjuuri eco shop, a photo studio and a bike repair shop 1990–2006

Eco Festival 1991

Marski fleamarket 1992–1998
- as many as 400,000 visitors per year (warm season)
- 200 sales booths

Various company events during the 1990s

Night basketball for ethnic minority groups

Forces of Light since 1997
- first serious winter time use of the unheated halls and courtyard

Club Lux 1998–2002

The real estate transferred from State Railways to Senaattikiinteistöt 1999

Middle Ages festival 1999; other festivals and popular events

Red Bull City Flight snowboarding event 2000

Key site of the Helsinki 2000 programme:
- Töölönlahti Art Gardens
- Artgenda Biennial: Intencities
- Exhibitions, clubs etc.

Human Wall demonstration for Makasiinit 17 September 2000
- 7,000–8,000 people
- biggest ever demo on an urban issue in Helsinki

Alternative use and repair plan by Oranssi and Livady 2000

Aurora Ravintolat became the main tenant of the whole of Makasiinit 2001
– Gallery Jangva moved out, the space became Bar Alahuone

Various independent clubs 2001–2003
– important venue for electronic music

Leningrad Cowboys bought 80% of the shares of Aurora Ravintolat in April 2003
– refurbishment of the interiors
– large scale entertainment and corporate events
– e.g. Tropicana Show 2003

Bad summer season 2004 makes Leningrad Cowboys to rethink their programming of Makasiinit, focus solely in corporate events

Southern wing of Makasiinit destroyed in a spectacular fire, 5 May 2006
– no-one is prosecuted for the demonstration-like arson, authorities close the case silently during the summer
– Makasiinit demolished

Official Planning since the mid-1980s

Different plans have been proposed for the Töölönlahti Bay area for almost a century. The most important of these include Pro Helsingfors by Eliel Saarinen and Bertel Jung dating from 1918, P.E. Blomstedt's open and modernistic proposal from 1933 and Alvar Aalto's city centre plans from the 1960s, which developed Blomstedt's scheme (Haarni 2000: 133). For different reasons, the plans have largely remained on paper, and the area has been in prolonged temporary use. The number and weight of successive unrealised plans is such that Nikula has called Töölönlahti Bay 'a black hole of Finnish urban planning' and 'a soldiers' grave for unrealised architectural utopias' (Nikula 1990: 5, 9).

The current planning cycle started with a big planning competition in 1985–1986. The result of the competition was a compromise. Three designs were awarded first prize. Each project reiterated the basic ideas of Blomstedt and Aalto. The park-like 'green wedge'[3] coming from the north to the very heart of Helsinki's centre remained unquestioned. Each project was monumental in character, suggesting large ensembles of public, cultural buildings and wide, open spaces. The main difference of the three awarded entries was the amount of new floor area around the park.

---

3   The southern end of the 'green wedge' was called 'Terassitori' by Aalto. This fan-shaped large open space was actually a deck that covered car parks and a bus station.

The 1985-86 competition did not take the existing situation into account. The site was assumed to be empty, a *tabula rasa*. In retrospect that is a mistake, but in mid 1980s terms the approach may be understandable. Firstly, the layers of old plans were regarded as a more real context than the existing built form. Secondly, the taken-for-granted symbolic importance of the planned ensemble of state and cultural buildings probably made it difficult for the architects to imagine any use and value for the existing industrial and railyard landscape. This is a very interesting case about the force of professional, formalised representations of space! For architects and decision-makers, the existing site was quite literally invisible, unseen.

Since the State Railways vacated the goods yard (including Makasiinit) in the late 1980s, planning of Töölönlahti Bay has continued as a mixture of an effort to sustain the comprehensive visual idea and a newer, incremental process to construct the area building by building. The results of the incremental approach include completions of the Museum of Contemporary Art Kiasma in 1998 and the HQ of the Sanoma publishing company in 1999. Both were based on architectural competitions. As a step to sustain the comprehensive process (and to fullfil the judicial requirements), the component master plan of Kamppi and Töölönlahti Bay was accepted in 1991. The plan was diluted and uninspired, but it nevertheless formalised the idea of a green wedge, overrunning Makasiinit. Another comprehensive plan, the long-debated detailed town plan for the whole Töölönlahti Bay area, was accepted in 2002.[4]

The competition for the museum of contemporary art (1993) was rather openly and interestingly programmed. The competition offered opportunities to propose alternatives for the component master plan. The winner, Steven Holl's 'Chiasma' (later called Kiasma), can be seen as veiled criticism against the underlying component master plan. Holl's project, for example, made obsolete the idea of constructing monumental terraces (cf. Terassitori) in front of the Parliament building. Kiasma takes the existing situation as its starting point, not the insecure plans. Therefore the Makasiinit buildings, too, could have worked with the new museum, and the planning of Töölönlahti Bay area could still have taken other routes. However, the subsequent architectural competitions (Sanoma HQ, Töölönlahti Bay park areas and Music Hall) were systematically used to reinforce and beautify the component master plan. Both briefs and juries suppressed interesting alternatives, and the winners can be seen as faithful 'renderings' of the component master plan. Their merit is that they prove that the problematic and uninspiring plan works at least somehow. The cross-routes and huge semi-public spaces of the Sanoma HQ are even a small innovation. The Music Hall is very sad example, however. Because of the tight 3D envelope of the component master plan and later studies, the large programme will be squeezed mostly underground. This

---

4   The detailed town plan for Kamppi, the other half of the planning area inside the built structure, was accepted much earlier. The construction of Kampin keskus, a huge traffic node and commercial complex, was completed in 2005.

must be considered a fundamental mistake, both symbolically and technically. Almost all the working and education spaces of Sibelius Academy will be below the surface, several floors below the ground!

The 'new' incremental approach was personified by vice mayor Pekka Korpinen, while Paavo Perkkiö, the head of City Planning Office, vocally supported the comprehensive ideal. The incremental approach received much criticism, and the debate grew to an open conflict between the two men (Mäenpää et al. 2000). In retrospect it is clear that the seemingly incremental process of planning through competitions without a detailed town plan was actually 'comprehensive'. The distinction was a decoy and the bitter argument about the process was largely a false one. Planning of Töölönlahti Bay area did have a vision and direction. The incremental moves and plans were rather well coordinated to support the underlying overall plan. The main difference to the comprehensive ideal is that the vision was not formalised to a judicially binding plan (until 2002). From a certain point of view, this sustained, evolving work is admirable. Clearly, the criticism since the early 1990s (e.g. Mäenpää et al. 2000: 161–7), claiming that the planning of Töölönlahti Bay would have been shortsighted and arbitrary is mistaken. Market-led it has been, though. On the other hand, it was not truly 'flexible', 'innovative', 'complexly processual' or positively 'experimental', either, as the supporters of incrementalism would like to present it (e.g. Korpinen 2000).

The Logic of the Official Representation of Töölönlahti Bay Area

The interesting question is what is the substance of the official, comprehensive vision and plan compilation of Töölönlahti Bay? What are the ingredients of this representation of space? What are its internal reality and the logic of the process behind it? Furthermore, how has the vision 'performed' the test of changing reality? How good is the result, evaluated from today's perspective?

In my view, the internal reality of the planning of the Töölönlahti Bay area is crystallised in three things. Firstly, there is the idea of the green wedge, inherited from Blomstedt and established by Aalto. This visual, map-based representation seems to haunt Töölönlahti Bay from decade to decade. During the subsequent plans, the idea has become strong and difficult to challenge, starting to live its own life. One reason for the strength of the green wedge is its visual simplicity. It is easy to draw and easy to remember, especially because since 1973 the eastern façade of Finlandia Hall, the only realised element of Aalto's plans, shows its edge and direction in the landscape. Another reason is a 'story', which provides the visual form with a meaning. The story says that from the heart of the capital city, there is a view to the north, to the rest of the country. Metaphorically, it is even possible to ski from Mannerheim statue to the forests beyond the city. This story lives on in national symbolism and myth. Its power lies in the combination of the Finnish nature ideology and the assumed role of Töölönlahti Bay as the new monumental centre for the country, a dream nurtured since the decision to build the Parliament

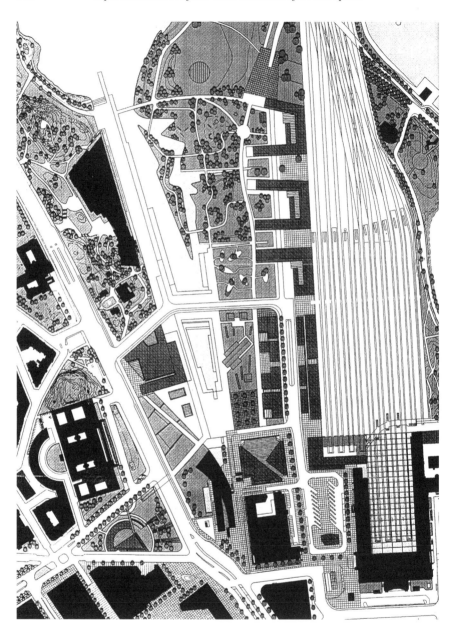

Figure 8.3   Illustration (excerpt) of the Töölönlahti detailed town plan (Helsinki City Planning Office 2000)

Note: small fragment of Makasiinit is visible in the middle of the plan.

House there, completed in 1931. In the story, Töölönlahti is a representative space for Finland, not a public space of the citizens of Helsinki. Names betray this, too: in the 1980s the open area in front of the Parliament was often referred to as 'Vapauden aukio' (Freedom Square); later in the planning process it was baptised as a more democratic but still stately 'Kansalaistori' (Citizens' Plaza).

The second key ingredient is the land policy agreement between the city and the state. The agreement dates from the 1986 planning competition. The main point is that the city gets 62 and the state 38 per cent of the total building right (certain coefficients weigh the floor areas of different functions, shopping, offices, cultural and housing) in Kamppi and Töölönlahti Bay. The purpose of the agreement was to free planners from the boundaries of landownership and to leave the decision about the final amount of building rights open. The agreement has given a strong frame for the economic process of urban construction. The city has been successful in developing Kamppi and selling the lot for Sanoma HQ. The city's share of the building right is more or less used, and the commercial developments, which moreover have a high coefficient in the agreement, have 'fixed' the total amount of anticipated building right, thus rendering ideas to enlarge parks and reduce the amount of built in Töölönlahti Bay part of the area virtually impossible. Programmatically significant is that the state has not had 'enough' projects, which has led to a risk that the state will not be able to build its share. This might prompt demands for the city to financially compensate the state. The city has a formal monopoly to plan, but nevertheless an effort to avoid compensation has strongly influenced the programming of Töölönlahti Bay since the mid-1990s (first visible in the detailed town plan draft of 1996). City planners have tried to find appropriate State projects and situate them inside the boundaries of the land policy agreement. Therefore, the Parliament extension was planned in an area that is marked as a park in the component master plan. The rationale to enlarge the programme of the Music Hall by putting Sibelius Academy there, partly also comes from the agreement. No other locations for the much expanded programme were taken into consideration, because the city's planners wanted the state project inside the agreement's area. Furthermore, the designated use of the planned city blocks next to the railyard has also changed because of the need to support and attract state projects. In the 1985–1986 competition and the 1991 component master plan the area is designated for mixed use. In the 2002 detailed town plan, the area is zoned for offices only to facilitate the state institutions' projects, such as ministries, and minimise 'non-state' spaces, such as shops and restaurants.[5] This is clearly disadvantageous for the resulting urban space. The originally fairly reasonable real-estate agreement has turned into a problem. During the debate about the detailed town plan several politicians proposed to renegotiate the agreement, to change its boundary, for example, but the city administration

---

5   The explanatory text of the plan refers to an opportunity to build apartments in the upper floors of the office blocks. In practice, however, such mixed programmes have proved to be difficult to realise.

did not want to start such a process. The currently (2009) discussed idea to put the Central Library in the office lots would again change the balance, for the better. At the time of writing, the negotiations between the city and the state are ongoing. Despite good intentions, solving the judicial and economic knot will not be easy, as the city likely has to find replacing lots for the State Real Estate Authority, or even pay compensations in cash.

The third element of the official plan's logic is a notion of what is important and acceptable in a city. Traffic infrastructures, big commercial projects and visible cultural monuments are seen to form a city centre. Somewhere in-between there may be well defined squares, 'plazas' and parks. Soft, changing and underdefined spaces, such as Makasiinit or the mixed, semi-industrial park space of the former railyard, are seen only as problems. They are said to be 'inappropriate' or 'ugly'. The city should be clean, clear and ordered, planning ideology pointing to a 'neat' city with little room for spatial disorder and roughness (Hentilä in Groth 2002, 18–19). Public appropriation and grassroots activity certainly is very low on the list of priorities of the official planning.

In all these three respects – green wedge, land policy agreement and a more general view about 'appropriate' elements of a city centre – Makasiinit were inconvenient. They were 'in the way' of something. Makasiinit buildings blocked the imaginary vista from the south towards the north and the desired water pool. They occupied an expensive plot, which the city's real estate people wanted to use to balance the land policy agreement. Their versatile, alternative uses did not seem to fit into the official cityscape dominated by the Parliament Building. This is why it was in the interests of Helsinki city planners and many politicians to demolish them.

Fourthly, the 'weight' of the planning process itself is an important part of its 'logic'. The long, two-decades process is contingent. Previous decisions are hard to change, increasingly so because of the constantly growing number of evaluations and other paper work that slow down planning processes. At later stages of the slow and hierarchical, even painfully heavy, process, planners are understandably not too interested in starting everything from scratch again. It also concerns the 'competence' and 'reliability' of the city and city planning as an institutional partner. If everything in a city plan can change at any moment, the actors that have an interest to develop their land (state, big firms) may draw the conclusion that the system is not credible.

According to the detailed town plan, which was finally approved in February 2002, the Makasiinit buildings were to be replaced by the new Music Hall. From the planners' point of view, an annoying obstacle was to be 'cleared'. But it is necessary to ask, if it is really such a problem that something is 'in the way'? The problem lies rather in the representation of space than in actual reality. The green wedge is a virtual sword, living only in the minds of planners. The real activities and deeply felt significance of Makasiinit were a manifestation of lived space, the Helsinki of its citizens. If the city was regarded as constant change and happening instead of frames carved in stone, the picture could have become different.

During the long planning process, Makasiinit had gradually become popular and much used. For the official planning machine, the emerging and intensifying public appropriation were a surprise difficult to handle. Already in the early 1990s, vice mayor Korpinen claims to have been interested in the 'social psychology' of Makasiinit and the surrounding landscape, leading to the founding of 'Korpisen nurmikko' (Vice Mayor's Grassland) in the vacated railyard. By 2000–2001, Makasiinit were widely accepted by the public. But the fact that despite the lengthy interest and strong appropriation, Makasiinit were not integrated in the detailed town plan, shows that the planners' vision and method were not flexible enough. Clearly, the logic of the official plan was too rigid. Planning did not fulfil the promise of an incremental or evolutionary ideal, reacting quickly to emerging opportnities. Essentially, the detailed town plan for Töölönlahti Bay area is a *museum piece*, a historical document. It is not so much a plan anticipating the future, as a backward-looking compilation of official decisions and reinterpretations since 1985, referring to even older plans and ideas.

Values the Official Process Failed to Notice

Contrary to the assumptions of the official planning, the Töölönlahti Bay area was full of interesting opportunities and cultural resources, only waiting to be raised to public consciousness. Quite likely Töölönlahti is the most symbol-laden area in the whole of Finland. In Helsinki, it belongs to the very few landscapes that still contain visible, concrete traces of *all the important historic layers of the city*. The area has been virgin nature, then modest agricultural land with huts and pastures. Road lines that cut this landscape derive from the time of Swedish rule, and Kaisaniemi park is an integral part of Engel's and Ehrenström's plan for the capital city of the Russian Grand Duchy, originated in 1810s. Finlands oldest railway starts from Töölönlahti Bay. Before industrial development reached its shores, Töölönlahti Bay was the summer villa colony of the industrial middle-class. Industry was followed by massive, Berlin-style urbanisation in the early 20th century, which almost wiped out the bay, as Saarinen's Pro Helsingfors plan with its monumental 'Kuningasavenyy' testifies. Postindustrialism, the city of leisure and culture, has advanced slowly in the Töölönlahti Bay area, because the railyard has inhibited development. Some large cultural buildings (Finlandia Hall, City Theatre, National Opera and Kiasma) have been realised, though.

Importantly, each wave of change has been partial and incomplete. Even the oldest stages, the site before the founding of Helsinki, can be felt there. While industrialism and the landscape of rail traffic are most visible, the landscape carries traces of all past moments. This co-presence of historical layers and partially realised plans creates the unique atmosphere of the Töölönlahti Bay area. Makasiinit were an undispensable part of the layered landscape, and their demolition was a turning point in the character of the place. As noted in the previous Chapter, urban culture was looking for a new direction in the 1990s. The city centre based on monumental cultural buildings started to feel like a worn-out idea. Makasiinit were a sign of grasping the moment to rethink what is a European, Finnish, and locally-rooted city centre like at the dawn of the twenty-first century. But the opportunity was not well used.

Public Appropriation of Makasiinit – Space In-between

The Makasiinit buildings became empty in 1987. For some years it was a closed 'no-go area', littered with the vestiges of its industrial use. In 1990, the artists' collectives Vapauden Aukio and Muu ry installed themselves in the buildings and were given a temporary lease by the State Railways. The same year, Muu ry founded its alternative art gallery Jangva in the northern wing of the buildings. Other early users included dance company Zodiac, photo studio Magito, Ruohonjuuri, Helsinki's first shop selling ecological and fair trade products, a bike repair and rental place Greenbike and Solar Café. These uses gave Makasiinit an artistic, 'green' and alternative character. Not accidentally, the name 'ruohonjuuri' translates as 'grassroots'. Makasiinit was, in particular, a place for artistic production and consumption. Its underdefined spaces allowed artists to do unusual projects. In 1990, Muu ry organised in Makasiinit and the surrounding wasteland the Muutospuisto event, which is said to be the first environmental art project in Finland. According to Kaarina Katajisto, one of the Muu ry artists, Makasiinit 'allows certain things to happen which would not happen anywhere else' (Katajisto interviewed by Groth 2002: 22). There was also a pronounced concern for networking and exchange of the art scene. With the organisation of debates, clubs, parties and exhibitions Makasiinit was turned into 'the most important place for alternative arts in the city centre' (ibid.: 23).

The alternative art scene has a small audience, though, and during the first years the use of Makasiinit was rather restricted. Popular events, such as Eco Festival (1991), started to make Makasiinit more widely known. The single most important function was the Marski flea market, which was the most popular in Helsinki between 1992 and 1998. In the first years, its 200 sales booths attracted some tens of thousands of visitors per annum, but its popularity grew so that eventually the annual number of visitors was as high as 400,000 (April–October) (Kajas interviewed in Makasiinit … 2000). The flea market became an institution in the life of the city. The artistic definition of the space evolved towards popular and open.[6] People from almost all social and age groups felt that Makasiinit were an inviting place (Makasiinityöryhmä 2001). The area started to be defined as a common people's place. The flea market greatly supported the appropriation of Makasiinit and their change into a popular lowbrow public space. They became a space of low thresholds,

---

6   In 1994, many members of Muu ry, for example, moved to the Cable Factory, which had become the new focus of art and cultural production. However, some of the early users stayed in Makasiinit until 2006.

sometimes even no thresholds – an unaffected place with a clear distinction from the rest of Helsinki's city centre. While the flea market certainly entails commerce, the ambiance was not commercial. Rather, the halls, platforms and courtyard became an easy place to hang out, meet others and have a cup of cheap coffee.

Besides the flea market, there were both public and corporate events of many kinds. As the gallery, studio and shops took up only a small fraction of the total area of Makasiinit, the large halls and the courtyard between the wings have from the beginning been open for temporary uses. Thanks to their rough quality and functionally versatile configuration and size of spaces, Makasiinit became one of the city's most popular venues for events. The broad courtyard had provided a stage for a snowboarding competition (2000) and a Middle Ages festival (1999); the halls had housed business promotion events, raves and night basketball for ethnic youth alike (Makasiinit … 2000).

In 1997 the Forces of Light festival, organised by Helsinki International Production Office led by Bo Karsten, started to use the cold halls and courtyard of Makasiinit during the winter. The programme included a new circus (e.g. Zirkus Lokomotiv 1997), light installations (Rauta-tie 1998), fire and dance shows (Punainen tanssi 1998) and experimental art events (Maximus Manicus 1999). Club Lux, a venue for progressive dance music, operated in the southern hall from 1998 to 2002. Year after year, Makasiinit became more important for the Forces of Light event. Club Lux proved that with some extra heaters and a big dancing crowd, the halls are also usable in the cold season (Makasiinit … 2000).

Helsinki's cultural year 2000 was a culmination, as well as a turning point, of the public appropriation of Makasiinit. The City of Culture Foundation rented the whole space (except the small premises of the old tenants) to be able to provide space for bigger events and to orchestrate a lively programme for the whole year. For the first time there was one actor 'curating' Makasiinit. Artgenda 2000, a Baltic biennial for young artists, was the biggest summer event. Intencities, a multi-art project by the Finnish Artgenda group, made the building and courtyard unusually visible and accessible. Besides, another City of Culture project, the Töölönlahti Art Gardens, increased the attractivity of the area surrounding Makasiinit. As a light 'rendering' of the plan for the future park Art Gardens (Diiva Productions/ Seppo Vesterinen, architects Hannu Tikka and Kimmo Lintula and several Japanese environmental artists) was part of the 'official' planning. Therefore Makasiinit were not integrated in the park scheme. Nevertheless, Makasiinit and the temporary park design formed an interesting juxtaposition.

Sundman describes the effects of the Art Garden, saying that

> the event resulted in a physical and mental appropriation of public space. Until
> now, Töölönlahti Bay has not been a common urban space … Now it has become
> an urban space, where people have been, where they have met others and learned
> to use the walking routes. Many have realised the nature of the area in the heart
> of [Helsinki's] public urban space. (Sundman 2000: 13)

Figure 8.4   Intencities project in Makasiinit in summer 2000

Source: Photo: Laura Mänki.

With very similar words, Mäenpää tells about Makasiinit during the intense summer of 2000. According to him, 'in the Töölönlahti Bay, an important appropriation of public space is going on. Why do people suddenly love old warehouses, which they hardly noticed before?' (Mäenpää 2000b, 8).

Together, Makasiinit and the Art Garden were the key sites of the Helsinki 2000 programme. They were active from spring till winter. If not earlier, now the area became widely known, often visited and very much liked among citizens.[7] The year opened the eyes of ordinary people – and many planners and decision-makers, too – to the great potential of Makasiinit and the surrounding open park space as a new kind of cultural venue and city centre public space. Suddenly it seemed just the right answer to the question 'how to develop a liveable city centre that is also internationally interesting'. For a passing moment, the Music Hall, grey office blocks and an over-designed 'Citizens' Plaza' seemed obsolete ideas.

In fact, the success of the Art Garden showed that the official town plan draft was mistaken. Even though the park design was an 'image' of the plan draft, in reality it did not prove that the underlying plan is good. This is because the park was several times more extensive than it would be if the plans were built. In the

---

7   In 2000, 94 per cent of the inhabitants of the Helsinki region knew where Makasiinit is situated and 44 per cent had visited Makasiinit during the year. One citizen in 20 was a frequent visitor (Makasiinityöryhmä 2001: 13).

Art Garden both the planned water pools and all office blocks were usable park surface, not to mention Makasiinit that would be replaced by the mass of the Music Hall. This much bigger park, with Makasiinit as its central hub and service point, would be a working and versatile urban park for Helsinki. Events and temporary uses of 2000 actually showed that the official plan was formalistic and cramped.

The planners, however, did not draw this conclusion. Planning continued as if nothing had changed. Helsinki City Planning Office and vice mayor Korpinen tolerated and sometimes vaguely supported the temporary uses, but they did not take any significant initiatives to change the detailed town plan draft to accommodate Makasiinit. It became evident that when making the detailed plan for the Makasiinit site, planners would follow the guidelines set in the component master plan a decade earlier. Makasiinit would be replaced by the Music Hall and the now popular green area close to Makasiinit would be built on. For some years, some professionals and activists had protested against the proposed demolition of Makasiinit, but now the scattered protest grew to a major movement. The insensitivity of politicians and City Planning Office sparked one of the biggest planning conflicts in recent years in Helsinki. After intense op-ed discussion, countless seminars and debates and many alternative plans, the popular protest culminated in the 'Human Wall' demonstration in 17 September 2000. Two to three continuous rows of people hand in hand surrounded Makasiinit, forming a dancing fortress around the buildings. Actors and small circus performances kept the mood. Oranssi activists, dressed in colourful protective coats, washed the brick walls in a symbolic act of caretaking. With its 7,000–8,000 participants, the Human Wall became the biggest demonstration about urban planning issue ever held in the city.

The demonstration showed that Makasiinit conflict may be a source of political support. Makasiinit became an important, maybe even definitive, theme in the municipal elections the same autumn. The Green Party took Makasiinit as its favourite theme, and the voters of Helsinki awarded them with a large victory. The Greens became the second biggest group in the City Council, passing the Social Democrats. An urban conflict was moved to the political theatre. This shift proved counterproductive for the case of keeping Makasiinit (Haukkala 2003).

Politics and Commerce Take Over

After 2000, Aurora Ravintolat, a group of experienced producers and restaurant owners,[8] bought the lease of Makasiinit from Senaattikiinteistöt. They planned to continue ambitious programming in the spirit of the cultural year, but this proved impossible because the extra public funding for cultural projects did not continue after 2000. Makasiinit was now 'owned' by a private company, and after the heated municipal election the public interest had slightly decreased. Makasiinit was more an issue of party politics, less a public concern and an embodied, evolving conflict.

---

8   Laura Hakamo, Erkki Kallunki, Bo Karsten and Stiina Seppälä.

Aurora Ravintolat ran Makasiinit with small resources. Economic profit was almost the only guide, and therefore Bar Alahuone (in the former space of Gallery Jangva) became important. Selling beer was now a key thing, and even though there was no obligation to consume to be allowed to stay in Bar Alahuone, the place was a much more 'normal' city centre commercial space now. The large halls and courtyard were programmed on a commercial basis. During the IT boom, Aurora Ravintolat very successfully organised PR events for bigger companies, which justifies calling Makasiinit 'the corporate living room of Helsinki' (Karsten interviewed by Groth 2002: 25).

Certainly there were also highlights. Many events did well. Independent clubs gathered niche audiences, and in 2001–2003 Makasiinit established itself as an important venue for the emerging Helsinki-based electronic music. But the inviting, popular atmosphere was slowly eroding. On the one hand Makasiinit was appropriated by small subcultures, as in the early 1990s, and on the other the space was used in a commercial, culturally uninteresting way. Strangely, the flea market that the City of Culture Foundation had tried to reinvigorate in 2000, never really recovered.

Meanwhile, the political battles about the detailed town plan and funding of the Music Hall continued. In 2001, Pro Makasiinit published a leaflet called 'Makasiinimanifesti' [Manifesto for Makasiinit]. The leaflet gathered an impressive list of cultural figures supporting Makasiinit. It also reproduced the optimistic spirit of autumn 2000, showing a positive vision of the future Makasiinit. The City Planning Office, too, finally took Makasiinit seriously. It published studies that confirmed the importance of Makasiinit (Makasiinityöryhmä 2001). Based on the 'scientific' verification of the value of Makasiinit, planners made some minor changes to the plan 'to keep a memory of Makasiinit' and to please its supporters. According to the adjusted plan, a fragment of the southern wing was supposed to be kept and a couple of other fragments should have been moved or reconstructed next to it, to form 'Makasiinipuisto' [Warehouse Park] surrounded by the glass facades of Music Hall, Sanoma HQ and other office bloks. In February 2002, the City Council approved this slightly modified detailed town plan of Töölönlahti Bay (vote 49:36). The political importance of the issue is reflected in the fact that the session was record long, over six hours. Before the decisive session, Pro Makasiinit and other supporters delivered a protest petition with 41,000 names to the City Council. As the last available move after the City Council vote, Oranssi ry together with Dodo ry, as well as the Greens of the Student Union of the University of Helsinki and the residents' association of Kruununhaka and some other associations filed judicial complaints about the plan. In spring 2004, the Supreme Administrative court dismissed the last of the complaints. The heated process seemed to be over.

In an important sense, the democratic planning and decision-making machine failed in the case of Makasiinit, because it was unable to recognise *emergent values*. The single formal planning process took 17 years (!). The planners' analysis of the urban situation was locked in a limited set of morphological and programmatic ideas. It did not significantly change, while the city experienced a major change in the form of the 'Europeanisation' of urban culture and the collapse of state-led modernisation and welfare projects. The official recognition of Makasiinit in 2001 was too late, leading to an unhappy and artificial compromise in the form of the mediocre Makasiinipuisto plan.[9]

Haukkala (2003) claims that because the Makasiinit conflict was politicised in the 2000 municipal election, it lost its value as a novel public space for negotiation. In a sense, the representative democracy 'ate' Makasiinit twice. First the professional planning systematically refused to 'see' them. Then the representative politics took Makasiinit as an 'issue', moving the conflict from urban space to the formalised space of political system and hugging it to death.

To me it seems that the chance for a proactive 'project identity' that challenges the established positions (Castells 1997, Cantell 2001) is linked to the 'bricks and mortar' of the site and the dynamics of its use. Only in real, lived space did the Makasiinit conflict evolve and take innovative turns. In the chambers of power, the project identity cannot be sustained and the dry duel of the legitimating and counter identities take over. The Music Hall, in contrast, was not politicised (many Pro Makasiinit supporters do support the Music Hall, but in some other location). Further, it could grasp onto the image and economic importance of classical music, and render the scheme as a showcase of the Nokia-land, at least to some extent. While many decision-makers realised the value of Makasiinit (referring to London's popular Covent Garden for example) in this strategic and marketing sense, too, the arguments for an ambivalent and changing urban space cannot easily be as clear as for an institution for an established art form.

In April 2003 Leningrad Cowboys Ltd, a globally operating show and music producer, bought 80 per cent of the lease of Makasiinit from Aurora Ravintolat. From the previous group, only Bo Karsten was left to continue there. If Aurora Ravintolat had minimal resources, now there was rather much money flowing in. The project to create a popular, vaguely cultural venue had a new take, so to say.

Leningrad Cowboys invested some €300,000 to refashion the interiors of the buildings and repair it technically (roof, toilets). The new tenants imported big and famous shows, such as the huge Tropicana Show from Cuba in 2003. They organised large, multi-stage music festivals with a populistic profile, including singing beauty queens and humorous bands. Company events remained the most important programme, however. While the operation has been fairly insensitive and very commercial, Cowboys say they still want to save some of the rough character and low thresholds. In words at least they acknowledge the importance of Makasiinit as a public space. Executive director Markku Mäntymaa has stated that 'Makasiinit is indeed the brand. We will not put any Leningrad Cowboys ads on the roof. We aim at operating in a consumer-oriented way, and this place has a strong, character in the eyes of the consumers' (Neuvonen 2003).

---

9   Planners' lack of belief in this compromise was shown later, as they supported the idea of an entrepreneur to replace the Makasiinit ruin and planned small buildings by a new rather large (1800m[2]) Dance Pavilion.

The success of the Cowboys style in running Makasiinit was not impressive. Non-commercial space worked better than pure commercial. The early Nights of the Arts provide a good comparison. Cantell (1999: 173) stresses that the uniqueness of the Night of the Arts was the absence of consumption. Because there was nothing to buy, the audience could not 'demand' anything from organisers, either. The event was self-made. Makasiinit had the same aura until 2000. It was popular and liked because of the non-commercial underdefinition and relative lack of codes of behaviour. The Cowboys, on the contrary, tried to turn Makasiinit – or the visitor's experience there – into a product. The users and visitors of Makasiinit were not active citizens or actors anymore, but consumers.

And the consumer is hard to satisfy. Summer 2004 was fairly bad for Makasiinit. Rainy weather made sure that people did not come in large numbers to outdoor events, but I do think that the bigger reason was that the too straightforward commercialisation has spoiled the unique and inviting atmosphere. A mega screen for viewing the Olympic games was shouting to a totally empty courtyard (*HS* 28 August 2004). As if to underline the change, Makasiinit were surrounded by high fences. As a social space it resembled the multi-purpose hall, Hartwall Areena: you need a ticket, making it another covenanted non-place.

The evolution of Makasiinit had travelled a long road. Groth notes that during the first ten years 'the warehouses have moved from absolute non-presence in the flows of the city centre of Helsinki to a heavily exposed position, not just in terms of cultural life' (Groth 2002: 24). If 2000 indeed was a culmination, after that Makasiinit were witnessing a downward tendency in popularity and in cultural significance. The conflict about their future was moved to the political arena, and the complexity, freedom and underdefinition of the space had largely evaporated. On the other hand, the actions of Leningrad Cowboys could be seen as a 'logical' continuation of the process from the experimental uses of pioneers (Muu ry) to common people's place (Marski flea market), the corporate living room (company PR events), the cultural icon and institution (forum for the Cultural year 2000) and finally a 'brand', a reified crust/fixed image of the social process. In a space of ten years, Makasiinit had become a strong phenomenon. The Cowboys simply exploited the meanings of the Makasiinit phenomenon commercially in a more efficient way than the first owner group Aurora Ravintolat. Efficiency, in this case, did not go well with keeping, not to mention developing further, those meanings, the 'roots of the brand'. The urban audience had been robbed of its agency, a shift that was very counterproductive for both cultural and economic success.

Final Act

The summer 2005 was another quiet and failed year for the Cowboys, and the last concert of Makasiinit was held on New Year's Eve 2005. The State Real Estate Company ended the last rental agreements, including ecoshop Ruohonjuuri, during that winter, aiming to start the preparatory works for the Music Hall as

Figure 8.5   The Makasiinit courtyard is covered for the Tropicana Show, brought from Cuba by Leningrad Cowboys

early as possible. In the eve of 1 May 2006, a group of young people went in to the Makasiinit courtyard, celebrating the carnivalesque night around a bonfire. Police were called in, stopping the party in a heavy-handed manner and locking in several people. In the same week, the demolition of Makasiinit was prepared by starting to fence the whole site. But Makasiinit still had a surprise to offer.

On Friday evening, 5 May 2006, someone set the southern wing of Makasiinit alight. It became a spectacular and festive event. The 120m long building, with wooden roof structures, created a massive wall of fire, smoke filling the whole city centre. Thousands gathered to view the fire, in enjoyment or awe. The immediate feeling of the crowd was that of relief and joy: Makasiinit got the spectacular end it deserved, instead of just being dismantled. People photographed the event with mobile phones, sending pictures to friends, so much so, that between 8 and 9 p.m.

the multimedia traffic in the mobile networks was doubled compared to the normal.[10]

There are no scientific studies about people's reactions. In the immediately following, lively internet discussion, both opinions that understood the fire and that doomed it were expressed. The official opinion of course stressed the criminality of the arson. City's representatives also pointed to the loss of historic values – an unbelievable argument from the party that had worked years to get through the plan to demolish Makasiinit. Probably the most accurate interpretation is linked to the political importance and symbolic value of Makasiinit. Koskela (2006) claims that the fire was a sign of popular discontent of the young towards the increasingly controlled and commercial urban space in general and Helsinki's strict zero-tolerance policy against graffiti in particular. Several marginalised groups had appropriated Makasiinit; it had become a symbol and actual arena for the struggle of the voiceless in urban space. The needs of those groups do not disappear by demolishing the buildings. Koskela then asks if the arson was 'a sign of defiance' (*uhopoltto*), resulting from too hard policies against youth and their alternative, non-commercial uses of space. More tolerance would be needed. After some weeks of intense effort to find the culprit(s) of the arson, the police quietly dropped the effort. No-one was prosecuted.

Why Makasiinit Was So Important 1: Debate

> The debate around Makasiinit ... can be seen as the momentary crystallising point of these tendencies towards the 'awakening of the civil society'. (Groth 2002: 19)

> The Makasiinit question is interesting, because in it different elements of the production of space meet in a way unseen in Finland before. (Cantell 2001: 22)

> Public space is not something essentially defined through 'space', but through 'public'. (Rajanti 1999)

What after all was so special about Makasiinit? Following the trail of the dispute concerning the warehouses reveals something new about Helsinki, something that is not obvious, something that is only just emerging. Perhaps a seed of an urban community was germinating in the warehouses. Perhaps Helsinki was given a public space in all its intrinsic complexity as if by accident. Perhaps Helsinki, the urban experience and the social reality, was about to change. I believe that for a while Makasiinit indeed was a truly new kind of public space, a 'metaspace' (Chora 2001) of pending possibilities, suspension and evolutionary games. It was a public space in the sense of Rajanti, opening up 'wherever there is a dispute to be resolved,

---

10   *Helsingin Sanomat*, 7 May 2006.

Figure 8.6   Makasiinit on fire

Source: Photo: Petteri Sulonen.

where the clash of different desires hangs over and penetrates into the space and connects some of the desires' (Rajanti 1999: 61). The question is, firstly, which moment in the process of public appropriation was most interesting? Secondly, in what sense Makasiinit provided greater socio-spatial complexity, openness, ambiguity and spatial centrality than its surroundings? Thirdly, how to reinstall and keep a 'metaspace'? Or is such keeping and freezing fundamentally impossible?

Many of the qualities in Makasiinit resemble my observations about Senate Square and other successful event venues in Helsinki. The event potential of Makasiinit consisted of underdefinition, rich historical layers and configurational ambivalence between centrality and marginality. What is interesting and special is that in Makasiinit these same qualities seemed to support the emergence of a new, well-appropriated public urban space, not only a suitable venue for one-off events. It seems that Makasiinit offered an example of a middle ground between event venue and permanent public space. For some years it became a metaspace. It acted as a truly political space not only in the sense that it offered a concrete forum/issue for debate but also in the deeper sense of demonstrating the malleability of urban space, the softness of arguments producing and regulating it and to an extent the weakness of official institutions. The weakness was felt (probably also by planners and politicians *in* those institutions) but it did not lead to a 'success', as the official planning alternative won in February 2002.

From the urban cultural point of view, the importance of Makasiinit was precisely in the political protest. 'In Töölönlahti Bay, an important claiming of public urban space is taking place' (Mäenpää 2000b: 8). Mäenpää sees 'a dialectic of the discussion' in the citizens' two ways to give meanings to Makasiinit. Firstly, meanings are constructed in relation to the place and its present use. Secondly, they are in relation to its planned future uses. So it is about elites, political power and high culture (Music Hall) against grassroots level, democracy and popular culture (Makasiinit); about historic layers against new. Both arguments would not be believed without the other.

When analysing the conflict, Cantell (2001) claims that planning is producing abstract and thus global space, while users defend their own experience and thus local place. However, it is far from clear how apt this interpretation is. I think that Lefebvre's spatial terminology works better than Castells' here. Certainly users' lived space fighted planners' conceived space in Makasiinit, but just as clear is that the lived included non-local ideas, memories, networks and social bonds. The 'space of places' cannot be geographically local, as I discussed above in Chapter 4. The defenders of Makasiinit were not (only) local or self-centred, but had strongly the idea of European city and urban culture in mind (Manninen and Villanen 2001). They even thought that keeping Makasiinit would prove a productive alternative from the 'strategic' point of view, stressing international competitiveness and tourism flows. Manninen and Villanen (2001) highlight the non-local aspects of the argument, supporting Makasiinit. Based on opinions collected in the 'info box' of Töölönlahti Bay planning project in 1998–2000, the authors discuss what Makasiinit signified and meant for Helsinki citizens. From the text material, they find eight viewpoints that help analyse the discussion about Makasiinit. Those are: 1) the relation of Makasiinit and the surrounding visual townscape; 2) straightforward statements about the buildings; 3) the relation of Makasiinit and experienced urban space; 4) the functions of Makasiinit; 5) Helsinki and the rest of the world; 6) history and the relations between generations of urban dwellers; 7) elites against the people; and 8) financial costs and benefits. The authors suggest that the points 1 to 4 would form the level of 'living in the city' and points 5 to 8 the level of 'societal structures' (Manninen and Villanen 2001: 23–4). Furthermore, Manninen and Villanen claim that those who defend Makasiinit, support a 'European' way to be in the city and use it. The European 'urbanism' is combined with continental understanding of democracy and social life, stressing direct participation and appropriation of urban space more than the traditional 'Nordic' reliance on representative democracy and rational decision-making (ibid.: 30). Groth, too, finds in Makasiinit a realisation of a new, ambivalent urbanism or 'creative disorder' that connects Helsinki to urban culturally significant places in the Continent, such as RAW-Tempel in Berlin and the temporary occupation of Leopold Station in Brussels (Groth 2002: 73, also Lehtovuori et al. 2003, *Shadow City* … 2004).

On the other hand, while the planners' representation of space may be seen as 'abstract' and 'global' in terms of economic constraints, the logic of profit and a (in this case imagined) land rent, it is rather *local* in terms of simplified image about 'appropriate' culture to be cultural monuments for the nation state. Even more markedly local, strongly place-bound in fact, is the compilation of older plans, which form an invisible layer of professional discourse about that specific site as discussed above.

The crux is ambivalence. According to Cantell (2001: 29), the Makasiinit conflict is unique because it is the first large project in Helsinki, linked to 'project identity'. Project identities are not simply opposing the legitimating identities, but manage to *question the basis of the legitimating identity* (Castells 1997). Mäenpää, too, claims that a deeper urban cultural change would explain why people defended Makasiinit and fighted the Music Hall. He recognises a shift in how citizens relate to the city, what they expect and what they believe is a good, real and right city. Makasiinit were 'good' because they represented open and enabling urban space. Things happened in Makasiinit. The Music Hall, in contradistinction, seems closed, stable and final kind of urban space (Mäenpää 2000b: 8). Users and the Pro Makasiinit movement had proactively produced not only an alternative vision about the site, but also an ambivalent situation that exposed the problematic, weak and fundamentally contractual foundation of urban planning and political decision-making in general. In that sense the political debate is the important thing about Makasiinit.

Why Makasiinit Is So Important 2: Material Shell Dynamised

> ... I regard space, like other actants (including the non-human) as performative,
> constitutive as well as constituted. (Hillier 2007: xiii)

The opinions of the National Board of Antiquities, regarding the value of Makasiinit and its public uses, warrant a mention. Principally, the Board is interested in the preservation of material artefacts (Härö 2004). Makasiinit buildings were not very valuable or unique from that point of view. So, during the preparation of the 1991 component master plan, the Board did not propose to protect the Makasiinit buildings. Neither, were they part of the Board's large programme to protect railway-related areas nationwide.

The citizens' activities to form a forum for alternative politics and the emerging cultural importance of Makasiinit influenced the Board, so that it revised its view and started to voice that they should be protected. Another reason for the changing opinion was that against the hope and advice of the Board, the detailed town plan for Töölönlahti Bay area was developed without orders to protect Makasiinit. In 1996, the Board made a statement about the protection proposal by Pro Töölönlahti ry, saying that 'the buildings are a historic, still expressive document about the history of the last 130–140 years in Töölönlahti Bay and about Finland's finest railyard of its time'. In 1998, the Board wrote a letter to the City of Helsinki, stating that 'the area in front of the Parliament is most suitable for free citizen activities'. The same year, the Board also tried to influence the Ministry of Environment (Makasiinityöryhmä 2001). Tommi Lindh, an architect with the Board of Antiquities, stated that '[t]he new uses that have taken root in Makasiinit during the last ten years is the best, and actually even the only, reason to save the buildings' (Lindh 2000: 5). The National Board of Antiquities used many means to influence decision-makers, but could never take a fully supportive official position, because it would have lost its credibility as an expert organisation. In that sense its position resembles that of the City Planning Office: for an expert, supposedly using 'objective' criteria, it is hard to change minds.

The difficulty of the Board of Antiquities to value Makasiinit as a material, historical artefact provides us with an interesting theoretical lesson. The Board felt it awkward and difficult to say the artefact should be protected *because of its use*. That is because the institution has a long tradition of viewing artefacts in an archaeological context, as 'dead' relics and subjects of research. The artefacts and their evaluation are disconnected from the present-day life, with historical and documentary values foregrounded. In Makasiinit, however, the material artefact was valuable precisely and only in the present context, as a 'living' and connected socio-spatial (socio-material) reality. The artefact, the 630,000 hand-made bricks, 56 steel trusses made in Peiner Walzwerke somewhere in Germany, the scars of time, the smell of wood and tar, the size, form, direction, configurational qualities, such as the fluid, sieve-like order to facilitate quick movement of goods through the warehouses to trains and horse-carriages – all that was important, suitable and productive in the new situation *precisely as it is* (Livady 2000). In that sense the archaeological view would have been very apt. But the Board could not make the conceptual leap to understand material space as a unified, or dialectically connected, quasi-object with emerging future practices and significations.

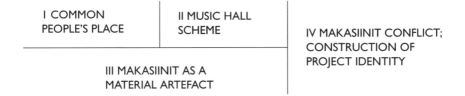

| I COMMON PEOPLE'S PLACE | II MUSIC HALL SCHEME | IV MAKASIINIT CONFLICT; CONSTRUCTION OF PROJECT IDENTITY |
| III MAKASIINIT AS A MATERIAL ARTEFACT | | |

Figure 8.7   The material artefact (buildings, courtyard, their configuration and material qualities) was dynamised in the Makasiinit conflict

From this theoretical observation I would like continue to a preliminary conclusion. Namely, in Makasiinit the material space turned out to be the carrier of the project identity, to use Castells' term, or the focal point of urban centrality, to use Lefebvre's notion. In Makasiinit, the material space became the hinge or the third term of spatial dialectics. After a decade of public appropriation, it was not just a site or just an empty building providing cheap space to do something. Mäenpää (2000b) claims that the cultural process that made Makasiinit significant is in a certain sense independent of the buildings. While it is true that the Makasiinit debate retains its importance even though the buildings will be demolished, the actual conflict and space in all its complexity was 'carried' by the material situation. Groth aptly observes that Makasiinit in their post-2000 state still offered socio-cultural structures, which are more complex than the well-defined surrounding spaces (Sanoma HQ, Glass Palace Media Centre), and that this is because of their *physical nature* (Groth 2002: 25, Groth and Corijn 2005: 514). It is the rough surfaces, quietness, freedom to loiter, ambiance. This is not an essentialising notion, though. Makasiinit were a quiet oasis in comparison to the traffic-dominated surroundings. They were old and worn-out, again in comparison to the shiny city around it.

The structural forces explaining the 'new urban culture' (above page 150) were there like a thundercloud, but Makasiinit, the physical buildings and site in its particular context or set of relations to its surroundings, triggered the blitz. From an essentialist and historicist valuation of the physical structures, this idea moves to their relational valuation. *The material substance and artefact was dynamised in the case of Makasiinit.* While it is true that the uses and new forms of culture created the value of Makasiinit during the 1990s, it is not so that those uses would have standed without the material space they offered. This may seem self-evident, but it is not so, as the semi-serious suggestion by the City Planning Office to move the shells of Makasiinit to another location, graphically shows. Such an idea shows that the point of the indispensable connection of the site and its use was not understood, even though the debate was lengthy and the more progressive planners finally in 2000–2001 took seriously the possibility of saving them.

Conclusion of Part 4

Physical/visual space and its culture of use, space as container and what it contains, public architecture and public life are different things – yet inseparable and in dialectical relation to each other. In Helsinki, urban events have since the late 1980s used space in novel ways, reinterpreting its layered symbolisms. Spatial analysis reveals a duality or tension in their location. Events seek central and symbol-laden urban spaces, but simultaneously, they seem to benefit from a certain peripherality or edge quality of urban space. A centre-periphery ambivalence seems to be the core of the event potential of Helsinki's urban space. In this respect, Töölönlahti Bay area has very high potential. During the 1990s the area acted as an urban playground or 'metaspace', nurturing an alternative ambiance and use.

The public conflict about Makasiinit, situated in Töölönlahti Bay area, finally verified the *political significance* of the new urban cultures. The conflict opened a utopian space. Makasiinit became a political forum – resembling the ancient Greek *agorà* – to express opinions about the site but also to influence wider urban agenda. Even though the planning conflict was lost and Makasiinit buildings were demolished, I find the struggle and conflict very important in a wider sense, not least because it showed the malleability of the urban reality (cf. Lefebvre 1996, Gottdiener 1994 [1985]: 18, 128). The ephemeral, commonly produced public space of Makasiinit as both political and practical project, as a unique moment or time-place, provided the urban community of Helsinki with an opportunity to discuss its values and visions. It also showed that the centre-periphery tension may be crucial not only for events but also for new forms of public urban space.

PART 5
Towards Experiential Urbanism

Chapter 9
The Experiential Approach
to Urban Planning

In a city you must always take what already exists as the point of departure: it is not possible to simply empty the table, start from scratch and create something entirely new on your own terms. A city that is a work of art or a monument is distant, self-absorbed and unsuitable for living. (Rajanti 1999: 15)

The observation that in Makasiinit the material space had such importance in the formation of a point of urban centrality leads to the concluding discussion about planning, urban design and architecture. Much of what I have said so far has been critical towards planning, its means, practices and possibilities. I have claimed that urban design and planning, as we know them, cannot proceed without the self-contradictory double illusion of the simultaneous transparency and opacity of space. Thereby, any plan, and any professional representation of space in fact, by necessity entails simplification, distortion, omissions and violence against the dominated, lived space. All too often, this representation, the Concept City, is substituted for the complex urban reality. Will this set of critical ideas lead to 'planning nihilism'? Will it lead to a position that nothing should be planned? To a position that, if practised, planning can only do evil? I hope not.

How to Generate Potential?

Rem Koolhaas has expressed well the idea that planning, ideally, produces opportunities, while architecture consumes them. According to him, '[u]rbanism generates potential, creates possibilities and causes events, whereas architecture is a discipline that exhausts this potential, exploits the possibilities and restricts events' (Koolhaas 1995). On the one hand, the imagination of urbanism is the indispensable complement for the seductive but consuming process of architecture; on the other, urbanism is elusive, weak and hard to define. It seems that the 'urbanism' of Koolhaas is clearly a more cultural, mixed and experimental activity than planning as it is commonly practiced.[1] It must accept the surprising

---

1 When discribing Euralille, Koolhaas tries to redefine urban plan. 'Fuck the context', he shouts, stating that '[w]hat we're interested in is the development of new urban models; in the wake of the urbanism of the eighties and nineties, we should now be focusing on the discovery of new type of urbanism, which opposes the concept of the city as an ordered

urban realities, act flexibly and in new ways. Urbanism is more about surrender than victory, more about game than control – it is a *Gay Science*.

I have claimed that one important reason, nullifying the possible distinction between the two, is that planners' space-conception is too architectural. As far as the structures of thinking are concerned, the two disciplines can hardly be separated. This has reduced planning to architecture on a large scale, a practice restricting events instead of opening up oportunities. I believe this distinction should be re-established. But what can planning do? How to generate potential?

1. In general terms, planning should become an enabling urban practice, a research interpreting possibilities, foregrounding symbolic layers, refining atmospheres, finding actors and giving them a voice. Firstly, the 'extended spatial analysis' of the socio-spatial condition of the site, surrounding city and society, addressing spatial configuration, symbolic layers, actors and their scenarios and any other potentially relevant 'material', refers to the belief that if the analysis is narrow, superficial or biased, there indeed is a high risk that planning does evil and harms important values, intruding into lived space. Every act of planning and urban construction both produces and consumes, but bad analysis means that the balance of production and consumption is negative. Secondly, each situation is unique. I do not think that a formula, applicable everywhere, can be found. Rather, any 'good' plan is a prototype, suggesting a new synthesis of the complex issues and actors. Thirdly, the 'power' of the existing material space should not be underestimated. In the condition of increasing 'aesthetic reflexivity' (Lash and Urry 1994), subtle phenomena and small details may be of paramount importance. These minute aspects easily escape the means of planning, and even architecture, pointing to a need to refine their tools. Difference is potential.

   The case of Makasiinit shows clearly that in developing underdefined sites and old structures, subtle and aesthetically sensitive treatment of material surfaces and constructions is of paramount importance. A unique atmosphere is hard to create and easy to wipe away. The dismantling of the rails of the Makasiinit courtyard was a blow to the atmosphere and symbolic layers, but as long as the buildings were let on their own, without repairs, the special, different and free feeling persisted. The material shell

---

series of objects; we should be promoting forms which are rarely expressed and which have no architectural relation whatsoever with one another' (Koolhaas cited in Espace Croisé 1995). Koolhaas ironically discusses the current planning/urbanism, where '[t]he professionals of the city are like chess players who lose to computers' and 'specialists in phantom pain' (Koolhaas 1995b). Instead of order and control, the aim of urbanism should be to accept realities and its own weakness, to deny paternalistic responsibily and become a fan or supporter of the city, relating to the forces of *Groszstadt* like 'a surfer to the waves' (Koolhaas 1995).

'carried' the socio-spatial difference vis-à-vis the surrounding city, and Makasiinit retained the Otherness and character as a 'quasi-object' until the renovations by the Leningrad Cowboys. With some buckets of paint on the interior walls, Cowboys may have done more harm than with the two years of fairly boring programming. Material features are irreplaceable. The worst thing one can do is to change or destroy features of buildings and material landscape without precisely knowing why and how. Obviously, bricks and steel trusses do not organise urban demonstrations or write protest petitions. It is the weak place, the personal momentary experience and signification that is able to dynamise the material condition, articulate its links to other spheres of the particular social situation, and start a process possibly leading to conflict, assembly and the production of a new public urban space. The point is that in this process the Material is not innocent, but mixed and active, in its 'weak' contingency. This is why, in the present condition, forgotten material, lost objects and empty sites are powerful. Taking care of that fragile power – subtly and analytically – creates potential.

2. Referring to Häussermann (1992) Groth claims that the Urban[2] is contradictory in itself, since it implies that for a city to be urban it must provide the space, both physically and socially, for the different claims and interests to be articulated. A truly urban situation arises from the juxtaposition of order and chaos. The Urban always contains a residual, resistant, unintended or anarchistic element (Groth 2002: 73). The approach to public urban space I have developed in this study refers precisely to the site and the moment of such juxtaposition, socio-spatial articulation. Public urban space is both the product and condition of production of the Urban. This leads to another set of ideas concerning the task of urban planning and design.

The Urban cannot be seen as a stable state; its 'ingredients' cannot be exhaustively defined. Urbanism (as an umbrella practice) should deal with the presence of historical memory in a way that exceeds the mere preservation of monuments, to support a new unity of daily life and help overcome the strict regulation of time and space. The mixity and unity should characterise any part of the extended spatial analysis. This call comes close to the Lefebvrean idea of *homme totale* and the Situationists' 'unitary urbanism' (Shields 1999: 49–50, Sadler 1998: 117–22). In this context, planning practice should deliberately maintain contradictions, which cultivate encounters with the 'stranger'. The notion of 'metaspace' by the Chora group refers to such real life assembling of urban potential. 'Metaspaces are spaces of possibilities, spaces of holding ... A metaspace

---

2   In German the term is *Urbanität*. Some, Groth included, use 'urbanity' in English, but the linguistic problem notwithstanding I prefer 'the Urban', following many translations of Lefebvre.

allows us to play with complex relationships and their mutual development in time ... When part of a city is designated a metaspace, it becomes an Urban Gallery – a fluid form of public space that evolves in time ...' (Chora 2001: 151, 409). Makasiinit, for example, was momentarily a metaspace. The question becomes, how to best maintain or 'curate' the fluid and volatile socio-spatial condition of emerging space. In such situations, planning should be understood as an open process, which allows for evolution and contradictions and does not impose a polished final result. Irritatingly open situations rather than clear-cut solutions create potential. Love unsolved problems; avoid decisions!

3. Lefebvre, in an interview[3], strikingly says that '... today the city is above all considered according to a historicist model and there are masses of studies on the origins of the evolution of cities. But studies looking into the future are rather few and tentative. This is a serious error ... [U]rban thinking is at its beginning. It is still a thinking attached to the land, to the logic of agricultural production which leaves traces, outlines. One continues to think in forms shaped by this social base: the land and not the city' (Lefebvre 1996b [1989]: 211–12). This critique is still highly relevant, and applicable to urban planning. The whole map-based practice of planning indeed is tied to the land, to former 'outlines' of urban form, and disconnected from the complex, changing, non-local and partly non-material socio-spatial reality that is the Urban. Planning does not have 'the sense of possibility' but looks down to the surface of the Earth, working in 'the rational sense of reality'.[4]

Urbanisation that since Lefebvre's time has reached new levels so that the horizon of a completely urbanised world is very imaginable does not necessarily lead to 'urban society' in a qualitative sense. For Lefebvre, urban society is a possibility that requires a dialectical change, 'an urban revolution', that overcomes the countryside-city or rural-urban distinction. There is a historical and spatial sequence from rural to industrial and from industrial to urban 'continent', or realm. In this dialectical view, urban conflicts are not against urbanisation, but against the lack of urban lifeforms in the city (Schmid 2005: 153). The conflict about Makasiinit is again an illustrative example. The appropriation and experimental uses of Makasiinit can be seen as truly urban phenomena, momentarily lived realisations of the potential urban life and space.

What is the 'form of the city', then? How could a planner think in the forms of the city? In *Right to the City*, Lefebvre discusses a scheme of forms. In his long list,

---

3   Société Francaise in 1989.
4   *Möglichkeitssinn* and *Wirklichkeitssinn* (Häussermann and Siebel 1987).

'urban form' is the most concrete and immediate.[5] Mentally, urban form concerns simultaneity of events, perceptions and elements of a whole in the 'real'. Socially, urban form presents itself as the encounter and the concentration of what exists around, in the environment. Through concentration of assets and products, acts and activities, as well as wealth, urban society becomes the privileged social site (Lefebvre 1996 [1968]: 137–8). This privilege is not just that of an easy life or material wealth. Urban form is the 'meeting between the *oeuvre* and the product' (ibid.). The point is, that unlike the countryside and unlike a factory, the *urban form allows people to produce their own social conditions*. This voluntary social production, facilitated by a relatively rich material condition (product), is the 'work', the *oeuvre*, which essentially is the meaning of urban society. This *meeting* of abstract and concrete should be the focus of planning-thought.

***

Space; place; the Urban. Besides its qualitative definition as coexisting chaos and order, the Urban can secondarily be seen as a 'statistical' background factor. In large concentrations of people, cultures and wealth, the emergence of conflict and the existence of spatial artefacts that may become quasi-objects, carrying new project identities, is more likely.

The Theses of Experiential Approach

Let me condense the ideas of 'experiential urban planning', a new type of professional, urbanistic activity, into a manifesto, a set of theses (Lehtovuori 2002: 74).

1. Urban planning has forgotten the social space of the city, the lived and experienced city. It is pathologically stuck in the visually biased representations.
2. The experienced city consists of places. The place is the moment of signification, and it cannot be drawn.
3. Experiential planning means the discovery and supporting of these momentary, weak places. Planning must seek the largest possible number of ways to see an area as meaningful, seek people, both local and visitors, and to inscribe their urban experiences.

---

5   Each form in Lefebvre's grid has a mental and social existence. This duality is supposed to help in deciphering the relationship between the real and thought, abstract and immediate. Lefebvre discusses logical form, mathematical form, form of language, form of exchange, contractual form, form of the practico-material object, written form and urban form (Lefebvre 1996: 133–8).

4. Each interpretation can result in a separate project. Urban planning is always in the plural, in multiplicity.
5. Interpretations and projects may clash in locations that belong to the life orbits of many people and are meaningful to many. In these loci the public nature of the city, public space, is like a darkening cloud from which the rain of significant discussion may fall at any time.
6. In the clashes of personal places, the concept and praxis of participation gain a new, constitutive role. Participation is not commenting in retrospect, but an integral part of the changing of a city. The planning of a city proceeds in conflict.
7. Images must arise from experienced realities, and not from other images. The moment the planner puts pen to paper to draw the first line, or clicks the origin of the first vector with the computer mouse, must be postponed as long as possible.
8. Reason and emotion are not opposites; new phenomena call for new ways of seeing. An emphasis on personal experience and signification does not mean an abandonment of reason.
9. A picture never represents a city.
10. The city happens.

In Practice: New Tools, New Focuses

Theories change; manifestoes are written and forgotten. However, the professional fields of planning, architecture and real estate development change slowly. Their practices are supported by a thick web of habits, cultures and technical tools that make rethinking and redoing difficult. So how, in practice, to refocus from built space to social space, from traces on land to potentials of the Urban? What might be the concretely useful intellectual tools? An interesting set of concepts that help to rethink architectural knowledge, site analysis and development, is that of configurations, experientality and experimentation.

How to See

Configurations refer to *conceived space*. If, instead of visual representations (maps, plans, elevations, perspectives), configurations (as unearthed by space syntax for example) were to form the core of the representation of space, architectural knowledge would have made a small quantum leap. Configurations (and also typologies if interestingly used) do provide planning with a surprising and largely untapped area of imagination and new solutions. Configurations are on another level of abstraction than images, producing a novel 'layer' of spatial knowledge. They provide the socio-spatial representation of urban space, which nevertheless seems to be nearest the built space and therefore easiest to accept by planning professionals. Configurations are more practically applicable than the other socio-spatial approaches I discuss above in Chapter 3.

What to Take Seriously

Experientiality refers to *lived space*. Experiential planning is about finding and supporting meanings, individual perceptions, weak places. It also touches upon participation and the multiplicity of urban space. Those issues, the differences, subtleties, revelations and creative misunderstandings of everyday life, should form the focus – and source – of urbanism.

How to Act

Experimentation is about *spatial practice*. Here I do not mean spatial practices in general but the practice or agency of real-estate sector, which according to Gottdiener (1994 [1985]) is the most important actor in the production of urban space. Experimentation in the real-estate sector would call for internal R&D. In a conservative and norm-bound professional milieu, these are big challenges. Actor-based approaches are needed, so are new business models. The question of experimentation is how to bring elements together in new ways, in a non-simplified manner, so that key aspects are not lost. It is about translation (cf. Latour 1996) and speaking new 'languages' in planning, participation, realisation, marketing.

Some Further Approaches

Cultural Planning

'Cultural planning' is an alternative and integral approach to urban development. Ideas developed around that notion, mostly in Britain, Australia and the US, valorise further the possible subjects of the 'extended analysis' of urban situations. Cultural planning can be defined as: 1) the strategic use of cultural resources for the integrated development of communities at the local, regional and national level; 2) an action-research approach based on broad definitions of 'culture' and 'cultural resources', which encompass the heritage, local traditions, the arts, the media, the crafts, topography, architecture, urban design, recreation, sports, entertainment, tourism and the cultural representations of places; and 3) a culturally sensitive approach to urban and regional planning and to environmental, social and economic policy-making (European cultural … 2004). The key notion is that of 'cultural resources', in which Bianchini includes (local) skills in arts and media; youth, minority and occupational cultures; heritage and traditions; local and external perceptions of the place (jokes, songs, literature, myths, Lonely Planet, etc.); the qualities of the natural and built environment; the diversity of retailing, leisure, cultural, eating and drinking facilities; the repertoire of specific local products and skills (Bianchini 1996: 21).

Temporary Uses as a Tool

Above I already discussed temporary uses as public space producers. The results of the Urban Catalysts study further suggest that temporary uses could become much stronger parts of the urban planning and governance than is currently the case. In a complex and difficult planning situation, temporary uses can offer a 'third way' out. Instead of avoiding criticism by stepping back and doing nothing, the planner may propose temporary uses as a provisional solution. Temporary uses facilitate a *multiple coding of a site* and are, therefore, able to 'sniff the wind' in a conflict situation. Temporary uses may also provide an opportunity to preserve the existing values and interesting features of the site better than other development options. They are a research tool, which helps the planner in testing different uses and spatial patterns. After a while, the different situations can be analysed, leading to potentially wiser decisions. The Töölönlahti Bay Art and Flower Garden (2000-2002) can be seen as such a test – even though the planners of Helsinki did not dare draw conclusions from it (see above pp. 191–3; also Isohanni 2002). The park drew 350,000 visitors a year. The success proved that a much bigger park than the planned one would be necessary. A micro-example is provided by the Soundings for the Architecture 2002 workshop in Jyväskylä, which tested a new organisation of the pedestrian street by 1:1 section model of a building facing the street. This temporary tool helped to gather information about how people use the new configuration (Lehtovuori et al. 2003: 57–60).

Wikiplanning

Following the unprecedented success of Wikipedia and other forms of web-based co-creation, similar ideas have recently been experimented in urban planning. At the time of writing, there are rather established wikiplanning providers (for example http://www.wikiplanning.org) and academic development projects (for example Urban Mediator, http://mlab.taik.fi/urbanmediator/ and Opus http://opus.tkk.fi/) that frame their services as an alternative community creation and improved participatory planning. Staffans (2004) has approached the problem of participation in planning from the point of view of distributed and competitive knowledge production. Until now, the experiments have not been able to seriously challenge the professional city planning institution. While activists or residents can increasingly create alternative and competing knowledge, the power to decide (and to decide who to listen) has remained in the planning offices. There the legal framework of planning is of paramount importance, causing different situations in different countries. Legal responsibility to achieve certain criteria (such as equal services for all) can – often with good reason – be used to legitimate the power to decide. In non-conflictual situations, however, wikiplanning can work well, producing better ideas than the ordinary top-down process and engaging different actors. In recent experiments by a Finnish NGO Dodo,[6] the problem of 'translating' from the users' language to the professional language (again necessitated by the legal ramifications of plans) was overcome by making the participatory phase on big-scale physical models, which are fun to work with and understandable to most people. After a series of participatory workshops, students of architecture made professional renderings and drafts of plan documents, based on pictures and videos of the workshop.

Urban Curation

One of the most thorough recent attempts to create a new methodology of urban planning is the work of the Chora group of architects. Chora comprehends the city to be a life form with emotions. It is a second skin covering nature or the ground. The metaphors of nature and man employed by Chora do not refer to the modernist idea of the city as an organism, with roads as arteries and parks as lungs. The feeling city is above all a city of people. It is the social space of the city with its spatial practices, actors and meanings assigned by them. The city is a field of many opportunities waiting to be realised. Chora refers to a budding opportunity for a public space or urban phenomenon as a 'proto-urban condition'. The planner's (curator's) task is not to introduce from somewhere outside a new order, to engender an artificial project or take command of the city with visual tools, but to support and refine these urban proto-phenomena and opportunities. The planner is someone who senses and surmises and can launch a new course of developments with small moves. 'Architects are designers of spaces for emergent phenomena, for social, political, economic and cultural change' (Chora 2001: 27). In addition to the proto-urban condition, the thinking of the Chora group employs central concepts such as 'caretakers' of arising phenomena, 'epic geography' as the urban concretisation of the 'metaspace', 'urban icon' as a social collector and point of assembly and 'liminal body', as the self-organising new actor or participant in the process of change (Chora 2001, Chora 1996: 152–61, Lehtovuori 2001b). 'Urban Curation' is the practice of maintaining the metaspaces; overseeing, organising and supporting their contents (Chora 2001: 446).

The projects of Chora rarely lead to built results. Therefore, it is impossible to evaluate them directly in relation to the mainstream urban planning. The approach is interesting, because it shows a way in which the social space can be taken as the starting-point and goal of planning instead of the visual. Instead of drawing pictures, planning entails conversations, assembling people, the planning of experimental games and playing them with different actors. Change and sensitivity to things new, as well as co-operation with real people, are the core of the approach. 'Processes are the substance of the second skin's flux; they create its form in time and space'. The series of processes of change, with which Chora

---

6   http://www.dodo.org/english/, visited 20 April 2009.

constructs scenarios, are Erasure, Origination, Transformation and Migration (Lehtovuori 2002: 78–82).

Weak Form-giving

To end this listing of practical approaches that can act as tools of experiential urbanism, I would like to refer to an own experience as planner and urban designer. While working with an ideas competition in Joensuu,[7] our team was faced with the difficulty of final form giving. We had made a rich 'extended analysis' of the site and whole city, created programmes and a zoning based on morphology, green spaces and urban atmospheres, but finding the form for the new urban blocks was difficult. We had in mind an echo of wooden Joensuu, its morphology, rhythm and scale, but new sources were needed for the actual design. The ideas about feelings and identity did not alone help.

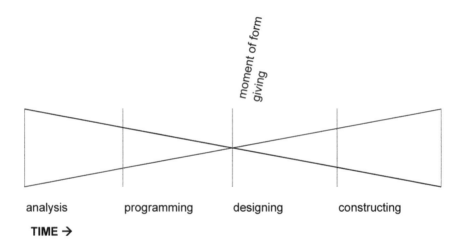

Figure 9.1   The singular moment of form giving

In the end, the solution was 'weak form giving'. We had the historic morphology 'in the corner of the eye', not really looking at it, but looking past. The first instantiation of the new form was 'a badly memorised past form'. It was then overlaid by two new themes, resulting in a second instantiation based on irregular 3D treatment (cutting) of the buildings and a third, final instantiation based on a continuous wooden skin delineating the buildings to sculptural entities. This process was very fast, Katri Pulkkinen being mainly responsible for that stage.

----

7   The Open Ideas Competition for 'Rantakortteli' [urban waterfront] in Joensuu (2002). Team: Sirpa Laaninen, Panu Lehtovuori, Mikko Mälkki and Katri Pulkkinen, assistant Ari Bungers. Third prize entry 'Pop'.

The generalisable lesson was that form giving is a singular moment in the design process. The new form cannot be directly 'derived' from any source, which would be concretely connected to the site. It cannot be derived from a past form (as criticised in Chapter 2), neither from a wider socio-spatial analysis. We wanted to avoid the 'transplantation' of form based on a modern typology, economic calculus, fashion or personal taste, and in this case the selected strategy was 'weak form giving', which allowed some links to the analysis to be sustained, while also allowing for innovation. The problem of form became the 'joker', the Other and the mover of the design process.

Excursion 7: Alternative Use Plan of Makasiinit

> Form and content are inseparable; Makasiinit and its culture can only be saved as a unitary whole. (Makasiinit … 2000: 12)

The study and alternative project[8] was made after the 2000 municipal elections. Its aim was to provide balanced information for the municipal decision-makers about the use of Makasiinit, its present condition and the cost of its reparation. The waves of the Makasiinit conflict were running high, and the study attracted a fair amount of media publicity. The idea came from Vesa Peipinen of Oranssi ry, an NGO best known for promoting alternative youth housing policies. Oranssi had realised that even though the Makasiinit debate had lasted for years, there was not a single study or plan available that would take *Makasiinit itself* as its starting point. The discussion was framed by the proposals and calculations of the City's planning and real estate sector, which were taken as givens – or fiercely and negatively questioned. The representatives of both positions put the present, interestingly evolving socio-spatial conditions in brackets.

Now it was time to provide a realistic plan, starting from the existing uses, actors, values and material conditions. Much as in the Töölönlahti Bay competition, the objective of the Makasiinit study was to ascertain and valorise the existing values and uses of the site, and envision a realistic path to sustain those uses. The project was formulated as stepping-stones towards a 'metaspace' (Chora 2001). The stepping-stones simultaneously built a path of analysis and rhetorics, aiming at an alternative representation of space.

----

8   'Makasiinit, A Study for the Re-use and Rehabilitation of the State Railway's warehouses' (2000). Authors: Livady Architects: Mikko Bonsdorff, Marko Huttunen, Pekka Lehtinen, Panu Lehtovuori, Juulia Mikkola, Mikko Mälkki, Janne Prokkola. Oranssi ry: Vesa Peipinen, Lissu Lehtimaja.

Analysis: Stepping-stones⁹ Towards a Metaspace

1   A Space that is not a Product

There is something special about the site: the space, the old halls, the grass springing up between the stones, the sounds of the city somewhere in the distance … Although the rails have been dismantled, it is not difficult to imagine the clinking sound of wagons being joined together, men shouting, the steam and the smell of coal. And weighers warming by their stoves in winter in their tiny cabins, and forklift truck drivers so drunk or tired that they bump into the doorframes, explaining the damage to the frames at fork height.

Brave New Helsinki is growing around Makasiinit. It is a booming city with expensive business palaces, fancy cafés and cultural livingrooms. All that is new in Helsinki is eager to assure its openness. The Museum of Contemporary Art has no thresholds, bringing art close and making it accessible. The glazed façade of the Sanoma HQ is likewise open and its corporate plaza invites everyone to drop in. A shopping mall is a street and a street is a shopping mall. Yet there are a number of codes in both shopping malls and museum cafés. You have to dress the right way, you must know how to conduct yourself, you have to be interested, you must fit in. In Makasiinit, the codes are not equally clear: the place is neither fixed nor defined. This is what makes Makasiinit unique, and every fully developed city centre plot and finished 'public space' only adds to its value. Unbranded, undefined spaces, wastelands are being weeded out in today's Helsinki.

Cities are being turned into products, something that can be easily bought, sold and exchanged. Wastelands remain beyond this logic – for the time being. Wasteland is something that you can experience, something with which you can gradually build a relationship, something, which you can hug, a place where you can dance. The warehouses provide a 'wasteland' with a form.

2   Space of Happening

As discussed already, Makasiinit belongs to the most frequented event venues in Helsinki. Events started the process of public appropriation of Makasiinit, and they sustain its changeable character.

3   History Carved in Stone

Makasiinit was designed by Bruno F. Granholm, the favourite architect of the State Railways, and completed in 1899. They became a synapse linking the railways to the street system of the city. Goods arrived from around the world and left the city

---

9   The 'stepping-stones' are modified excerpts from the original project description by Mikko Mälkki and the author. A version published in Lehtovuori and Mälkki 2002.

for faraway places. During the Second World War, Makasiinit provided temporary accommodation for Karelian refugees and storage room for their belongings.

Makasiinit are a document of the industrialisation of Helsinki, a manifestation of the production flow of a city that industrialised at a fast pace. The form of the buildings was dictated by the aim of the maximum amount of goods passing through a minimally short route. Makasiinit are a sieve, a space of flows. Moreover, they are a living document of work and work methods.

The features of industrial architecture contribute to the practical side of the event potential of Makasiinit. It is well suited to mass events: external and internal spaces are feasibly connected; all spaces are highly versatile thanks to their rawness; there is plenty of covered outer area, and it can accommodate events of all sizes. Moreover, rents have remained at a moderate level because of the lack of heating and the rough overall appearance of the place.

4   Central Margin

Makasiinit is a textbook example of an ideal space for urban events. As discussed in Chapter 7, urban events of Helsinki have found their way to a small number of centrally located venues, all characterised by symbolic and configurational ambivalence. Töölönlahti Bay is emblematic in this respect. Furthermore, the more recent development underlines the juxtaposition of central and marginal values in Makasiinit. There is a clash of conceived and lived spaces: Many people who want to replace Makasiinit with something more prestigious or more orderly – more 'appropriate' for important and central site – do actually not see Makasiinit. They literally and figuratively overlook the low, shabby roofs and cannot even start grasping their possible importance.

5   Take Seriously what Already Exists

Any given space is a convergence of multiple elements and agents. Similarly, to experience a space or a city is a phenomenon of convergence. There are directions and intentions, yet no one has total control over what actually happens. Both spaces and experiences are related to skills and survival in the labyrinth of Daedalos, a change in time. Why can we not accept this reality in city planning?

These stepping-stones lead to conceiving Makasiinit as a 'metaspace'. It is a 'proto-urban space' (Chora 2001), because its position in the minds of the people of Helsinki manifests something essential about this city. The dispute over the warehouses is an expression of affinity, of love. Contrary to the claims of the Helsinki planning authorities, the demolition of the warehouses is hardly an uncontroversial issue, and definitely not inevitable. An apparent basis for seeking the convergence of elements in this case would be the dynamic dialogue between the Parliament Building and the warehouses, for example.

Method: Everyday Urbanism

As Hentilä (2002: 21–2) insightfully notes, the Makasiinit study represents 'everyday urbanism'. According to Douglas Kelbaugh, three paradigms – new urbanism, everyday urbanism and post urbanism – cover most of the contemporary theoretic approaches in the field of architecture and urbanism in the USA. Even though the European context differs from that of the USA, Kelbaugh's frame has explanatory power. It seems that the experiential approach to planning is quite near his 'everyday urbanism'.

NEW URBANISM	EVERYDAY URBANISM	POST URBANISM
utopian	situated	heterotopian
inspirational	conversational	sensational
structuralist	utopian	post-structuralist

Figure 9.2   The three urbanisms

Source: modified after Douglas Kelbaugh.

Everyday urbanism[10] is *situated* since 'it builds on everyday, ordinary life and reality, with little pretence about the possibility of a perfectible, tidy or ideal built environment'. It is also *conversational* since it is open to populist informality. It is furthermore *non-structuralist* because it downplays the direct relationship between physical design and social behaviour. Everyday urbanism, 'for instance, delights in the ways migrant groups informally respond in resourceful and imaginative ways to *ad hoc* conditions and marginal spaces'. More than design, culture is highlighted as a determinant of the behaviour. The aim is to reassemble and intensify the existing everyday conditions (Lehtovuori et al. 2003: 60–61, Hentilä 2002: 21–2, cf. Kelbaugh 1997: 2000).

In the Makasiinit study, everyday urbanism appeared in two ways. Firstly, much emphasis was placed on studying the history of the railyard and Makasiinit buildings and in measuring the construction. This belongs to the normal practice in inventories of the built history. Here it was applied to a rather mundane construction so that atmospheric and configurational qualities became more important than stylistic. Secondly, an important theme was to map the existing use patterns and interview users to create an idea as to what would best serve precisely such use. This actor-oriented approach seemed to us natural and evident, but in planning and urban design it is exceptional. The end result is an original *and* organic plan,

---

10   Instead of 'situated' Kelbaugh uses term 'non-utopian' which I find problematic.

proposing that not much needs and should be done. Instead of grand gestures, the new cultural venue and public urban space is best helped by refraining from big new constructions. If it ain't broke, don't fix it!

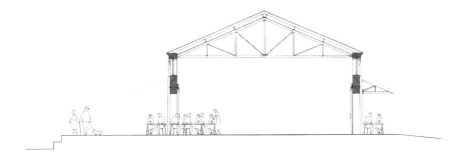

Figure 9.3   Adaptive re-use. Section of the southern Makasiini hall, showing the small but important changes (e.g. lightweight awnings, natural seating, repair of doors to restore the sieve-like quality of the space) that facilitate continued, versatile event use

Source: Livady Architects.

Plan: Adaptive Reuse

Makasiinit as it stood in 2000, is an excellent example of adaptive reuse. With almost no renovations or investments, the old storage buildings have served as a key event venue and public space in the city centre. An independent do-it-yourself mentality and scarce fiscal resources have characterised the users of Makasiinit (except the Leningrad Cowboys). This has led the users to adapt their activities to the potential of the existing buildings. There has been little need to extensively refurbish or add air conditioning, insulation and other modern building technologies in the old structure. Such adaptive reuse is well founded from the ecological point of view. It is the best way to ensure that the historical values of the buildings are saved.

Furthermore, in the study of different kinds of event that had used Makasiinit, the main finding was that while the use had changed from railway storage to a venue for public events, the use pattern had remained surprisingly the same. Makasiinit was a sieve through which goods had flowed in the original use and through which people and ideas flow now. If physically the buildings are long and wall-like, functionally they are open and permeable. This became the key urbanistic idea of the project: Makasiinit is more a roof in the park than a building. It is a sieve, not a wall. If the many doors are repaired, the building will get back its openness, becoming a node of flows. This ease and logic of the proposal is also the key artistic idea.

Figure 9.4   Makasiini hall in use

Source: Livady Architects.

It became clear that it is easy to reinforce the prerequisites of current uses with minor actions. Excessive refurbishment and use of money would actually do more harm than good, turning a spontaneous sprout into an institution. Therefore, the central qualities of our proposal were openness and accessibility, and with regard to the extent of renovation, lightness, feasibility and economy.

Accessibility and visibility would be improved by removing unnecessary fencing, protective walls and level differences. The area between Mannerheimintie road and the warehouses would be made into a single, open surface. The wide eaves obstructing the façades would be replaced by lightweight awnings facilitating the easy change of appearance according to season or event. Appropriate lighting would be provided.

The interiors, the courtyard and its extensions would form a coherent venue for events. The basic surfaces – the hall and platform levels as well as the courtyard – would be clarified. The level difference between the platforms and the yard would be retained, but the edges would be turned into seating stairs which would not require railings. The platforms would also be made broader and extended towards

Töölönlahdenkatu street. The raw, open, quality of the yard would be retained. Movable bridges contributing to the adaptability of the space would be a new introduction.

The warehouse halls would be provided with light thermal insulation and windows and doors would be renewed, thus creating a semi-warm space. The renovation would be inexpensive and cause no problems related to either aesthetical or technical issues such as humidity. The sliding doors would be repaired so as to make them easy to use. Warm and technical spaces would remain at the ends of the wings, as today.

A renovation such as this would further contribute to the attraction potential and usability of the warehouses, making them a true, viable constituent of the new city centre. The price difference between renovations for adaptive re-use, starting with the needs of the actual temporary users, and a total modernisation of the premises for speculative 'high' uses, such as offices or shopping, is in this case eight- to tenfold (Lehtovuori and Mälkki 2002).

Chapter 10
A New Paradigm

Experiential Urbanism, A New Paradigm in Planning

Rational-comprehensive planning and communicative planning[1] are ideal types that repeatedly appear in European and North American planning theoretical texts (Healey 2007, Sandercock 2001, Staffans 2004). The 'communicative turn' of planning has also been critically compared to the notion that science progresses through sudden and radical paradigm changes (Taylor 1998), originally proposed by the philosopher of science Thomas S. Kuhn (1962). Looking primarily from the British perspective, Taylor doubts that changes in planning are rather organic and gradual than in Kuhn's sense paradigmatic. I believe, on the contrary, that the question is open for debate. Experiential urbanism can be seen as a new paradigm.

To understand what a paradigm change in planning might mean, I have to shortly discuss Kuhn's basic concepts. According to him, scientific knowledge is not only cumulatively added, but there are sudden ruptures in the development of a discipline. Paradigm is the dominant, non-questioned basic view of a discipline, and scientific revolution denotes the change from one to other mutually exclusive paradigm. The concept of paradigm has different definitions, but usually it refers to the 'disciplinary matrix', or the whole of 1) symbolic generalisations (laws), 2) exemplars (historically significant solutions of scientific problems) and 3) values shared by the scientific community (Pihlström 1996). Paradigm thus concerns ontology, methods, value-laden aims and the most important scientific problems.

In philosophy of science, Kuhn's ideas raise the question what is the relationship between science and reality. Kuhn appears to be a constructivist, because for him paradigm constitutes a world. On the other hand, observations that deviate from the theory held by any current, dominant 'normal science', coming from reality outside the world constituted by the paradigm, are the necessary condition for a paradigm change – a view that comes close to philosophical realism.

I think that the problem of the relationship between (scientific) theory and reality offers a workable link from Kuhn's ideas to urban planning. A paradigm change in science entails both ontological and epistemological shifts. In other words, the scientific community changes both the object of knowledge and ways to gain knowledge. We do not need to discuss how scientific urban planning is to analogically suggest that any well-established planning practice and community

---

1   In communicative planning we include also advocacy planning and radical planning. The rational-comprehensive ideal was most clearly defined by the Chicago School in 1950s and 1960s (Sandercock 1998).

holds a certain way to conceptualise its object, city or region, and a related way to understand how it can influence urban development and change. As Dear and Häkli (1998) note, the practices of planning constitute the 'city of urban planning' as a special urban reality intelligible for planning.

Regarding any possible new planning paradigm, the interesting observation is that while the conceptualisation of the city/the urban and its planning always are related, *the relation rarely is clearly thought and expressed*. In the rational-comprehensive that was the case, which is a reason to count it as a paradigm. The city was conceptualised as a system or an organism, which parts and internal relations were in principle knowable. Planner's assumed superior knowledge of that system / organism was the foundation and legitimation of planning, operating neutrally in public interest (Sandercock 2001). The communicative ideal, for its part, stresses the actors, especially residents. Concrete cases or situations of planning are viewed rather from inside than outside. But this new emphasis is not anchored to a well-articulated conception of the object of knowledge, the city.

I claim that a paradigmatic change in urban planning is possible, but its ontological articulation is not ready. The problem can be phrased so that when moving from rational-comprehensive to communicative, the idea about the object of planning has indeed changed. Faludi's (1973) distinction between substantive and procedural planning theories points to that: the former focus on the normative aims while the latter focus on planning practices. Because communicative theories are rather procedural than substantive, the conceptualisation of the city – the object of rational-comprehensive theory – has got little attention. Communicative theory has been busy with methods and processes, while neglecting the theory of space, city and the Urban. This neglect has deep ramifications. Firstly, it has emptied the possibility of a paradigm change of planning in the Kuhnian sense. The possible, indeed necessary, change of the disciplinary matrix has been left half-way. Secondly, the neglect may explain why, in communicative practices, there is a continuous fight about the 'right' or best representation of the object of planning, fight about right knowledge and conceptualisation (Staffans 2004), eroding the political legitimacy of new, alternative approaches.

If the analogy with revolutions in science holds, the 'matrix' of planning, including generalisations about the object of planning, exemplary models as well as values shared by the profession, should have changed or be changing. I hope that my work on social space, weak place, the dialectical assemblage of public urban space gives material for rethinking the theory. Regarding values, I wish that my work points towards sensitivity to differences and potentials of the Urban. Together with models and exemplars, briefly studied in Chapter 9, these elements could start to come together as a new paradigm. An interesting proposition for a new paradigm is Jean Hillier's (2007) 'multiplanar theory of spatial planning', which problematises representation with reference to Deleuzian ideas.

Produced Knowledge

What does it mean to say that a picture never represents a city? The soundings to the experiential approach to planning still call for an epistemological note about the possibility of production of knowledge as part of the wider production of space.

Knowledge conceived in Constructionist terms does not consist of objective discoveries but is rather made or produced. Therefore, the context of knowledge is *within* it, not outside. Knowledge is not a piece of a greater reality or context. Rather, it can be understood as a set of chosen approaches and an (ongoing) construction, employing subjects of attention. The end result, knowledge, changes according to choice of approaches (Kuoppamäki 2001: 31–2, Knorr-Cetina 1999). If urban planning adopts new approaches and new focuses of interest, the knowledge that planning has about the city will change. Because of the dialectical link between conceived, perceived and lived, the city, both present and future, will simultaneously change as well.

The Constructionist conception of knowledge appears to be relativist, because knowledge seems to be dependent only on the author, on his or her choices. In *Understanding the Urban* (2001) David Byrne criticises the relativistic position. Byrne states that in order to think, communicate and act at all, we must assume that it is possible (through a careful realist methodology) to obtain at least *local* objective knowledge. This position is possible in science, if we manage to conceive of science as neutral and proceeding purely towards truth, but in urban planning, which always deals with issues of power, the idea of a single true, and thereby better, knowledge, even local, is problematic. I think that it is better to accept the challenge of competing and conflicting constructions of knowledge. Byrne is correct, however, in noting that '[t]he important thing about the urban … is that we will only understand it by changing it …' (2001: 195). Again: the city happens.

So far, in both architecture and urban planning the main bearer of information and knowledge is the drawing. According to Kuoppamäki, architectural knowledge is produced in the act of drawing, in which the designer mixes things of his own with things that have been adopted (Kuoppamäki 2001: 40). This idea does not alter the role of drawings in Lefebvre's triad of space-concepts. Constructionist drawn knowledge is no less a 'conceptualised space' than if it had been thought through the terms of some other epistemology. It is still true that a place cannot be drawn. But this idea adds a new tone to the visuality of urban planning and the conception of architecture or urban planning as art. It is customary to think that urban planning operates between science and art, or that it 'needs' both (see e.g. Sandercock 1998: 27). According to Kuoppamäki drawings do not represent their subject but present knowledge in themselves with the altering of reality as the objective (Kuoppamäki 2001: 148, on interests of knowledge, see Häkli 1999: 31, Varto 2000: 98–9). A drawing can contain a variety of material, such as moods, humour and recollections extending above and beyond the visual. Seen in these terms, planning does not balance between science and art. Instead, art and (scientific) knowledge may both reside in the drawings. It is not at any rate easy to distinguish, for instance, 'the art of space' from other deliberations, skills and even random occurrences belonging to planning. This idea points to a need to create new hybrid visual languages in planning.

Nor is Constructionist produced knowledge relativistic to the extreme. Its social and shared nature can be understood through the concept of epistemic culture. 'The drawing is a gate "into" the culture of drawing, the social state and situation where drawing takes place' (Kuoppamäki 2001: 32). The important consideration is what goes into the drawings, in what culture and from what elements they are made. The drawings of the Chora group of architects, for example, are truly different pictures, because they are made within a different epistemic culture, experiential instead of visual, and local and living instead of universal. The approach and means of planning in relation to all three aspects of social space, perceived, conceived and lived, can and must be enlarged, as also strict urban knowledge and its applications in planning. The experiential approach is a true expansion and not a zero sum game.

Experiential Urbanism and Art

When evoking 'art', I do not imagine great artworks hanging in museum walls neither ordered City Beautiful vistas. Instead, I am interested in the moments of creation, the edges, thresholds or singular moments (cf. critical moments in Bourdieu), which I personally feel to be important and necessary in evaluating the projects. My focus is the artistic content and the design method, a new kind of conceptualisation of planning and design. The examples of this chapter have primarily been about subtle, cultural values and only secondarily about practical benefits, economic efficiency or the political success of plans and designs. There is an important reason for this focus. I think that in the pressures of economy on the one hand and public participation on the other, the art of both architecture and planning is too easily lost from view. Architects and planners are seen as strange and secretive users of power. They are more often than not rendered as a problem *both* from the point of view of streamlined money-making *and* inclusive participation of lay-men (as users, residents). I would like to voice two distinct reactions to that negative view. Firstly, there is no doubt that the art and practice of architecture and planning could and should change to better 'serve' whatever is the configuration of actors in a specific case. Architecture can become an organiser of a social process, a 'facilitator' if you wish; participation can become much more central to the art of planning than it is now. Urbanism could and should recognise the energy of conflict and live on it (Thesis no. 6 above). Secondly, as an important complement to the humble first statement, all actors – society at large – should recognise the independence of architecture and urbanism as art. This is not so much a personal or professional point (an effort to establish a *refugio* or boost self-esteem), but a cultural one. The history of architecture, its present education, the professional codes and the relations between building and professional publicity constitute the 'rules' of architecture. Because the field is complex, it may indeed seem secretive or odd. I strongly argue, however, that in all its intricacy architecture as art is an important part of our culture. It is part of us, and it should be loved, not hated. With all its weaknesses, this rooted web of architectural judgement, after all, is one *counter-force to the 'abstract space'* of economic values, which is constantly eating away the differences and uniqueness of urban space and buildings. Only the notion of art, in my view, secures this possibility. If architecture, urban design and planning are considered loyal servants of the real-estate sector, only, they cannot sustain this role at all. In that case, architecture and planning, indeed, are the 'façade of power', nothing else (cf. Gottdiener 1994 [1985]: 18).

Conclusion of Part 5

I have presented some versions of the extended socio-spatial analysis and some methods to facilitate and rehearse planning and architecture. If every project is a *prototype* and *experiment*, more projects would result in more ideas and findings. I nevertheless hope that the complex relationship between planning, urban design and architecture has been valorised. The notion of urbanism can be seen as a cultural umbrella for these converging/diverging disciplines.

It has become clear that while the game of appropriation is about diversions (*détournement*), in architectural and planning practices it is hard to avoid the 'violent' moment of creation, proposing a new form. And it should not be avoided, even though it can be pushed much further in the design process than is normally done. Nevertheless, the moment of form creation has its own singularity. In its ostensible freedom and contentlessness (as an 'image'), form is the tiny and difficult eye of the needle every architect has to push through. However, what I have presented in the previous pages shifts the ground of form giving. If architectural form and spatial configuration are 'mixed' with social and mental, taking case-by-case different and unique positions in the spatial dialectic, the whole meaning of form giving changes. Like weak place, form cannot easily be 'drawn'. Rather, it may be obliquely found/produced.

Planning and design process should be seen as a sustained effort to bring together qualitatively differing socio-spatial 'materials'. The process itself can be seen as dialectic. The 'concept' in the architectural sense of the word, is a dialectic movement, not an image or 'vision' of the future project. This makes clearer the idea that 'concept cannot be drawn'. In the Makasiinit study, the creative assembly took place in the middle, with the realisation that the old use and new use share the same logic and pattern, thereby confirming that the configuration of Makasiinit is superbly suitable for the new event use and simultaneously the new use cannot exist without the old configuration. This finding was then condensed in the maxims: 'Form and content are inseparable; Makasiinit and their culture can only be saved as a unitary whole' and 'If it ain't broke, don't fix it!'

Finally, to come back to the distinction between urbanism and architecture: It may be that 'planner' should be redefined as 'interpreter' of urban situations, more a researcher than designer, maybe even a 'switch' of multifarious social and cultural currents, while 'architect' may more easily continue in his seductive consumption of the potentials produced by the newly defined planner. However, I resist the idea that the singular moment of form giving would mark the boundary between planning and architecture, the disciplines of creating opportunity and consuming it. No, the art of planning should be understood structurally (cf. Stenros 1992: 271–3), so that good quality is a multilayered resonance of differing elements influencing many levels from analysis to final built artefact. This idea is difficult to verbalise. It is more a feeling of joy, an insight or a revelation an urbanist may experience. It is a lived moment that can be recollected but not represented.

Afterword
Experience and Conflict

In a field between science and art, being right cannot be the only aim. Rather, the aim should be to be different, to open new possibilities for thought and action. In thinking theory, practice and their relationships, my primary aim has been to reform the planning-thought by providing an alternative to the established but inherently problematic chain of ideas from Concept City to the visual bias in representing space and the resulting belief that urban space can be designed. If knowledge indeed is produced as the constructionists claim, I believe that this theoretical work would open up opportunities for new knowledge and thereby new lived realities. While I have used the notion of space as my passage to the field, I have maintained that the conceptual work is a tool to propose new avenues for the practices of planning, urban design and architecture. The new enabling, culturally and emotionally sensitive practice I call 'experiential urbanism'.

In the effort to 'relearn to think about space', my eye has been in finding differences, foregrounding the not-yet-existing and allowing for inventions. To do that, I have addressed ontological, epistemological and methodological challenges. Becoming has been in focus instead of Being, change instead of stable things and moments instead of *dureés*. Ontologically, the key notion has been the moment of coming-together, the dialectical point of (urban) centrality in Lefebvre's spatial dialectics. Epistemologically, the ideas of Vattimo and Benjamin – weak thought and dialectical image – have offered some possibility to know the unknowable, think the unthinkable. Both modes of thought look backwards, but there is a difference between mere describing the past and re-living, recollecting and reinventing the past. My methodological solution to carry out the task has been to create trans-discursive work, a mixture of qualitatively different approaches and texts, structured like the game 'paper, stone, scissors'.

If Part 1 was a preparatory speech, a critique opening the discussion, Parts 2 and 3 monologues developing the point and Part 4 a coda, confirming what was said before, the projects in Part 5 provided a 'test' of experiential urbanism. After the three challenges of scientific methodology, projects brought in the fourth one, that of action. I asked, what would be a planning practice, analogous to weak thought, weak place, dialectical image and spatial dialectics, suggesting that planning and urban design should also somehow be *Andenkend* and facilitating – a tensioned assembly or a dialectic past and future. A certain structural similarity cuts through the layers of conceptualisation and action. If public urban space is approached as a point of assembly, the art and aesthetics of an urban project become redefined, too. I would say that art and beauty reside in the *moment when the qualitatively different elements come together beautifully*, in a clear, revealing or liberating manner. It is the moment of Odysseus stringing the bow and sending an arrow straight through the sockets of twelve axe heads lined in a row – through all layers of social space, perceived, conceived, lived – to open the eyes, and heart, of Penelope

The moment has nothing to do with drawing or predicting, but with sensing, tasting, experiencing, acting. In such a moment, the architect, designer or planner – urbanist – is like the conductor leading an electric current from clouds to earth, and vice versa. Sometimes, this moment can be sustained in space. That is the subtle task of experiential urbanist, necessitating all the devices of Daedalus: assembling space, not bricks.

***

The evolution of urban events from the Night of the Arts to the Human Wall mark the 'human process' of appropriation of Helsinki's urban space, while the process from the Total Balalaika Show to Global Balalaika Show (with the role of the Cowboys) emphasise the 'commercial process' of domination. There have constantly been competing and contradictory processes during the studied period, constituting a 'game'. The Total Balalaika Show was a unique event that featured in the development of Senate Square and the general *festivalisierung* of Helsinki. From the point of view of genuine public urban space production its effects may have been adverse, however. Spectacles that 'hi-jack' meanings are complex interpretations of layered symbolisms but they cannot be very subtle. The line from the Total to the Global Balalaika Show and the Leningrad Cowboys commercialising Makasiinit has shown that urban innovation is, after all, a scarce resource. In the first years of the 2000s, Helsinki's urban event scene has been 'more of the same'. However, without Makasiinit Helsinki would be a different city, with a different urban agenda. In that sense the public conflict about the fate of Makasiinit ensures it a longer-term importance, even though the process was cut and the quasi-object was not let to gather more elements around it. The two lines, spectacle and appropriation, are constantly present in events and spaces. It is a delicate question, which of the two extremes becomes dominating.

***

As referred to in the Introduction, I believe that personal signification, attachment and action are connected, playing a role in a variety of urban conflicts. Not just people with architectural or aesthetic education and sensibility make the link between weak places and tensioned conflicts that produce public space. On the contrary, besides creating new, temporary project communities, urban conflicts of differing time-scale and intensity open up opportunities for a number of 'publics' to influence (produce) space, while reinforcing and expressing their own identity. Graffiti and Helsinki's exaggerated fight against it under the banner 'Stop töhryille' is a case in point. After years of surveillance, data gathering and new prosecution practices to track down the painters and curb graffiti as a youth cultural phenomenon, the problems of the ideal graffiti-free 'abstract space' promoted by real estate owners, city authorities and security companies are slowly being exposed. The assumed connection between clean walls and safety of the streets is understood to be futile, while the negative effects of suppressing the conflict, criminalising 'the Other' and sanitising public space are increasingly felt (Koskela 2003). This example foregrounds the issue of societal domination: without doubt, when searching for a wall to paint, imagining and planning the mural and executing it the graffiti painter feels strongly. In a 'normal' situation, without conflict, this feeling or interpretation would be simply neglected by the city authorities (and also probably by a large fraction of urban dwellers). Conflict makes a difference, shifting the clear-cut power hierarchy. Paradoxically, the official, heavily executed anti-graffiti policy and the resulting 'low-intensity' urban conflict, move or 'raise' the acts of appropriation of graffiti painters from 'private' or 'parochial' to 'public' and 'political'. Without the conflict, graffiti would be a quite stable and limited insiders' thing. But the disputed frontier in metro stations, court rooms and alternative press is to some extent able to 'operationalise' the painters' deeply felt moments and lend them power to influence the constellation of perceived-conceived-lived of a larger public. For example, without graffiti, metro stations and the commuters' every-day landscape of noise control fences and rock slopes along the line would be a single identityless 'non-place'. The ephemeral murals, painted grey by the City's anti-graffiti unit in a day or two, revalorise and 'activate' them. Non-place is turned to a public battlefield. Therefore, I claim that a conflict in public urban space does have some progressive / liberating potential, even in a situation where the dominating actor does not acknowledge the existence of the conflict and the consequences for individual painters may be severe. Obliquely, the suspended conflict between graffiti painters and the security company City has hired to fight graffiti is feeding a political discussion about good policy, good city and, ultimately, good life.

An important question is, which issues and strongly felt moments do *not* spark public, urban conflicts. A potential example might be immigrants' problem in finding cultural 'pockets' in Helsinki. According to Rob Shields, Helsinki is culturally rather 'cold' and its urban space is so programmed that immigrants' cannot easily integrate (Ilmonen and Lehtovuori 2002: 34–5, see also Hynynen 2002). Currently this is a latent question, not a conflict. Probably, immigrants do not have the societal and cultural resources to raise their concern to an urban conflict. This 'silence' most likely concerns many other weakly positioned groups and 'publics'. Children and very old people, for example, can be assumed to have a higher threshold to act in public space than well-educated professionals, with more valid networks and skills. I have to conclude that while urban conflict can be a vehicle for the dominated to produce space and, thus, gain power, the differences between age, occupation, ethnic background and probably gender do play a role.

Planners, therefore, should be sensitive towards signals of conflict and tension. Knowing that planning can never collect the experiences of all people, and knowing, too, that the story told about one's experience loses the acuteness of the lived situation, urban conflict appears to be a valuable 'asset' for the new planning practice. In conflict, individual experiences become public and shared in such a way that the directly lived is not lost. The tensioned moment and community, tied together in a conflict, is indeed acutely lived and active. This is why conflicts are so interesting from the point of experiential urbanism.

***

The whole project to elevate Experience and Conflict to the constituents of urbanism posits itself as an alternative, critique or marginal, both in the field of theory and practice. In both realms, my ideas foreground the Other, the strange and the weak, but in those two fields this marginality is not the same marginality. I hope that theory and practice offer a cross-valorisation, starting another round of the stone-paper-scissors game. A game played in meeting rooms and building sites, lived constantly feeding conceived space and the other way round.

Concerning Lefebvre's theory of space, I offer a set of fresh ideas and translations. My work recontextualises his ideas, shifting them from the wide societal plane and the horizon of urban revolution to the architectural plane and that of a specific project. This shift raises the most unremarkably and concretely material thing to a status Lefebvre did not expect it might have. Lefebvre conceptualised everyday life in a dual and complex manner, so that it simultaneously is both boring, banal and dominated by structurally superior forces and surprising and full, opening possibilities to challenge the societal domination. But I do not think Lefebvre ever thought a mere object could have the dual nature and potentiality. He maintained the distinction between *oeuvre* and product. However, in the conceptual frame developed above, it is correct to state that a product, a building for example, in its relational field may be dynamised so that it reaches *without mediation* to the social and mental. This can be seen as the urban equivalent to the Marxist notion of commodity form condensing social relations. However, in the urban/architectural realm, many aspects are not interchangeable with the notion of commodity. Urban artefact as a quasi-object is unique. It has the potential to become the 'white object' opening itself to countless (new, innovative, daring) definitions and claims, thus gathering momentary, conflictual community.

Such an assembly took place in Makasiinit, but it seems a rather rare occurrence. While many other temporarily used buildings and sites provide fascinating examples of innovative uses, such a closely knit socio-material connection is not that common. In Berlin Mitte in the mid-1990s, the nomadic clubs could use almost any space and move freely in the urban labyrinth. The fight over the unique and politically heavy shell of *Palast der Republik*, on the other hand, might be a fairly comparable case with Makasiinit. The material space, its spatial configuration and the experience it may evoke, may indeed have the potential to trigger change, to be the Other of spatial dialectics. It not only 'facilitates', but also really 'creates', simply by being what it is. In this specific type of dialectical constellation, the

Material is not contingent, but necessary, thus momentarily overturning my basic argument about the relation between signification and its material condition.

***

The most important question is beyond the professional field. I think that the notions of Experience and Conflict reframe our way of relating to the world. Instead of opportunistic, life should be actively political. Yi-Fu Tuan maintains that experience cannot be passive and internal, but refers to a daring conduct of life, venturing in the unfamiliar and gathering skills. 'Experience is the overcoming of perils. The word "experience" shares a common root (*per*) with "experiment", "expert", and "perilous" … To become an expert one must dare to confront the perils of the new' (Tuan 1977: 9). The Finnish language has a parallel connection. While *kokemus* is chiefly a positive term, also signifying 'a magnificent experience', other 'perilous' concepts such as *koe* (experiment) and *koettelemus* (trial, tribulation) belong to the same family of words. Experience is linked to confronting the world. In that sense it is something public.

Experience and conflict are the sides of the coin of active life. Underdefined and marginal, but symbolically central and rich spaces invite active people to divert them further and create something new. The experiential urbanist should join those people, stop trusting in distanced representations and try to suspend the unfolding conflict.

Bibliography

Allmendinger, Philip (2002). Towards a Post-Positivist Typology of Planning Theory. *Planning Theory*, Vol. 1, No. 1, pp. 77–99.

Ameel, Lieven and Tani, Sirpa (2007). Säröjä kaupunkitilassa. Parkour. *Alue ja ympäristö*, vol 36, No. 1, pp. 3–13. [Cracks in urban space. Parcour.]

Andersson, Harri (1997). Kulttuuri ja paikan politiikka kaupunkiuudistuksessa. In Haarni, Tuukka; Karvinen, Marko; Koskela, Hille and Tani, Sirpa (eds), *Tila, paikka ja maisema. Tutkimusretkiä uuteen maantieteeseen*. Tampere: Vastapaino, pp. 107–28.

Andreotti, Libero (1996). Introduction. The urban politics of the Internationale Situationniste. In Andreotti, Libero (ed.), *Situationists. Art, Politics, Urbanism*. Barcelona: MACBA and ACTAR, pp. 11–35.

Ahlava, Antti (2002). *Architecture in Consumer Society*. Helsinki: Publication series of the University of Art and Design Helsinki A 36.

Archis 2/2004.

Arendt, Hannah (1958). *The Human Condition*. Chicago: University of Chicago Press.

Arendt, Hannah (1999) [1970]. Introduction. In Benjamin, Walter, *Illuminations*. London: Pimlico, pp. 7–58.

Argan, Giulio Carlo (1996) [1963]. On the typology of architecture. In Nesbitt, Kate (ed.), *Theorising a New Agenda for Architecture Theory*. New York: Princeton Architectural Press, pp. 240–47.

Arkkitehti, kilpailuliite 5/1972.

Atkinson, Rowland (2001). Domestication by cappuccino or a revenge on urban space? Paper presented at the Institute of British Geographers, Plymouth January, 2001.

Augé, Marc (1995). *Non-places. Introduction to an Anthropology of Supermodernity*. London: Verso.

Bauman, Zygmunt (2001). Uses and disuses of urban space. In Czarniawska, Barbara and Solli, Rolf (eds), *Organizing Metropolitan Space and Discourse*. Malmö: Liber, pp. 15–32.

Beauregard, Robert (2002). New urbanism: ambiguous certainties. *Journal of Architectural and Planning Research*, Vol. 19, No. 3, pp. 181–94.

Beauregard, Robert (2003). Positioning Urban Theory. *Antipode*.

Bello, Mafe (2004). RIPped Places. Cemeteries as Cultural Landscapes and Heterotopias. Unpublished master's thesis, Polis European MA in Urban Cultures.

Bengs, Christer, Hentilä, Helka-Liisa and Nagy, Daniel (2002). *Urban Catalysts. Workpackage 3, Analysis Report*. Espoo: YTK E2. <http://www.hut.fi/Yksikot/ YTK/julkaisu/E2Urbancat_wp3.pdf> (visited 14 January 2005).

Benjamin, Walter (1979) [1927]. Moscow. In *One-Way Street and Other Writings*. London: Verso, pp. 177–208.

Benjamin, Walter (1979b) [1928]. One-way street [Einbahnstrasse]. In *One-Way Street and Other Writings*. London: Verso, pp. 45–104.

Benjamin, Walter (1999). *The Arcades Project*. Cambridge, MA: Harvard University Press.

Benjamin, Walter (1999b) [1935]. Paris, capital of the nineteenth century. Exposé of 1935. In *The Arcades Project*. Cambridge, MA: Harvard University Press, pp. 3–13.

Benjamin, Walter (1999c) [1936]. The work of art in the age of mechanical reproduction. In *Illuminations*. London: Pimlico, pp. 211–44.

Benjamin, Walter (1999d) [1950]. Theses on the philosophy of history. In *Illuminations*. London: Pimlico, pp. 245–55.

Benjamin, Walter and Lacis, Asja (1979) [1924]. Naples. In *One-Way Street and Other Writings*. London: Verso, pp. 167–76.

Berger, Peter L. and Luckmann, Thomas (1967). *The Social Construction of Reality. A Treatise in the Sociology of Knowledge*. New York: Doubleday.

Bhaskar, Roy (1986). *Scientific Realism and Human Emancipation*. London: Verso.

Bianchini, Franco (1996). Cultural planning. An innovative approach to urban development. In Verwijnen, Jan and Lehtovuori, Panu (eds), *Managing Urban Change*. Helsinki: UIAH Publications, ss. 18–25.

Blinkenlights. <http://www.blinkenlights.de/> (visited 10 January 2005).

Boeri, Stefano (2000). Notes for a research program. In Koolhaas, Rem, Boeri, Stefano, and Kwinter, Sanford (eds), *Mutations*. Bordeaux: ACTAR, pp. 356–77.

Boeri, Stefano (2004). Eclectic atlases. In Graham, Stephen (ed.), *The Cybercities Reader*. London: Routledge, pp. 117–22.

Böhme, Gernot (1989). *Für eine Ökologische Naturästhetik*. Frankfurt am Main: Edition Suhrkamp.

Böhme, Gernot (1995). *Atmosphäre. Essays zur neuen Ästhetik*. Frankfurt an Main: Edition Suhrkamp.

Böhme, Gernot (1998). *Anmutungen. Über das Atmosphärische*. Stuttgart: Edition Tertium.

Böhme, Gernot (2001). *Aisthetik. Vorlesungen über Ästhetik als allgemeine Wahrnehmungslehre*. München: Wilhelm Fink Verlag.

Bonsdorff, Pauline von (1998). *The Human Habitat: Aesthetic and Axiological Perspectives*. Lahti: International Institute of Applied Aesthetics, series Vol. 5.

Braga, Andréa da Costa and Falcão, Fernando A.R. (1997). *Guia de Urbanismo, Arquitectura e Arté Brasília*. Brasília: Fundação Athos Bulcão.

Broadbent, Geoffrey (1990). *Emerging Concepts in Urban Space Design*. London: Van Nostrand Reinhold.

Buck-Morss, Susan (1989). *The Dialectics of Seeing. Walter Benjamin and the Arcades Project*. Cambridge, MA: MIT Press.

Burgin, Victor (1996). *In/Different Spaces*. Berkeley, CA: University of California Press.

Byrne, David (2001). *Understanding the Urban*. New York: Palgrave.

Cantell, Timo (1992). *Valoa yössä. Taiteiden yö kaupunkikulttuurin uudistajana*. Keskustelualoitteita 1992:4. Helsinki: Helsingin kaupungin tietokeskus.

Cantell, Timo (1993). *Kannattaako kulttuuri? Kulttuurisektori ja kaupunkien kehityshankkeet*. Helsinki: Helsingin kaupungin tietokeskus.

Cantell, Timo (1999). *Helsinki and a Vision of Place*. Helsinki: City of Helsinki Urban Facts.

Cantell, Timo (1999b). *Helsinki suurtapahtumien näyttämönä*. Tutkimuskatsauksia 1999:1. Helsinki: Helsingin kaupungin tietokeskus.

Cantell, Timo (2001). Paikan henki globaalisten virtojen tilassa. In Makasiinityöryhmä (eds), *VR:n makasiinit pääkaupungin ytimessä*. Helsinki: Helsingin kaupunkisuunnitteluviraston julkaisuja 2001:14.

Carr, Stephen, Francis, Mark, Rivlin, Leanne G. and Stone, Andrew M. (1992). *Public Space*. Cambridge, MA: Cambridge University Press.

Casey, Edward S. (1997). *The Fate of Place. A Philosophical History*. Berkeley, CA: University of California Press.

Castells, Manuel (1977) [1972]. *The Urban Question. A Marxist Approach*. London. [Original: *La Question Urbaine*.]

Castells, Manuel (1989). *The Informational City. Information Technology, Economic Restructuring, and the Urban-Regional Process*. Oxford: Blackwell.

Castells, Manuel (1992). *European Cities, the Informational Society, and the Global Economy*. Amsterdam: Centrum voor Grootstedelijk Onderzoek.

Castells, Manuel (1996). *The Rise of the Network Society*. Cambridge, MA: Blackwell.

Castells, Manuel (1997). *The Power of Identity*. Oxford: Blackwell.

Cavallaro, Dani (2001). *Critical and Cultural Theory*. London: Athlone Press.

Caygill, Howard (1998). *Walter Benjamin. The Colour of Experience*. London: Routledge.

Certeau, Michel de (1984*)*. *The Practice of Everyday Life*. Berkeley, CA: University of California.

Certeau, Michel de (1993). Walking in the city. In During, Simon (ed.), *The Cultural Studies Reader*. London: Routledge, pp. 151–60.

Ching, Francis D.K. (1979). *Architecture. Form, Space and Order*. New York: Van Nostrand Reinhold Company.

Chora (Bunschoten, Raoul, Hasdell, Peter and Hoshino, Takuro) (1996). Orchestrating negotiation. In Verwijnen, Jan and Lehtovuori, Panu (eds), *Managing Urban Change*, Helsinki: UIAH Publications, pp. 152–61.

Chora (Bunschoten, Raoul, Hoshino, Takuro and Binet, Hélène) (2001). *Urban Flotsam. Stirring the City*. Rotterdam: 010 Publishers.

Crang, Mike and Travlou, Penny S. (2001). The city and topologies of memory. *Environment and Planning D: Society and Space*, Vol. 19, pp. 161–77.

Crowhurst Lennard, Susan H. and Lennard, Henry L. (1984). *Public Life in Urban Places*. Southampton, NY: Gondolier Press.

Dangschat, Jens (1996). Lokale Probleme globaler Herausforderungen in deutschen Städten. In Schäfers, Bernhard and Wewer, Göttrik (eds), *Die Stadt in Deutschland*. Opladen: Leske + Budrich, pp. 31–60.

Davis, Mike (1990). *City of Quartz. Excavating the Future in Los Angeles*. London: Verso.

Dear, Michael (2000). *The Postmodern Urban Condition*. Oxford: Blackwell.

Dear Michael and Flusty, Steven (1997). The Iron Lotus. Los Angeles and postmodern urbanism. *Annals of American Academy of Political and Social Science*, Vol. 551, pp. 151–63.

Dear Michael and Flusty, Steven (1998). Postmodern urbanism. *Annals of the Association of American Geographers*, Vol. 88, No. 1, pp. 50–72.

Dear, Michael and Häkli, Jouni (1998). Tila, paikka ja urbanismi – uuden kaupunkitutkimuksen metodologiaa. *Terra*, Vol. 110, No. 2, pp. 59–68.

Debord, Guy (1994) [1967]. *The Society of the, Spectacle*. New York: Zone Books.

Deutsche, Rosalind (1996). Agoraphobia. In *Evictions: Art and Spatial Politics*, Cambridge, MA: MIT Press.

Doron, Gil M. (2002). The bad sheets. *City*, Vol. 6, No. 1, pp. 43–59.

Dzokic, Ana (2000). 'USE.01 Belgrade (Inundation).' In Koolhaas, Rem, Boeri, Stefano and Kwinter, Sanford (eds), *Mutations*. Bordeaux: ACTAR, pp. 380–81.

Eberle, Manfred (2002). *Temporary Spaces*. Berlin: Die Gestalten Verlag.

Elden, Stuart (2004). *Understanding Henri Lefebvre. Theory and the Possible*. London: Continuum.

Elmlund, Peter (2004). Vi behöver freda oss mot dem vi älskar allra mest. *Axess*, Februari 2004, pp. 16–18.

Eräsaari, Leena (1999). Helsingin strategiat ja Töölönlahti. *Yhteiskuntasuunnittelu*, Vol. 37, Nos 3–4, pp. 26–49.

Eskola, Hanna and Ruoppila, Sampo (1999). Snadista stadista cityn sykkeeseen. In Keskinen, Vesa (ed.), *Lama.nousu@hel.fi. Havaintoja vuosituhannen vaihteen Helsingistä*. Helsinki: Helsingin kaupungin tietokeskus, pp. 117–26.

Espace Croisé (ed.) (1995). *Euralille. The Making of a New City Centre*. Basel: Birkhäuser.

Espuche, Albert Garcia (ed.) (1994). *Ciutats: del globus al satèl-lit*. Barcelona: CCCB and Electa.

European Cultural Planning (2004). De Montfort University MA course pages. <http://www.dmu.ac.uk/faculties/humanities/pg/ecp.jsp?ComponentID=7045 &SourcePageID=6345> (visited 14 January 2005).

Faludi, Andreas (1973). *Planning Theory*. Oxford: Pergamon Press.

Flusty, Steven (1994). *Building Paranoia. The Proliferation of Interdictory Space and the Erosion of Spatial Justice*. Los Angeles, CA: Los Angeles Forum of Architecture and Urban Design.

Flusty, Steven and Dear, Michael (1999). Invitation to a postmodern urbanism. In Beauregard, Robert and Body-Gendrot, Sophie (eds), *The Urban Moment*.

Cosmopolitan Essays on the Late-20th-century City. Thousand Oaks, CA: Sage, pp. 25–50.

Foucault, Michel (1986). Of Other Spaces. *Diacritics*, 1.

Franck, Karen A. and Paxton, Lynn (1989). Women and urban public space. In Altman, Irwin and Zube, Erwin H. (eds), *Public Places and Spaces*. New York: Plenum Press, pp. 121–46.

Friedmann, John (1973). *Retracking America. A Theory of Transactive Planning*. New York: Anchor Press/Doubleday.

Forester, John (1989). *Planning in the Face of Power*. Berkeley, CA: University of California Press.

Gadamer, Hans-Georg (1979) [1975]. *Truth and Method*. London: Sheed and Ward.

Gardner, Michael (2000). *Critiques of Everyday Life*. London: Routledge.

Gehl, Jan (1987). *Life between Buildings. Using Public Space*. New York: Van Nostrand Reinhold.

Gehl, Jan and Gemzoe, Lars (2001). *New City Spaces*. Copenhagen: Danish Architectural Press.

Giddens, Anthony (1984). *The Constitution of Society. Outline of the Theory of Structuration*. Cambridge: Polity Press.

Gilloch, Graeme (1996). *Myth and Metropolis. Walter Benjamin and the City*. Cambridge: Polity Press.

Gottdiener, Mark (1994) [1985]. *The Social Production of Urban Space*. Austin: University of Texas Press.

Gottdiener, Mark (1993). Henri Lefebvre and The Production of Space. *Sociological Theory*, Vol. 1, No. 11, March 1993, pp. 129–34.

Gottdiener, Mark (1995). *Postmodern Semiotics. Material Culture and the Forms of Postmodern Life*. Oxford: Blackwell.

Gottdiener, Mark (1997). *The Theming of America: Dreams, Visions and Commercial Spaces*. Westview Press/HarperCollins.

Gottdiener, Mark (2001). *Life in the Air. Surviving the New Culture of Air Travel*. Lanham, MD: Rowman and Littlefield.

Gottdiener, Mark and Lagopoulos, Alexandros Ph. (eds) (1986). *The City and the Sign. An Introduction to Urban Semiotics*. New York: Columbia University Press.

Graham, Stephen and Marvin, Simon (2001). *Splintering Urbanism. Networked Infrastructures, Technological Mobilities and the Urban Condition*. London: Routledge.

Gromark, Sten (2004). Situations of urban architecture as cultural explorations. Manuscript to paper in The Congress CATH Philosophy of Architecture/ Architecture of Philosophy, Bradford, July.

Groth, Jacqueline (2002). Reclaiming urbanity. Unpublished Master's thesis, Polis European MA in Urban Cultures.

Groth, Jaqcueline and Corijn, Eric (2005). Reclaiming urbanity: Indeterminate spaces, informal actors and urban agenda setting. *Urban Studies*, Vol. 42, No. 3, pp. 511–34.

Haarni, Tuukka (2000). Unelmien Töölönlahti – painajaisten Kamppi? In Stadipiiri (eds), *Urbs. Kirja Helsingin kaupunkikulttuurista*. Helsinki: Helsingin kaupungin tietokeskus and Edita.

Hajer, Maarten (1999). Zero-friction society – the cultural politics of design. *Urban Design Quarterly*, 71, pp. 29–34.

Hall, Peter and Ward, Colin (1998). *Sociable Cities*. Chichester: John Wiley and Sons.

Hall, James (2000). *World as Sculpture. The Changing Status of Sculpture from Renaissance to the Present Day*. London: Pimlico.

Harvey, David (1973). *Social Justice and the City*. London: Edward Arnold.

Harvey, David (1989). *The Condition of Postmodernity*. Cambridge, MA: Blackwell.

Harvey, David (1996). *Justice, Nature and the Geography of Difference*. Malden, MA: Blackwell.

Haukkala, Ville (2003). Musiikkitalo vai makasiinit? Erään symbolisen kamppailun anatomia. *Tiede and Edistys* 4/2003, pp. 314–25.

Havik, Klaske (2004). Subcultuur als generator voor stedelijke activiteiten-onverwachte allianties tussen subcultuur en instanties [Subculture as generator of urban activities – unexpected alliances between subculture and authorities.] *de Architect*, July–August 2004, The Hague: Ten Hagen&Stam publishers, pp. 30–33.

Healey, Patsy (1997). *Collaborative Planning. Shaping Places in Fragmented Societies*. Basingstoke: Macmillan.

Healey Patsy (2006). *Urban Complexity and Spatial Strategies: A Relational Planning for our Times*. London: Routledge.

Heikkinen, Timo (2000). Odotus, lupaus, lunastus. Helsingin kulttuuri-kaupunkitapahtuman tuottaminen. In Stadipiiri (eds), *URBS. Kirja Helsingin kaupunkikulttuurista*. Helsinki: Edita, pp. 137–47.

Helin, Heikki (1999). Kriisissä, kriisiytymässä, lähestymässä kriisin esiastetta. In Keskinen, Vesa (ed.), *Lama.nousu@hel.fi. Havaintoja vuosituhannen vaihteen Helsingistä*. Helsinki: Helsingin kaupungin tietokeskus, pp. 11–18.

Helsingin imago Lontoossa. Research report, no printing year.

Helsingin yleiskaava 1992: Kehityskuva. (1992). Helsinki: Kaupunginkanslian julkaisusarja A.

Hemment, Drew (2004). The locative dystopia. <http://amsterdam.nettime.org/Lists-Archives/nettime-l-0401/msg00021.html> (visited 7 April 2005).

Hentilä, Helka-Liisa (2002). Urban Catalysts Work Package 4: Potentials. Helsinki Local Report. Helsinki University of Technology, Centre for Urban and Regional Studies (unpublished report).

Hillier, Bill (1996). *Space Is the Machine. A Configurational Theory of Architecture*. Cambridge: Cambridge University Press.

Hillier, Bill and Hanson, Julienne (1984). *The Social Logic of Space*. Cambridge: Cambridge University Press.

Hillier, Bill, Stonor, Tim et al. (1998). From Research to Design. Re-engineering the Space of Trafalgar Square. <www.spacesyntax.com/publications/traf.htm> (visited 27 January 2004).

Hillier, Jean (2007). *Stretching Beyond the Horizon*. Aldershot: Ashgate.

Holden, Adam and Iveson, Kurt (2003). Designs on the urban: New Labour's urban renaissance and the spaces of citizenship. *City*, Vol. 7, No. 1, pp. 57–72.

Hubacher, Simon (1999). Weak urbanism. Schwäche(n) mit Zukunft. *Daidalos* 72, 10–17.

Hynynen, Ari (2002). Kotoutumisen paikat – kaupunkitila maahanmuuttajien integraatioprosessissa. *Yhdyskuntasuunnittelu* Vol. 40, No. 3–4, pp. 40–59.

Häkli, Jouni (1997). Näkyvä yhteiskunta. Kansalaiset ja kaupunkisuunnittelun logiikka. In Haarni, Tuukka, Karvinen, Marko, Koskela, Hille and Tani, Sirpa (eds), *Tila, paikka ja maisema. Tutkimusretkiä uuteen maantieteeseen*. Tampere: Vastapaino, pp. 37–52.

Häkli, Jouni (1999). *Meta Hodos. Johdatus ihmismaantieteeseen*. Tampere: Vastapaino.

Häkli, Jouni (2002). Kansalaisosallistuminen ja kaupunkisuunnittelun tiedonpolitiikka. In Bäcklund, Pia, Häkli, Jouni and Schulman, Harry (eds), *Osalliset ja osaajat. Kansalaiset kaupungin suunnittelussa*. Helsinki: Gaudeamus, pp. 110–24.

Härö, Mikko (2004). Museovirasto kaupunkikulttuurin toimijana. *Yhdyskuntasuunnittelu* Vol. 42, No. 2, pp. 24–32.

Häussermann, Hartmut (ed.) (1992). *Ökonomie und Politik in alten Industrieregionen Europas*. Basel: Birkhäuser Verlag.

Häussermann, Hartmut and Siebel, Walter (1987). *Neue Urbanität*. Frankfurt am Main: Suhrkamp.

Ilmonen, Mervi (1999). Helsingin Senaatintori muistiteatterina. In *Näkyvän taa/ Beyond the Visible*. Helsinki: Helsingin kaupungin tietokeskus, pp. 28–32.

Ilmonen, Mervi (2000). Helsingin Senaatintori muistiteatterina. In Stadipiiri (eds), *Urbs. Kirja Helsingin kaupunkikulttuurista*. Helsinki: Helsingin kaupungin tietokeskus and Edita, pp. 91–103.

Ilmonen, Mervi and Lehtovuori, Panu (2002). Tila on merkityksellinen ja suhteellinen. Rob Shieldsin haastattelu. *Yhdyskuntasuunnittelu*, Vol. 40, Nos 3–4, pp. 23–37.

IS #3 = Internationale Situationniste #3 (1959). Unitary urbanism at the end of the 1950. In Andreotti, Libero and Costa, Xavier (eds) (1996), *Theory of Derivé and Other Situationist Writings on the City*. Barcelona: MACBA and ACTAR, pp. 83–8.

Isohanni, Tuula (2000). Helsinki, Arabianranta: about art and wasteland. *The Finnish Journal of Urban Studies* [Yhteiskuntasuunnittelu], Vol. 38, No. 3, pp. 76–83.

Isohanni, Tuula (2002). Helsinki, Arabianranta – through layers and data into a place of the arts. In Isohanni, Tuula, Lehtovuori, Panu, Vikberg, Jukka and Ylimaula, Anna-Maija, *Urban Adventures*. Helsinki: University of Art and Design.

Isohanni, Tuula (2006). *Arabia, Arabia. Taiteellinen toiminta osana asuinalueen suunnittelua*. Helsinki: Taideteollinen korkeakoulu A 66.

Jacobs, Jane (1961). *The Death and Life of Great American Cities*. New York: Vintage.

Joensuun rantakortteleiden yleinen ideakilpailu. Palkintolautakunnan arvostelupöytäkirja (2002). Joensuun kaupunki.

Joutsiniemi, Anssi (2002). *Accessibility in Helsinki Metropolitan Region*. <http://butler.cc.tut.fi/~joutsini/aesop/atj_2002volos.pdf> (visited 16 January 2005).

Kaliski, John (1999). The present city and the practice of city design. In Chase, John, Crawford, Margaret and Kaliski, John (eds), *Everyday Urbanism*. New York: Monacelli Press, pp. 88–109.

Karjalainen, Pauli Tapani (1987). *Ympäristön eletty mieli*. Joensuu: Joensuun yliopisto, kulttuuri- ja suunnittelumaantieteen julkaisuja 2.

Karjalainen, Pauli Tapani (1997). Aika, paikka ja muistin maantiede. In Haarni, Tuukka, Karvinen, Marko, Koskela, Hille and Tani, Sirpa (eds), *Tila, paikka ja maisema. Tutkimusretkiä uuteen maantieteeseen*. Tampere, Vastapaino, pp. 227–41.

Karres, Sylvia and Brands, Bart (2000). Object trouvés. A strategy for Park van Kraal. *Mama – magasin för modern arkitektur* 26/2000, pp. 56–7.

Keinänen, Olli (1992). *Kumpulan kyläkarnevaali*. Keskustelualoitteita 1992: 1. Helsinki: Helsingin kaupungin tietokeskus.

Kelbaugh, Douglas (1997). *Common Place. Towards Neighbourhood and Regional Design*. Seattle: University of Washington Press.

Kelbaugh, Douglas (2000). Three paradigms: New urbanism, everyday urbanism, post urbanism. <http://www.periferia.org/3000/3paradigms.html> (visited 14 January 2005).

Keskuskatu (1995). *Quaderns*, 200, pp. 64–77.

Klasander, Anna-Johanna (2003). *Suburban Navigation. Structural Coherence and Visual Appearance in Urban Design*. Göteborg: Chalmers tekniska högskola, Sektionen för arkitektur 2003: 13.

Knorr-Cetina, Karin (1999). *Epistemic Cultures. How the Sciences Make Knowledge*. Cambridge, MA: Harvard University Press.

Kofman, Eleonore and Lebas, Elizabeth (1996). Lost in transposition – time, space, and the city. In Lefebvre, Henri, *Writings on Cities*. Oxford: Blackwell, pp. 3–60.

Koolhaas, Rem and Mau, Bruce (1995). *Small, Medium, Large, Extra Large*. Rotterdam: 010 Publishers.

Koolhaas, Rem (1995b). What ever happened to urbanism? In Koolhaas, R. and Mau, B., *Small, Medium, Large, Extra Large*. Rotterdam: 010 Publishers, pp. 960–71.

Koolhaas, Rem (1995c). Generic City. In Koolhaas, R. and Mau, B., *Small, Medium, Large, Extra Large*. Rotterdam: 010 Publishers, pp. 1248–64.

Koolhaas, Rem, Boeri, Stefano and Kwinter, Sanford (eds) (2001). *Mutations*. Bordeaux: ACTAR.

Kopomaa, Timo (1997). *Tori, marginaali, haastava kaupunki. Tilatapauksia julkisten ulkotilojen käytöstä ja reunimmaisista käytännöistä*. Helsinki: SKS.

Korpinen, Pekka (2000). Jälkikirjoitus ja vastalause. In Mäenpää, Pasi; Aniluoto, Arto; Manninen, Rikhard and Villanen, Sampo (2000), *Sanat kivettyvät kaupungiksi. Tutkimus Helsingin kaupunkisuunnittelun prosesseista ja ihanteista*. Yhdyskuntasuunnittelun tutkimus- ja koulutuskeskuksen julkaisuja B 83. Espoo: Teknillinen korkeakoulu.

Koskela, Hille (1994). *Tilan voima ja paikan henki*. Publications of the Department of Geography, B 42, Helsinki: University of Helsinki.

Koskela, Hille (1999). Fear, control and space – epilogue. In *Fear, Control and Space. Geographies of gender, fear of violence, and video surveillance*. Publicationes Instituti Geographici Universitates Helsingiensis A 137, Helsinki: University of Helsinki.

Koskela, Hille (2003). Pelon politiikka ja vaarojen hurma. *Oikeus*, Vol. 32, pp. 278–85.

Koskela, Hille (2004). Webcams, TV shows and mobile phones. Empowering exhibitionism. *Surveillance and Society*, Vol. 2, No. 2/3, pp. 199–215. <http://www.surveillance-and-society.org/articles2(2)/webcams.pdf> (visited 16 January 2005).

Koskela, Hille (2006). Oliko tuhopoltto uhopoltto? *Helsingin Sanomat*, Vieraskynä 9 May 2006 [Was the arson a sign of defiance?.]

Kostof, Spiro (1992). *The City Assembled. The Elements of Urban Form through History*. London: Thames and Hudson.

Krier, Rob (1979) [1975]. *Urban Space*. London: Academy Editions.

Krumholz, Norman and Forester, John (1990). *Making Equity Planning Work. Leadership in the Public Sector*. Philadelphia, PA: Temple University Press.

Kuhn, Thomas S. (1962). *The Structure of Scientific Revolutions*. University of Chicago Press.

Kuoppamäki, Riitta (2001). *Viivan selitys. Arkkitehti hahmo-orientoituneessa kulttuurissaan*. Helsinki: Albion.

Kuusamo, Altti (1991). Typologioiden kehittämismahdollisuudet tietokone-avusteista suunnittelua varten. In *Työkalut ja tietojärjestelmät. Valtion teknillinen tutkimuskeskus tiedotteita 1236*. Espoo: VTT, pp. 100–20.

Landry, Charles (1998). *Helsinki: Towards a Creative City. Seizing the Opportunity and Maximising Potential*. Helsinki: City of Helsinki.

Landry, Charles and Kelly, Owen (1994). *Helsinki: A Living Work of Art. Towards a Cultural Strategy for Helsinki*. Helsinki: City of Helsinki Urban Facts.

Latour, Bruno (1996) [1992]. *Aramis or the Love of Technology*. Cambridge, MA: Harvard University Press.

Latour, Bruno (2005). *Reassembling the Social: An Introduction to Actor-network Theory.* Oxford; New York: Oxford University Press.

Latour, Bruno and Steve Woolgar (1986). *Laboratory Life: The Construction of Scientific Facts.* Princeton, NJ: Princeton University Press.

Lash, Scott (1999). *Another Modernity, A Different Rationality.* Oxford: Blackwell.

Lash, Scott and Urry, John (1994). *Economies of Signs and Space.* London: Sage.

Leach, Neil (ed.) (1997). *Rethinking Architecture. A Reader in Cultural Theory.* London: Routledge.

Lefebvre, Henri (1991) [1974]. *The Production of Space.* Oxford and Cambridge (MA.): Blackwell. [*La production de l'espace*, English translation by Donald Nicholson-Smith.]

Lefebvre, Henri (1991b) [1947]. *Critique of Everyday Life.* London: Verso. [*Critique de la vie quotidienne I: Introduction.*]

Lefebvre, Henri (1996) [1968]. Right to the city. In *Writings on Cities.* Oxford (MA): Blackwell, pp. 61–181. [*Le droit à la ville*, English translation by Kofman, E. and Lebas, E.]

Lefebvre, Henri (1996b) [1989]. The urban in question. In *Writings on Cities.* Oxford: Blackwell, pp. 209–15.

Lefebvre, Henri (2003) [1971]. Beyond strcturalism. In Elden, Stuart, Lebas, Elizabeth and Kofman, Eleonore (eds), *Key Writings.* New York: Continuum, pp. 37–41.

Lefebvre, Henri (2003b) [1980]. Triads and dyads. In Elden, Stuart, Lebas, Elizabeth and Kofman, Eleonore (eds), *Key Writings.* New York: Continuum, pp. 50–56.

Lehtonen, Hilkka (1994). *Perspektiivejä arkkitehtuurisuunnitelmien esityskäytäntöihin.* Espoo: Yhdyskuntasuunnitteluntäydennyskoulutuskeskuksen julkaisuja A 22.

Lehtovuori, Panu (1999). Two creative cases: the Glass Palace Media Centre and the Cable Factory. In Verwijnen, Jan and Lehtovuori, Panu (eds), *Creative Cities. Cultural Industries, Urban Development and the Information Society.* Helsinki: UIAH Publications, pp. 212–33.

Lehtovuori, Panu (2000). Weak places. Thoughts on strengthening soft phenomena. *City*, Vol. 4, No. 3., pp. 398–415.

Lehtovuori, Panu (2000b). Tapahtuma – toinen paikka?. In Stadipiiri (eds), *Urbs. Kirja Helsingin kaupunkikulttuurista*, Helsinki: Edita, pp. 104–17.

Lehtovuori, Panu (2001). Public space as a resource for urban policy – notes on 1990s Helsinki. In Czarniawska, Barbara and Solli, Rolf (eds), *Organizing Metropolitan Space and Discourse.* Malmö: Liber, pp. 67–89.

Lehtovuori, Panu (2001b). Metropolista identiteettiytimiin – pohdintoja Yleiskaavan 2002 päämääristä ja välineistä. *Yhteiskuntasuunnittelu* Vol. 39, No. 3, pp. 67–80.

Lehtovuori, Panu (2001c). From privatopia to liquid urban landscape. *Maja* 1–2001, pp. 21–6.

Lehtovuori, Panu (2001d). Warehouse utopia. In Sederholm, Helena (ed.), *Artgenda 2000 Helsinki. Alive in the City*. Helsinki: Helsinki International Production Office, pp. 36–41.

Lehtovuori, Panu (2001e). Review of Pred, Allan (2000). Even in Sweden. Racisms, Racialized Spaces and the Popular Geographical Imagination. Berkeley, CA: University of California Press. *Sociological Research Online*, Vol. 6, No. 1. <http://www.socresonline.org.uk/6/1/contents.html> (visited 16 January 2005).

Lehtovuori, Panu (2002). Place is the moment of signification. On the theory of an experiential approach to urban planning. In Isohanni, Tuula, Lehtovuori, Panu, Vikberg, Jukka and Ylimaula, Anna Maija, *Urban Adventures*. Helsinki: University of Art and Design, pp. 33–89.

Lehtovuori, Panu (2002b). Uljas uusi metropoli? Brave New Metropolis? *The Finnish Architectural Review*, 6/2002, pp. 16–27.

Lehtovuori, Panu (2003). Temporary uses as catalysts of new urban cultures. *Ptah* 2003:2, pp. 15–23.

Lehtovuori, Panu (2003b). Hajakeskittyvän kaupunkiseudun tuottaminen. *Yhdyskuntasuunnittelu*, Vol. 40, No. 3–4, pp. 108–13.

Lehtovuori, Panu (2003c). Aleksin musta joulu. *Yhdyskuntasuunnittelu*, Vol. 41, No. 2, pp. 86–7.

Lehtovuori, Panu (2005). *Experience and Conflict. The dialectics of the production of public urban space in the light of new event venues in Helsinki 1993–2003*. Espoo: Teknillinen korkeakoulu, Centre for Urban and Regional Studies Publications A 32. (A PhD book).

Lehtovuori, Panu (2008). Artifacts, oeuvre and atmosphere. Applying Lefebvre's spatial thinking in urban design. In: Avermaete, Tom; Havik, Klaske ja Teerds, Hans (eds), *Oase 77: Into the Open*. Rotterdam: NAI Publishers, pp. 58–70.

Lehtovuori, Panu and Havik, Klaske (2009). Alternative politics in urban innovation. In: Kong, Lily and O'Connor, Justin (eds), *Creative Economies, Creative Cities: Asian-European Perspectives*. Springer Verlag, pp. 207–27.

Lehtovuori, Panu and Mälkki, Mikko (2002). The City Happens. Some stepping stones in the argument for the railway warehouses. <www.panulehtovuori.net> (visited 14 May 2003).

Lehtovuori, Panu, Hentilä, Helka-Liisa and Bengs, Christer (2003). *Temporary Uses. The Forgotten Resource of Urban Planning*. Espoo: Publications in the Centre for Urban and Regional Studies C 58.

Liggett, Helen (1995). City sights/sites of memories and dreams. In Liggett, Helen and Perry, David C. (eds), *Spatial Practices*. Thousand Oaks, CA: Sage, pp. 243–73.

Linder, Mark (2004). Modeling urban spaces. Between GIS and CAD. Unpublished conference paper, AAG 2004, Philadelphia.

Lindh, Tommi (2000). Tavaramakasiinien käyttö tärkein syy säilyttämiselle. *Rakennustaiteen seuran jäsentiedote* 3: 2000, pp. 5–7.

Locative media. <http://locative.net/> (visited 10 January 2005) <http://www.pixelache.ac/locative/> (visited 10 January 2005).

Lofland, Lyn H. (1973). *A World of Strangers. Order and Action in Urban Public Space*. Prospect Heights, IL: Waveland Press.

Lofland, Lyn H. (1998). The Public Realm. *Exploring the City's Quintessential Social Territory*. New York: Aldine de Gruyter.

Low, Setha M. (1999). Spatializing culture. The social production and social construction of public space in Costa Rica. In Low, Setha M. (ed.), *Theorizing the City. The New Urban Anthropology Reader*. Piscataway, NJ: Rutgers University Press.

Lynch, Kevin (1960). *The Image of the City*. Cambridge, MA: The MIT Press.

Madanipour, Ali (1996). *Design of Urban Space. An inquiry into a socio-spatial process*. Chichester: John Wiley.

Makasiinit. Tutkielma VR:n tavaramakasiinien käytöstä ja korjaamisesta (2000). Livady Architects and Oranssi ry. Unpublished project description.

Makasiinityöryhmä (eds) (2001). *VR:n makasiinit pääkaupungin ytimessä*. Helsinki: Helsingin kaupunkisuunnitteluviraston julkaisuja 2001:14.

Manninen, Rikhard and Villanen, Sampo (2001). *Makasiinien alueen ja toimintojen merkitys kaupunkilaisille*. Helsinki: Helsingin kaupunkisuunnitteluviraston julkaisuja 2001:1.

Massey, Doreen (1993) [1991]. A global sense of place. In Gray, A. and McGuigan, J. (ed.), *Studying Culture*. London: Edward Arnold, pp. 232–40.

Massey, Doreen (1994). *Space, Place, and Gender*. Cambridge: Polity Press.

Massey, Doreen (1998). The spatial construction of youth cultures. In Skelton, Tracey and Valentine, Gill (eds), *Cool Places. Geographies of Youth Cultures*. London: Routledge, pp. 121–9.

Massey, Doreen (2005). *For Space*. London: Sage.

McCann, Eugene J. (1999). Race, protest and public space: contextualising Lefebvre in the US city. *Antipode*, Vol. 31, No. 2, pp. 163–84.

Menestyksen strategiat (2002). Joensuun kaupunki. <http://www.jns.fi/suomi_uusi/2002.html> (visited 16 January 2005).

Merrifield, Andy (2000). Henri Lefebvre. A socialist in space. In Crang, Mike and Thrift, Nigel (eds), *Thinking Space*. London: Routledge, pp. 167–82.

Milgrom, Richard (2008). Lucien Kroll: design, difference, everyday life. In Goonewardena et al. (eds) *Space, Difference, Everday Life. Reading Henri Lefebvre*. New York: Routledge, pp. 264–82.

Mommaas, Hans (1999). The Tilburg Pop Cluster. In Verwijnen, Jan and Lehtovuori, Panu (eds), *Creative Cities. Cultural Industries, Urban Development and the Information Society*. Helsinki: UIAH Publications, pp. 176–89.

Moudon, Anne Vernez (1994). Getting to know the built landscape: typomorphology. In Franck, Karen A. and Schneekloth, Lynda H. (eds), *Ordering Space: Types in Architecture and Design*. New York: Van Nostrand Reinhold.

Mäenpää, Pasi (1993). *Niin moni tulee vastaan. Katutason tutkimus kaupunkijulkisuudesta*. Helsinki: Helsingin kaupunkisuunnitteluvirasto.

Mäenpää, Pasi (1999). Tee työtä ja menesty, suomalainen! *Yhteiskuntasuunnittelu*, Vol. 37, Nos 3–4, pp. 7–25.

Mäenpää, Pasi (2000). Viihtymisen kaupunki. In Stadipiiri (eds), *Urbs. Kirja Helsingin kaupunkikulttuurista*. Helsinki: Edita, pp. 17–31.

Mäenpää, Pasi (2000b). Urbaani elinvoima ja dialektiikka. *Rakennustaiteen seuran jäsentiedote* 3:2000, pp. 8–10.

Mäenpää, Pasi (2005). *Narkissos kaupungissa. Tutkimus kuluttaja-kaupunkilaisesta ja julkisesta tilasta*. Helsinki: Tammi.

Mäenpää, Pasi, Aniluoto, Arto, Manninen, Rikhard and Villanen, Sampo (2000). *Sanat kivettyvät kaupungiksi. Tutkimus Helsingin kaupunkisuunnittelun prosesseista ja ihanteista*. Espoo: Yhdyskuntasuunnittelun tutkimus- ja koulutuskeskuksen julkaisuja B 83.

Mäkelä, Laura (1996). *Kulttuurin muuttuva kenttä – klustereita, sponsorointia ja kumppanuuksia*. Helsinki: Helsingin kaupungin tietokeskus.

Mäntysalo, Raine and Nyman, Kaj (2001). *Kaavoitus - suunnittelua? Suunnittelun patologioita maankäyttö- ja rakennuslain sovelluksissa*. Oulu: Oulun yliopisto.

Nesbitt, Kate (ed.) (1996). *Theorizing a New Agenda for Architecture Theory*. New York: Princeton Architectural Press.

Neuvonen Aleksi (2003). Leningrad Cowboys goes Makasiinit. <http://www.hels inki.fi/ylioppilaslehti/2003/030509/juttu_leningrad.html>(visited 11 September 2003).

Nikula, Riitta (1990). *Töölönlahti-suunnitelmia 1910–1990*. Helsinki: Suomen rakennustaiteen museo.

Norberg-Schultz, Christian (1971). *Existence, Space and Architecture*. London: Studio Vista.

Nowotny, Helga (1994). *Time. The Modern and Postmodern Experience*. Cambridge: Polity Press. [*Eigenzeit. Entstehung und Strukturierung eines Zeitgefühls*, 1989.]

O'Connor, Justin (1999). Popular culture, reflexivity and urban change. In Verwijnen, Jan and Lehtovuori, Panu (eds), *Creative Cities. Cultural Industries, Urban Development and the Information Society*. Helsinki: UIAH Publications, pp. 76–100.

Oldenburg, Ray (1989). *The Great Good Place*. New York: Marlowe and Company.

Pakkala, Pekka (2001). Katajanokan kärki – innoitteita ja vaikutteita. In Niskanen, Aino (ed.), *Antipasto Misto*. Helsinki: Yliopistopaino, pp. 155–65.

Palmesino, John (2000). USE.12 Helsinki (Clearing). In Koolhaas, Rem, Boeri, Stefano and Kwinter, Sanford (eds), *Mutations*. Bordeaux: ACTAR, p. 395.

Pérez-Gómez, Alberto and Pelletier, Louise (1997). *Architectural Representation and the Perspective Hinge*. Cambridge, MA: The MIT Press.

Paasi, Antti (1991). Deconstructing regions: notes on the scales of spatial life. *Environment and Planning A*, 1991: 23, pp. 239–56.

Pallasmaa, Juhani (2000). Hapticity and time. Notes on fragile architecture. *Architectural Review* May 2000, pp. 78–84.

Pevsner, Nikolaus (1976). *A History of Building Types*. London: Thames and Hudson.

Pirsig, Robert (1974). *Zen and the Art of Motorcycle Maintenance*. London: Vintage.

Plant, Sadie (1992). *The Most Radical Gesture. The Situationist International in a Postmodern Age*. London: Routledge.

Porteous, J. Douglas (1990). *Landscapes of the Mind. Worlds of Sense and Metaphor*. Toronto: University of Toronto Press.

Pred, Allan (2000). *Even in Sweden. Racisms, Racialized Spaces and the Popular Geographical Imagination*. Berkeley, CA: University of California Press.

Prigogine, Ilya and Stengers, Isabelle (1985). *Order out of Chaos. Man's New Dialogue with Nature*. London: Fontana.

Rajanti, Taina (1999). *Kaupunki on ihmisen koti*. Helsinki: Tutkijaliitto.

Reed, M. and Harvey, D.L. (1992). The new science and the old. Complexity and realism in social sciences. *Journal for the Theory of Social Behaviour*, 22, pp. 356–79.

Relph, Edward (1976). *Place and Placelessness*. London: Pion.

Romppanen, Mervi (2002). *The Impact of Ring Roads on City Structure*. Helsinki: Publications of the Uusimaa Regional Council E 78.

Rose, Gillian (1993). *Feminism and Geography*. Cambridge: Polity Press.

Rossi, Aldo (1982) [1966]. *The Architecture of the City*. Cambridge, MA: The MIT Press. [*L'architettura della citta.*]

Rossi, Aldo (1996) [1976]. An analogical architecture. In Nesbitt, Kate (ed.) (1996), *Theorizing a New Agenda for Architecture Theory*. New York: Princeton Architectural Press, pp. 348–52.

Ruoppila, Sampo and Cantell, Timo (2000). Ravintolat ja Helsingin elävöityminen. In Stadipiiri (eds), *Urbs. Kirja Helsingin kaupunkikulttuurista*. Helsinki: Edita, pp. 35–53.

Ruoppila, Sampo; Lehtovuori, Panu ja von Hertzen, Nina (2007). *Infrastructures for Innovation: Enhancing Innovation Activity through Urban Planning in Baltic Metropolises*. Helsinki: BaltMet Inno Project. <http://www.inno. baltmet.org/uploads/filedir/File/BM%20Inno%20Infrastructures%20for%20 Innovation.pdf>.

Saarikangas, Kirsi (1998). Tila, konteksti ja käyttäjä. In Saarikangas, Kirsi (ed.), *Kuvasta tilaan*. Tampere: Vastapaino, pp. 247–98.

Sadler, Simon (1998). *The Situationist City*. Cambridge, MA: The MIT Press.

Sager, Tore (1994). *Communicative Planning Theory*. Aldershot: Avebury.

Sandercock, Leonie (1998). *Towards Cosmopolis. Planning for Multicultural Cities*. Chichester: John Wiley.

Sandin, Gunnar (2003). Dealing with non-place in exploitation, belonging and drifting. *Nordisk Arkitekturforskning* 2:2003, pp. 67–84.

Sassen, Saskia (1991). *The Global City: New York, London, Tokyo*. Princeton, NJ: Princeton University Press.

Sassen, Saskia (1998). *Globalization and Its Discontents*. New York: New Press.

Sayer, Andrew (1985). The difference that space makes. In Gregory, Derek and Urry, John (eds), *Social Relations and Spatial Structures*. London: Macmillan.

Sayer, Andrew (1992) [1984]. *Method in Social Science. A Realist Approach.* London: Routledge.

Schmid, Christian (2005). *Stadt, Raum und Gesellschaft. Henri Lefebvre und die Theorie der Produktion des Raumes.* München: Frank Steiner Verlag.

Schmit, Carole (2000). USE.05 Benelux (Intensification). In Koolhaas, Rem; Boeri, Stefano and Kwinter, Sanford (eds), *Mutations.* Bordeaux: ACTAR, pp. 336–7.

Schmitz, Hermann (1969). *Der Gefühlraum.* Bonn: Bouvier.

Schulman, Harry (1990). *Alueelliset todellisuudet ja visiot: Helsingin kehitys ja kehittäminen 1990–luvulla.* Espoo: Yhdyskuntasuunnittelun täydennyskoulutuskeskuksen julkaisuja A 18.

Sebastiani, Chiara (2001). The idea of the public sphere and the politics of public space. In Czarniawska, Barbara and Solli, Rolf (eds), *Organizing Metropolitan Space and Discourse.* Malmö: Liber, pp. 90–114.

Sederholm, Helena (1994). *Intellektuaalista terrorismia: Kansainväliset situationistit 1957–72.* Jyväskylä: Jyväskylän yliopisto.

Sennett, Richard (1990). *The Conscience of the Eye. The Design and Social Life of Cities.* London: Faber and Faber.

Sennett, Richard (1992) [1974]. *The Fall of Public Man.* New York: Norton.

The Shadow City. Freezones in Brussels and Rotterdam (2004). Urban Unlimited Rotterdam with o2.consult; MUST; dS+V l OBR; VUB Brussels.

Shields, Rob (1991). *Places on the Margin. Alternative Geographies of Modernity.* London: Routledge.

Shields, Rob (1996). A guide to urban representation and what to do about it: alternative traditions of urban theory. In King, Anthony (ed.), *Representing the City.* London: Macmillan, pp. 227–52.

Shields, Rob (1999). *Lefebvre, Love and Struggle. Spatial Dialectics.* London: Routledge.

Sibley, David (1999). *Geographies of Exclusion.* London: Routledge.

Sitte, Camillo (1965) [1889]. *City Planning According to Artistic Principles.* London.

Smith, Michael Peter (1999). Transnationalism and the city. In Beauregard, Robert and Body-Gendrot, Sophie (eds), *The Urban Moment: Cosmopolitan Essays on the Late-20th-Century City.* Thousand Oaks, CA: Sage.

Smith, Neil (1992). New city, new frontier. The Lower East Side as wild, wild west. In Sorkin, Michael (ed.) (1992), *Variations on a Theme Park. The New American City and the End of Public Space.* New York: Hill and Wang, pp. 61–93.

Soja, Edward (1989). *Postmodern Geographies. The Reassertion of Space in Critical Social Theory.* London: Verso.

Soja, Edward (1996). *Thirdspace. Journeys to Los Angeles and Other Real-and-imagined Places.* Malden, MA: Blackwell.

de Solà-Morales, Ignasi (1998) [1987]. Arquitectura dédil/Weak Architecture. *Quaderns d'Arquitectura i Urbanisme* 175, pp. 74–85. (Republished in Hays,

Michael K. (ed.) (1998), *Architecture Theory Since 1968.* Cambridge, MA: MIT Press, pp. 616–23.)

Sorkin, Michael (ed.) (1992). *Variations on a Theme Park. The New American City and the End of Public Space.* New York: Hill and Wang.

Sotarauta, Markku (2004). Luova luokka, kulttuuri ja kaupunkien kehitys. <http://personal.inet.fi/tiede/markku.sotarauta/verkkokirjasto/Kulttuuri_ JKYLA_04_2.pdf> (visited 6 December 2004).

Spivak, Gayatri Chakraworty (1990). *The Post-Colonial Critic.* Sarah Harasym (ed.), New York and London: Routledge.

Staffans, Aija (2004). *Vaikuttavat asukkaat. Vuorovaikutus ja paikallinen tieto kaupunkisuunnittelun haasteina.* Espoo: Yhdyskuntasuunnittelun tutkimus- ja koulutuskeskuksen julkaisuja A 29.

Stenros, Anne (1992). *Kesto ja järjestys. Tilarakenteen teoria.* Espoo: Teknillinen korkeakoulu.

Stenros, Anne (1998?). The contemporary city: moments and monuments. Unpublished conference paper from proceedings of Kaupunki ja aika seminar, Espoo.

Stevens, Quentin (2007). *The Ludic City. Exploring the Potential of Public Spaces.* London and New York: Routledge.

Stevens, Quentin (2008). Why Berlin's Holocaust memorial is such a popular playground? In: Avermaete, Tom; Havik, Klaske ja Teerds, Hans (eds), *Oase 77: Into the Open.* Rotterdam: NAI Publishers, pp. 71–9.

Stoffen, Myriam (2004). The Zinneke Parade. An artistic citizens' parade? In INURA, *The Contested Metropolis. Six Cities at the Beginning of the 21st Century.* Basel: Birkhäuser, pp. 106–12.

Strassoldo, Raimondo (1993). *Tilan sosiaalinen rakenne.* Tampere: TTKK, A, Yhdyskuntasuunnittelun laitos, Julkaisuja 21.

Sundman, Mikael (1991). Urban planning in Finland after 1850. In Hall, Thomas (ed.), *Planning and Urban Growth in the Nordic Countries.* London: Spon, pp. 60–115.

Sundman, Mikael (2000). Töölönlahden taidepuutarhat: menestystarina. *Rakennustaiteen seuran jäsentiedote* 3:2000, pp. 10–13.

Söderlind, Jerker (1998). *Stadens renässans: från särhälle till samhälle. Om närhetsprincipen i stadsplaneringen.* Stockholm: SNS.

Söderlind, Jerker (1999). Culture as soft city infrastructure. Strategies for place-making for urban mines canaries. Conference paper, Conference on Cultural Industries in Europe, Essen Germany, 19–21 May.

Tani, Sirpa (1995). *Kaupunki Taikapeilissä.* Helsinki: Helsingin kaupungin tietokeskus.

Tani, Sirpa (1997). Maantiede ja kuvien todellisuudet. In Haarni, Tuukka, Karvinen, Marko, Koskela, Hille and Tani, Sirpa (eds), *Tila, paikka ja maisema. Tutkimusretkiä uuteen maantieteeseen.* Tampere: Vastapaino, pp. 211–26.

Tani, Sirpa (2000). Turistin katseita kaupunkiin. In Stadipiiri (eds), *Urbs. Kirja Helsingin kaupunkikulttuurista.* Helsinki: Edita, pp. 149–63.

Tapaninen, Jaakko (1994). Maalta kaupunkiin jakaupungista cityyn. In Haarni, Tuukka (ed.), *Ihmisten kaupunki? Urbaani muutos ja suunnittelun haasteet.* Helsinki: Stakes, raportteja 152.

Taylor, Nigel (1998). *Urban Planning Theory since 1945.* London: Sage.

Towards Urban Renaissance (1999). *Final Report of the Urban Task Force.* London: Spon.

Tschumi, Bernard (1996). *Architecture and Disjunction.* Cambridge, MA: MIT Press.

Tuan, Yi-Fu (1977). *Space and Place. The Perspective of Experience.* Minneapolis: University of Minnesota Press.

Töölönlahden puistoalueiden maisema-arkkitehtuurikilpailu. Palkitut työt (1998). Helsinki: Helsingin kaupunki.

Urbandrift. A Transcultural Platform for New Tendencies in Architecture, Design and Urbanism. <www.urbandrift.org> (visited 14 January 2005).

Uusitalo, Liisa (1998). Consumption in postmodernity. In Bianchi, Marina (ed.), *The Active Consumer.* London: Routledge.

Vadén, Tere and Hannula, Mika (2003). *Rock the Boat. Localized Ethics, the Situated Self and Particularism in Contemporary Art.* Köln: Salon Verlag.

Vari, Paolo (2000). USE.04 Raves (Eruption). In Koolhaas, Rem; Boeri, Stefano and Kwinter, Sanford (eds), *Mutations.* Bordeaux: ACTAR, p. 385.

Varto, Juha (2000). *Uutta tietoa. Värityskirja tieteen filosofiaan.* Tampere: Tampere University Press.

Vattimo, Gianni (1993) [1980]. *The Adventure of Difference. Philosophy after Nietzsche and Heidegger.* Cambridge: Polity Press. [*Le avventure della differenza.*]

Vattimo, Gianni (1988) [1985]. *The End of Modernity. Nihilism and Hermeneutics in Post-modern Culture.* Cambridge: Polity Press. [*La fine della modernita.*]

van de Ven, Cornelis (1978). *Space in Architecture. The Evolution of a New Idea in the Theory and History of the Modern Movements.* Amsterdam.

Venturi, Robert (1966). *Complexity and Contradiction in Architecture.* Chicago: Museum of Modern Art.

Venturi, Robert, Scott Brown, Denise and Izenour, Steven (1977) [1972]. *Learning from Las Vegas. The Forgotten Symbolism of Architectural Form.* Cambridge, MA: The MIT Press.

Verwijnen, Jan (1997). Tyyppi, typologia ja typomorfologia. In Mälkki, Mikko and Verwijnen, Jan (eds), *Avauksia. Kaupungin anatomiaa.* Helsinki: Helsingin kaupungin tietokeskus.

Vidler, Anthony (1996) [1976]. The third typology. In Nesbitt, Kate (ed.) (1996), *Theorizing a New Agenda for Architecture Theory.* New York: Princeton Architectural Press, pp. 258–63.

Vidler, Anthony (2000). Photourbanism. Planning the city from above and from below. In Bridge, Gary and Watson, Sophie (eds), *A Companion to the City.* Oxford: Blackwell, pp. 35–45.

Villanen, Sampo and Ilmonen, Mervi (2002). Henri Lefebvren keskeisiä käsitteitä. *Yhdyskuntasuunnittelu* Vol. 40, Nos 3–4.

Ward Thompson, Catharine (2002). Urban open space in the 21st century. *Landscape and Urban Planning*, Vol. 60, No. 2, pp. 59–72.

Whyte, William H. Jr (ed.) (1993). *The Exploding Metropolis.* Berkeley/Los Angeles: University of California Press. Reprint.

Wilson, Elizabeth (1991). *The Sphinx in the City: Urban Life, the Control of Disorder, and Women.* London: Virago.

Wilson, Elizabeth (2001). Against utopia. The romance of indeterminate spaces. In *The Contradictions of Culture. Cities, Culture, Women.* London: Sage, pp. 145–54.

Zukin, Sharon (1995). *The Cultures of Cities.* Cambridge, MA: Blackwell.

2000.hel.fi. Helsinki Euroopan kulttuurikaupunki vuonna 2000. Raportti. Helsinki: Helsingin Kulttuurikaupunkisäätiö.

Index